The Scro

Reference Library of Jewish Intellectual History

Zvi Mark

The Scroll of Secrets

THE HIDDEN MESSIANIC VISION OF R. NACHMAN OF BRESLAV

Translated by Naftali Moses

Academic Studies Press

2010

Library of Congress Cataloging-in-Publication Data

Mark, Zvi.
[Megilat setarim : he-hazon ha-meshihi ha-sodi shel R. Nahman mi-Braslav. English]
The scroll of secrets : the hidden messianic vision of R. Nachman of Breslav / Zvi Mark ; translated by Naftali Moses.
p. cm. -- (Reference library of Jewish intellectual history)
Includes bibliographical references and index.
ISBN 978-1-934843-93-2 (hardback) -- ISBN 978-1-934843-94-9 (pbk.) 1. Nahman, of Bratslav, 1772-1811. Megilat setarim. 2. Redemption--Judaism--History of doctrines. 3. Messianic era (Judaism) 4. Cabala. 5. Bratslav Hasidim. I. Moses, Naftali. II. Title.
BM645.R4N323613 2010
296.3'36--dc22

2010003570

ISBN

Book design by Olga Grabovsky

Published by Academic Studies Press in 2010
28 Montfern Avenue
Brighton, MA 02135, USA
press@academicstudiespress.com
www.academicstudiespress.com

CONTENTS

Introduction

Rabbi Nachman of Breslav (1772-1810) was one of the most enigmatic Chasidic masters. It is appropriate here to draw a distinction between "enigmatic" and "obscure." Nachman was anything but obscure. Beginning his short but audacious career as a Chasidic *zaddik* or holy man, Nachman made himself known as an precocious adolescent condemning many of the more well-respected Chasidic leaders of his time as mediocre in relation to his unique status. In a society where spiritual inheritance meant so much, where authority was largely relegated to disciples, Nachman claimed no such lineage. He was, of course, the great-grandson of the founder of Chasidism, the Baal Shem Tov, and his uncles were R. Baruch of Mezibush and R. Moshe Hayyim Efrayim of Sudlykov, two early masters and the grandchildren of the Baal Shem Tov. Thus he surely had strong family lineage and a brilliant if troubled mind, but he refused to accept any of these respected voices as his teachers. He was a self-made *zaddik*, a charismatic in the Weberean sense of the term.

The enigma stems in large part from the complex nature of his personality and the central role his self-fashioning played in his teachings. More than any other Chasidic master before or after, Nachman's teachings are largely about him; his homilies are an expression of his internal struggle to come to terms with his own self-image and its reception in the world around him. There is arguably no other Chasidic master whose teachings are more autobiographical in two ways: what he thinks of the world, and what the world thinks of him. This is all a frame for some of the most brilliant Torah insights in centuries. Many other masters, Chasidic and non-Chasidic, Ashkenazic and Sephardic, had mastered the large corpus of classical Jewish literature that seemed to be on Nachman's fingertips. But few, if any, had the intuitive, associative, and creative mind to weave complex patterns of color and texture that arise in his extended meditations, homilies, and stories on a variety of topics.

Perhaps like Mozart, Picasso, or John Coltrane, acutely aware of his own genius – a genius that could not be taught – he exhibited a strong sense of hubris, perhaps better coined as chutzpah, in almost everything attributed to him. His teachings were also laced with a deep melancholy and ambivalence about his own role in constructing his legacy. This dichotomy of suffering and exuberance is partly why he, more than others, became a leitmotif for modern Jewish thinkers who saw in him an embodiment of the existential master, one who captured something of the modernist struggle between hope and despair.

The world around him was in a state of transition: the enlightenment was encroaching on his environs, the Napoleanic Wars destabilized the continent, the industrial revolution was on the horizon, more developed roads between cities made it easier to explore worlds outside one's closed environment, the Sabbatean controversy was still burning a destructive path through Eastern Europe, and the messianic hope that ended so tragically with Sabbatai Zevi was transferred in a different hue to the Baal Shem Tov and his Chasidic movement. It is likely that Nachman viewed his role as the culmination of this seismic change serving as the messianic figure who would close the circle of Jewish, and world, history.

What makes this messianic figure so fascinating is that, unlike many other would-be messiahs, Nachman came to the realization that he was not, in fact, the messiah. Struggling to make sense of the tragic death of his infant son, Shlomo Efrayim (Nachman initially held some hope that it was Shlomo Efrayim who was the messiah), Nachman abandoned much of his messianic rhetoric. Soon after this tragic event he turned to storytelling. He told a series of thirteen original stories, some quite elaborate and complex, which were posthumously published in a bi-lingual Yiddish-Hebrew edition as *Sippurei Ma'asiyot*. Some of these stories contained veiled messianic hopes unrealized, the culmination of a short, intense, and hopeful life. The stories themselves became "torah" for his followers and to this day Breslav Chasidim study these stories on Shabbat morning after prayers. One scholar of Yiddish literature even argued that these stories serve as the template of modern Yiddish storytelling in the nineteenth and twentieth centuries.

He was surely not the first Chasidic thinker to view himself as the messiah, nor the last. What is so striking about Nachman in this regard is the energy he devoted to making his case, albeit doing so in a way that kept him inside, sometimes barely, the normative tradition of his youth. While his two-volume collection of homilies *Likkutei MoHaran* (the first volume published in 1809 and the second volume published posthumously in 1811) does not contain direct references to himself, it has been a long-standing Breslav tradition that when Nachman speaks of the unique *zaddik* in his *magnum opus* (which he does on almost every page) he is referring to himself and himself alone.

Given the proximity to the Sabbatean heresy and its aftermath, the audacity of this young genius's oblique references to what he believed was his messianic fate exacerbated by his seeming unwillingness to view himself as part of any living Chasidic lineage was troubling for many in the Chasidic and non-Chasidic communities where he lived. His untimely death from tuberculosis before the age of forty left much of his personal life shrouded in mystery. He also had a complicated relationship to books, ordering a disciple to burn one (it became known in Breslav circles as "the Burnt Book") and hiding various other manuscripts. Breslav lore suggests that the key to understanding the complexity of Nachman's self-fashioning, his true identity, was locked away in these hidden manuscripts. His published writings served merely as outer layers of what he really thought about himself and his relationship to the world.

This is precisely why Zvi Mark's book *The Scroll of Secrets: The Hidden Messianic Vision of R. Nachman of Breslav* is so important. The book begins with a discovery, a kind of "Raiders of the Lost Ark" or "Da Vinci Code" revelation on a much smaller scale. There has long been talk of a "secret scroll" that Nachman hid away before his death. It was never fully clarified whether the scroll was lost or was kept under wraps by the insular Breslav community. There are published reports of sections of this scroll that Nachman taught to various disciples, in one case, while riding in a carriage travelling somewhere in the Ukraine. But the scroll was never recovered. Throughout Breslav literary history, figures claimed to have seen the scroll, or parts of it, some even quoting short portions, but until now the scroll, like Nachman, remained shrouded in mystery. Could it be that the perpetuation of Nachman's own mystery was dependent upon the mystery of the scroll?

Some time ago Zvi Mark was told by people in the Breslav community in Jerusalem that the scroll did indeed exist. After considerable cajoling, Mark was able to gain access to a manuscript copy of the entire scroll from the Breslav community. As it turns out this discovery did not easily solve the mystery. The scroll was written in an esoteric style using obscure acronyms and abbreviated word forms (*roshei tavot*) that made deciphering its contents quite difficult, sometimes impossible. With the help of certain Breslav Chasidim who believed that bringing the scroll to light contributed to their belief that Nachman's teachings, even those hidden away, would procure the conditions for redemption, Mark was able to decipher most of the scroll. What he discovered was something not unexpected but remarkable nonetheless. In these writings, likely never meant to be read by those outside his small circle of followers (unlike many early masters, and despite his messianic inclinations, Nachman only attracted a very small circle of followers during his short life), we can see the extent to which Nachman did for a time view himself as the Messiah and believed he would usher in redemption. More striking, however, as Mark meticulously shows, are the unexpected dimensions of that messianic vocation. For example, the scrolls show that despite the insular nature of Chasidic pietism, Nachman viewed the role of the messiah (his role) as one who spent much of his time, perhaps most of his time, reaching out to non-Jews, in conversation and through teaching, in order to adequately prepare them for the messianic unfolding. And much of his time would also be spent engaging in healing the sick.

In any event, after deciphering and reproducing the scroll, Mark began the arduous work of examining and rethinking the entire Breslav corpus in light of his discovery. He makes some fascinating connections and clears up some inscrutable difficulties in Nachman's published works. In addition, he extends his analysis to engage the social framework of the contemporary

Breslav community, exploring its various, and sometimes odd, manifestations, revisited in light of a messianic vision that was, until now, obscured by the absence of this crucial document.

It is now almost two hundred years since Nachman of Breslav died in Uman, the Ukraine, on October 15, 1810. His circle of followers never chose another master, believing he was a unique *zaddik* who could not be replaced. His oblique comment at the end of his life that "my fire will burn until the coming of the Messiah" became a clarion call for his followers. Until now, the identity of that messiah in Nachman's comment remained unknown, or at least uncertain. It is perhaps appropriate that as we approach his 200th Yahrzeit, new dimensions of his enigmatic personality have come to light. Thanks to Zvi Mark (and all those who aided him on this Odyssean journey) we have a better sense of who Nachman intended in that comment cited above. This book will change the way scholars and non-scholars, disciples and skeptics, will read Nachman's literary corpus. To paraphrase Nachman's nemesis Moses Maimonides's comment on the messianic era, "nothing will be different, everything will be different."

Shaul Magid
Bloomington, Indiana

Translator's Introduction

While any translation requires walking the narrow path between literal and figurative meaning, the *Scroll* itself presented a special challenge. Working together with the author, Zvi Mark, I have attempted to render the *Scroll* into English which reflects the the meaning and feeling of the original Hebrew idiosyncratic text. The *Scroll* is a shorthand account of a longer oral discourse written using acronyms, abbreviations and sentence fragments. Its staccato style is difficult to read and difficult to interpret. The translation has attempted to transmit this same quality to the English reader. The rest of Mark's work serves to unpack this terse text.

The following abbreviations are used in the footnotes: TB for the Babylonian Talmud, YB for the Jerusalem Talmud and MT for the Mishne Torah.

I have omitted nearly all of the frequent appellations used in traditional Chasidic-Hebrew discourse as they are quite cumbersome when rendered into English. Only the occassional abbreviated 'of blessed memory' (obm) has been retained.

Naftali Moses

Foreword

The *Scroll of Secrets* is the innermost secret of Breslav. From the time I first heard of a *scroll* – esoteric and encoded – which dealt the coming of the messiah, it has occupied my thoughts and studies. It was through mere coincidence that a Breslav Chasid who would occasionally visit my home peddling books mentioned the *scroll*. He told me that it in fact existed and that he had actually seen it. When I asked him if he could arrange for me to view it myself, he pushed me off with any number of excuses. Only after much pleading did he agree to look into whether he could bring it to my home on his next visit. I excitedly prepared myself for his expected return and began to search through all mentions of the *Scroll* in the Breslav oeuvre and academic texts. The more I read, the more excited I became. Unfortunately, my Breslav friend kept putting off our meeting. After a good deal of time had passed, he thought that my interest had waned and returned to my home. When I brought up the *Scroll*, he told me that it was in the possession of his son – one of Breslav's "zealots". The son refused his request to lend it out. Only years later would the *Scroll* eventually find its way into my hands.

The second time I set out to discover this Breslav secret was already after I had published my book, *Mysticism and Madness: The Religious Thought of Rabbi Nachman of Breslav*,[1] an article on the "Tale of the Bread", and I had managed to collect a number of manuscripts containing the esoteric "Tale of the Armor". Professor David Asaf was kind enough to refer me to a number of Breslav Chasidim who were familiar with their rebbe's esoterica. At the same time, as a result of my book's publication, a number of Chasidim began to discuss my research with me and some suggested that I meet their

1 The English edition was published by Continuum Press, London in 2009.

own rabbis. These meetings continued, often focusing on manuscripts and their authenticity, the characteristics of the Breslav esoterica and the reasons behind their censorship. When I joined the traditional pilgrimage to Uman for Rosh Hashanah in 2005, I widened my circle of Breslav acquaintances. (This was, of course, in addition to the uplifting prayers and intense study which I enjoyed).

I received the manuscripts of the *Scroll* from Breslav Chasidim. They came to me piecemeal and not all from the same individual. I am grateful to them all. At first, I received a copy of one section of a manuscript belonging to R. Alter of Teplik. At first I believed that this was the complete text, but after much study, I felt that a part of it was missing. However, since the text is written in difficult-to-decipher code and shorthand, I was not sure whether the text was lacking, or just my understanding. After meeting another Chasid who owned a copy of the *Scroll*, I learned that one page was, in fact, missing from my copy. He was kind enough to supply the missing page. Afterwards, I came upon a facsimile of the *Scroll*. This was a later copy in which the copyist attempted to decipher a number of the coded acrostics. This manuscript was a great aid in my own attempts at deciphering the manuscript, even though my own conclusions often differed from those of its anonymous author. I was also able to read another late (and rather poor quality) manuscript, but I was not allowed to copy it myself. Thus it was of little help.

Over the course of my research I met with several central figures of the Breslav court. Some were more active in the court's leadership; some in its publishing arm. I was pleasantly surprised by their willingness to discuss Breslav esoterica with neither suspicion nor antagonism. I was also surprised by the initiative taken by one of the court's rebbes who invited me to meet a second time together with a number of Chasidim who were experts in R. Nachman's esoterica. During our meeting the subject of R. Nachman's strictures against disseminating these writings arose. The rabbi with whom I was meeting weighed the matter and decided that while R. Nachman did forbid the publishing of these writings, and as his disciples they were bound by his prohibition, it appeared that my interest was a propitious sign that the time had come to make them public.

Another leading Breslav rabbi with whom I spoke also felt that aside from tensions between competing Breslav courts, he could not find a reason to keep these texts hidden as they had been in past generations. He offered me his help in this project. So, it is with much gratitude that I can publicly thank my friend, R. Shmuel Tepilinski for all his trouble and dedication in assuring that the *Scroll* made its way to me. He also served as my guide in navigating the contemporary world of Breslav. I also thank R. Avraham Witzhandler, the editor of the Breslav publishing arm, *Meshekh Hanachal*, for our many warm and valuably edifying conversations.

I also want to thank the many Chasidim who upon hearing that the *Scroll* was in my possession offered their time, expertise and energy to help me decipher and interpret it. They, for reasons of their own, have requested to remain anonymous. Some of them went over the *Scroll* with me word by word, letter by letter; some read my own research and saved me from a number of mistakes. My book contains much that I distilled from our work together. I am grateful for both their help and the friendship which developed over the course of our work together.

Only after the Hebrew version of my book (based on a photocopy of R. Alter of Teplik's manuscript) was published, did I succeed in locating an original, authentic manuscript of the *Scroll*. This was found in the private collection of R. Leibel Berger. I hope, one day, to describe in detail this wonderful collection and its farsighted owner who invested much energy and expense in his diligent search and care for rare Breslav manuscripts. At present, though, I will be content with thanking R. Leibel Berger for sharing his collection, time and friendship with me. The photograph of the manuscript which appears in this addition is of that found in this collection and I appreciate his permission to print it here.

Additionally, I want to thank my friends and colleagues with whom I have discussed and sharpened many of my thoughts on the *Scroll*. To Professor Moshe Idel, Yonaton Meir, R. Yehoshuah Mondshine, Professors Elhanan Reiner, Avi Sagi and Dr. Elhanan Shilo and to my son Yehoshuah – many thanks. I am also indebted to the Shalom Hartman Institute, its fellows and executives, for the opportunity to participate in its challenging, yet supportive community. I am also grateful to my friend and translator, Dr. Naftali Moses. He worked hard on a difficult text, aided by deep familiarity with R. Nachman's writings. He found original solutions to the many challenges that this esoteric text presented in translating.

The research for this book was supported by the Israel Science Foundation. Its publication was made possible by a grant from the Hebrew Literature Department of Bar Ilan University's Isaac Akevyahu Fund and the Sznajderman Chair in the Study of Chasidism and to the Vice President for Research at Bar Ilan university, Prof. Harold Basch.

The *Scroll* is a sublime eschatological vision. Written in a concise style that encapsulates much, it relates to a wealth of topics connected with the messianic era and fundamental issues in the Breslav world, and can reveal both completely new and well-known facets of the bearer of this vision, R. Nachman of Breslav. The *Scroll* is written as a sort of code, as a random collection of letters, acronyms, and abbreviations. Whoever wishes to enter into its secrets must be armed with a great degree of patience and be ready to invest the labor entailed in the careful removal of veil after veil, letter by letter and word by word, in the attempt to combine them into a coherent whole. But beyond the mosaic of letters and fragmentary sentences, the reader will stand before a breathtaking and awesome messianic vision composed of poetry and prayer, desires and longings.

This book is lovingly devoted to my wife Ruth.

SECTION ONE

THE SCROLL OF SECRETS

Opening the Scroll

The Chasidic Movement opened up the world of the Kabala, in all its symbolic complexity, to the public. Drastic changes in religious thinking, ways of speech, writing styles and modes of leadership enabled the Chasidim to turn the Kabala into a way of life for their followers. Chasidic communities, as opposed to their then contemporary parallel religious fellowships, opened their ranks to new members. The former ethos of closed esoteric fellowship among mystical scholars was replaced by one that preached 'let the waters spring forth.'[1]

Constitutive Kabalistic concepts such as 'secrets of the Torah,' the 'secret' mode of interpretation and esoteric study all underwent radical reinterpretation in the hands and works of the Chasidim. In the world of the Chasidim, these ideas no longer only relate to Kabalistic texts or to esoteric knowledge, but rather to actual personal practice. That is, to the attempt at mystical union with God, whose hidden nature cannot be expressed in words.[2] The practical changes regarding questions of the nature of esoteric versus exoteric led to

---

1 See Martin Buber, *Bepardes HaChasidut* (Jerusalem: 1945). Rachel Elior, *Chasidic Thought - Mystical Origins and Kabbalistic Foundations* (Tel Aviv: 1999), 110-13. Gershom Scholem, "HeChasidut Hashalav Ha'acharon," in *Studies in Chasidism*, ed. Avraham Rubinstein (Jerusalem: 1977). I do not mean to stake a claim as to whether the Chasidic movement in its early stages turned to the masses or only to the more learned community members or to suggest when such a turn took place. Regarding these questions, see Immanuel Etkes, *The Beginning of the Chasidic Movement* (Tel Aviv: 1998), 59-67. Rayiah Haran, "*The Doctrine of R. Abraham of Kalisk*," *Tarbiz* 66, no. 4 (1971): 533-35.

2 Rav Meshulam Feibush Heller, *Yosher Divrei Emet* (Jerusalem: 1998), 122, paragraph 22. Rav Kolonimus Kalman Epstein, *Me'or Veshemesh* (New York: 1976), 232. Rav Kolonimus Kalman Shapiro, *Aish Kodesh* (Jerusalem: 1960), 69. On this subject and on the stance of R. Nachman himself, see Zvi Mark, *Mysticism and Madness in the Work of R. Nachman of Breslav* (Jerusalem: 2003), 154-57.

bitter controversy amongst Chasidim: What of the esoteric was permitted to expound? What was forbidden? At one time these questions shook the very foundations of the Chasidic world.[3]

However, despite the tendency to open the portals of once esoteric knowledge to the world, even among the Chasidim, the importance of the place given to the hidden throughout the mystical tradition was not completely forgotten. The tension between the concern that that which was traditionally secret should stay hidden and the strong desire to teach and even publicize this content (a tension that is the norm for esoteric knowledge in general),[4] accompanied the Chasidic tradition from its inception. In the epistle written by the Baal Shem Tov to his brother-in-law, R. Gershon of Kitov, he described a vision in which he asked the messiah when he would arrive. The reply was, 'When your studies are made known to the public and the waters of my teachings to you spring forth.' This answer became one of the very cornerstones of Chasidic thought. However, the Baal Shem Tov added that regarding the exact content of this messianic vision, 'permission was never granted him to reveal it.'[5] This paradox, in which the importance of revealing the secrets of the Torah is kept in tension with an imperative to guard the very same, continues to haunt the Chasidic world, as we will see below, to this very day.

In the world of R. Nachman of Breslav, the study of the esoteric held an important place.[6] An entire corpus of writings (and fragments) by R.

---

3 Haran, "*The Doctrine of R. Abraham of Kalisk*," 533-40.

4 Moshe Halbertal, *Concealment and Revelation: The Secret and its Boundaries in Medieval Jewish Tradition* (Jerusalem: 2001), 7-15, 96-100.

5 This quote is found in Immanuel Etkes, *Ba'al Hashem: The Besh – Magic, Mysticism, Leadership* (Jerusalem: 2000). 296-7.

6 The subject of the esoteric in Breslav Chasidism has been widely discussed in the literature. See Joseph Weiss, *Studies in Bratslav Hasidism* (Jerusalem: 1995), 181-258. Mendel Piekarz, *Studies in Bratslav Hasidism*, expanded ed. (Jerusalem: 1995), 10-17, 19, 51-3, 62, 111-17, 126-7. Arthur Green, *Tormented Master* (New York: Schocken, 1987), 8-9, 182-220. Yehuda Liebes, "Hatikun Haclali Shel R. Nachman Mebreslav Veyachaso Leshabta'ut," in *On Sabbateanism and its Kabbalah* (Jerusalem: 1995), 238-61. On 'The Tale of the Bread' as an example of the

Nachman has been covered with a veil of secrecy. Theoretical discussion of the exoteric and esoteric, of what is permitted and what is forbidden to teach, was given much attention as well.[7] R. Nachman himself practiced a number of different techniques aimed at secreting that which he wished kept hidden. Their variety reveals a new approach to the concept of esoterica. We know of one book which R. Nachman hid away,[8] another which he burnt,[9] as well as tales he forbade to reveal to outsiders.[10] So it was that Breslav Chasidim, as a group, enshrouded themselves within a certain air of mystery and kept up a continual discourse concerning hidden works and hidden meanings in their Rebbe's teachings.[11]

This book is devoted to the innermost of these mysteries – the *Scroll of Secrets*. Written using only acronyms and abbreviations,[12] this text details 'the coming of the righteous redeemer' and the secrets of the end of days. According to Breslav tradition, in every generation only one individual may know its secret.[13]

The very fact of the existence of this text was kept hidden for years with hardly any mention in the large Breslav corpus. The earliest sources in which it was mentioned, also pointed out that the scroll had been lost or stolen. In the

---

esoteric, see Weiss, *Studies in Breslav Chassidism*, 191-2. On *sod*, see Zvi Mark, "*The Tale of the Bread – a Hidden Story of R. Nachman of Breslav*," *Tarbitz* 72, no. 3 (2003).

7 Weiss, *Studies in Bratslav Hasidism*, 181-8.

8 Mendel Piekarz, *Studies in Bratslav Hasidism*, 63-4.

9 Weiss, *Studies in Bratslav Hasidism*, 215-44 and 245-8.

10 On 'The Tale of the Armor,' see Zvi Mark, "*Ma'aseh Mehashiryon (The Tale of the Armor) – from the Hidden Chambers of Breslav Censorship.*" *Zion* LXX, no. 2 (2005).

11 Mendel Piekarz, *Studies in Bratslav Hasidism*, 10-16 and 202; Arthur Green, *Tormented Master*, 4-5.

12 Weiss, *Studies in Bratslav Hasidism*, 189-214.

13 *Siach Sorfei Kodesh*, vol. 1-5 (Jerusalem: 1994), volume 2, 82-83 . On *Megilat Setarim*, see Weiss, *Studies in Bratslav Hasidism*, 189-214; Green, *Tormented Master*, 185 and 194-5. On esoteric readings in the Breslav oevre as they relate to messianism, see Weiss, *Studies in Bratslav Hasidism*, 189-248; Piekarz, *Studies in Bratslav Hasidism* 10-16; Liebes, "*Hatikun Haclali Shel R. Nachman Mebreslav Veyachaso Leshabta'ut*."; Green, *Tormented Master*, ibid.

academic world the importance of this text was recognized, but for quite some time no one was able to determine whether it was extant or not. Certainly, no one had ever seen it. Scholars could only speculate as to its actual content.[14]

Now that we have the actual text, aside from its own particular value, we also have an important hermeneutic tool with which to unlock other of R. Nachman's messianic works. His self-conscious vision of himself as a potential or virtual messiah (one of the foundations of both his literary and analytic works), the modalities of his leadership and the development of his court (up until our day) can all now be better understood.

In this first section of the book, I describe the background of the *Scroll's* original transcription. Who heard it, who transcribed it? Past evidence regarding its existence is brought, as well as the ways in which walls of subterfuge were built surrounding the history of its transmission from the time of R. Nachman himself until the present. At the end of this section, extant manuscript variations are discussed.

In the second section, after some two hundred years in hiding, the *Scroll* is produced. A photocopy of the manuscript is accompanied by a suggested decoding of its many acronyms and abbreviations. Despite much effort, some of these remain uninterpreted in their original enigmatic form. I hope that with its publication, other unknown copies of the Scroll may come to light and through comparisons, the rest of this manuscript can be deciphered.

The third section is devoted to interpreting the Scroll itself. Its messianic vision is laid out before the reader. The messianic theme as found here is compared with the rest of R. Nachman's oeuvre and with his actual

---

14 The most important study on this subject is that by Joseph Weiss, "*R. Nachman of Breslav's Hidden Book of the Advent of the Messiah.*" *Kirjath Sefer* 44 (1969). His article concludes: 'So long as the *Scroll* remains hidden we must remain satisfied with the few hints as to contents found in various printed works. Does this text actually no longer exist in manuscript among the Breslav Chasidim? If and when it is uncovered (assuming that the tale of its loss is just a fable) it will be possible to recognize it by the signs in the sources which we have discussed (Weiss, *Studies in Bratslav Hasidism,* 214). Now, when the *Scroll* has been uncovered, we find that most of Weiss' hypotheses were, in fact, correct and his descriptions accurate. This serves as another confirmation of the *Scroll's* identity.

biography. Here I also discuss new discoveries concerning the build-up of messianic tension towards the year 1806 and the place of the Temple in messianic times.

In the fourth section I discuss the *Scroll* in relation to the other secret works of R. Nachman. I offer a hypothesis as to why the *Scroll* was guarded in such secrecy for so long and how this affected both those who were privy to its secret and those who were never privileged to see it or to unravel its riddle.

The final section of the book describes the *Scroll's* history throughout the writings of the various Breslav sects. This discussion takes place against the backdrop of the rapid growth that the Breslav Court has undergone since the beginning of the twentieth century, as well as its growing presence in contemporary Israeli society. In the eyes of several Breslav sects, these phenomena themselves are tied to messianic tidings.

1. WHERE AND WHEN WAS THE SCROLL ORIGINALLY RELATED?

The first rumors concerning the existence of the Scroll and evidence as to the time and place of its original relation are found in *Yemei Moharnat (The Days of R. Natan),*[15] the autobiography of R. Natan of Nemirov, published posthumously by R. Nachman of Tscherin.[16] It appears that these mentions of the *Scroll* were not found in the original work written and prepared by R. Natan, but rather were additions added by its 'copyist,' R. Nachman of Tscherin. These were taken from other manuscripts of R. Natan which were in his possession.

---

15 Rav Natan of Nemirov, *Yemei Moharnat* (Jerusalem: 1982), Section 1, 20-1. Weiss dealt at depth with this source and its parallel in *Avneiha Barzel*, mentioned below. My discussion here rests upon his conclusions, with which the majority I agree.

16 The first section of the book, *Yemei Moharnat*, was first published by R. Nachman of Tscherin in 1876 in Lemberg. In 1903 the the book was again published in Lemberg, this time by R. Yisrael Halperin and Nachum Yehudah son of R. Aaron Shlomo. The second section was first published by Halperin in Jerusalem in 1904. See Rav Natan Zvi Koenig, *Neveh Tzadkim* (Bnei Brak: 1969), 138-9.

> Says the copyist: I saw fit to transcribe that which I found in the bundle of works…
>
> I also found written there, 'In the year 1806, on Sunday the fifth of Menachem Av, we heard from his holy mouth the details of the coming of the righteous redeemer (speedily in our day)…'
>
> I also found written there, 'On the following Sunday, he [commenced] to travel from here throughout the Ukraine[17] and we accompanied him until he departed from Ladazin and there, as he was leaving Ladazin, we sat in his wagon and then on the way he revealed to us the secret written here – things that have never been heard before, etc (that is the secret of the coming of the righteous redeemer mentioned above…).' He concluded: 'Much was immediately forgotten and not transcribed at all for the telling of this tale took more than two hours. He commanded us to never speak of it and to write it in code. Immediately most was forgotten for it wasn't put down at once.'
>
> Afterwards it was written there concerning that which they heard of this matter again on 'Friday, Sabbath eve, the eighth of Menachem [Av] in the year 1809 here in Breslav, etc… How wonderful that we were privileged to hear these hidden things the likes of which have never before been heard' (until here I copied from the manuscript mentioned above).[18]

We see that the text of the *Scroll* actually constitutes two different discourses given by R. Nachman on two different occasions concerning the coming of the messiah. It would appear that these discourses differed and that the second was not a mere rehearsal of the first, for they are brought in R. Natan's text one after the other and not as parts of the same text. The first discourse was told during a wagon journey on Sunday, 5 Menachem-Av 1806. Concerning it, R. Natan wrote that 'most was forgotten.' The second discourse took place in Breslav on Friday, 8 Menachem-Av, 1809.

---

17 Regarding the various journeys and the yearly travels throughout the Ukraine taken by R. Nachman, see Weiss, *Studies in Bratslav Hasidism*, 199-200.

18 Rav Natan, *Yemei Moharnat*, section 1, 20-21.

2. THE WALLS OF SECRECY: ON THE ESOTERICISM OF THE SCROLL AND ITS TRANSMISSION

THE FIRST TELLING

To whom was the secret hidden in the Scroll originally related? Who knew its secret? R. Natan describes hearing the contents of the Scroll in the first person-plural, but does not note who was present with him at each of it relations. Traditions which complete this picture are brought in *Kochav Or* (Star of Light) written by R. Avraham Chazan:[19]

> At the time that the secret concerning the coming of the redeemer was revealed to our teacher, R. Natan, and R. Naftali,[20] there sat next to him [R. Nachman] his son-in-law, Rabbi Yosef while two others from Teplik stood on the steps of the wagon, one behind the other facing our Master throughout the entire journey. His voice was so wondrously quiet while he was speaking that it was not clear to his son-in-law and to the two others whether he was speaking to R. Natan and R. Naftali who sat next to him. This I heard from several people and from my father[21] (may I be his atonement), who heard from those mentioned above, who spoke of this on many occasions.[22]

We see that the other listener privileged to hear the contents of the *Scroll* at its first telling was R. Naftali of Nemirov, one of R. Nachman's closer stu-

---

19 Regarding the additions and deletions made to this work, see David Assaf, *Breslav: an Annotated Bibliography* (Jerusalem: 2000), 22-3.

20 R. Naftali of Nemirov (Weinberg) was one of R. Nachman's closest disciples and a close friend of R. Natan of Nemirov; he died in 1860. For more on him, see Rav Noach Halevi Shternfeld, *Gidulei Hanachal* (Jerusalem: 1984), 81.

21 His father was R. Nachman of Tulchin, a student of R. Natan.

22 Rav Avraham Chazan, *Kochvei Or* (Jerusalem: 1961), 50-1. See also *Siach Sorfei Kodesh*, Book One, 141.

dents and a good friend of R. Natan. Three others, despite their presence on the wagon, miraculously heard nothing of what R. Nachman said.

In *Avneiha Barzel* (Its Stones are Iron), published in 1935 by R. Shmuel Horowitz, a number of traditions heard by the students of R. Avraham Chazan in Uman are collected. One of them recalled the following:

> The first *Scroll of Secrets*, during our Rebbe's journey from Ladazin to Breslav: Some Cossacks passed us and our Rebbe began to tell of us of Russia and what would transpire until the coming of our redeemer and from then until the resurrection of the dead. Seated by our Rebbe was Reb Yoske, his son-in-law, along with R. Natan and R. Naftali. Also two men from Teplik sat on the wagon's step – one on either side. Afterwards, when R. Natan engaged R. Yoske in conversation, he saw that he knew nothing of what had been told – only a story about a tree with golden leaves. The two others had also heard nothing. When R. Natan and R. Naftali saw this, they realized that our Rebbe wanted this kept a secret. And so it was. Therefore, R. Natan wrote the *Scroll* using acronyms.[23]

The description given here is parallel to that found in *Yemei Moharnat* and *Kochav Or* save for two points on which these versions differ. The first, and less significant for us, concerns the direction of travel: did they journey from Ladazin to Teplik (according to *Kochav Or*) or from Ladazin to Breslav (according to *Yemei Moharnat*)?[24] The second discrepancy, however, concerns the manner in which the esoteric nature of the *Scroll* was determined. In *Yemei Moharnat*, it was R. Nachman himself who 'commanded us to never speak of it and to write it in code.' The second version, however, attributes this to a decision made by R. Natan and R. Naftali themselves

---

23 R. Avraham Chazan, *Avneiha Barzel* (Jerusalem: 1983), 29-30. Joseph Weiss has compared and analysed the various traditions represented in *Yemei Moharnat*, *Kochvei Or* and *Avneiha Barzel* regarding the *Scroll*. I agree with most of his conclusions. See Weiss, *Studies in Bratslav Hasidism*, 189-214.

24 It seems that the version in *Kochvei Or* is the correct one. See Weiss, *Studies in Bratslav Hasidism*, 208-9.

based upon their discovery that the others in the wagon had miraculously heard nothing of R. Nachman's discourse.[25]

We might want to interpret the phrase used by Reb Avraham, 'and so it was,' as indicating what happened after the telling of the actual tale. That is, afterwards R. Nachman himself commanded that he 'wanted this kept a secret'. If so, then there are two distinct stages regarding the secrecy prescribed by R. Nachman. At first, R. Natan and R. Naftali understood on their own that what had been divulged should be kept secret. Consequently, however, either on R. Nachman's instigation or through their own inquiry of R. Nachman, it was made clear to them that R. Nachman desired to keep the contents of the *Scroll* hidden.

In 1984 a collection of Breslav traditions that had been orally transmitted by R. Levi Yitzchak Brand, one of R. Avraham Chazan's students and a leader of the court in Israel until his passing in 1989, was put to paper and published as, *Siach Sorfei Kodesh* (Speech of the Holy Fiery Angels). In the first volume, a copy of *Avneiha Barzel* was reprinted, 'for we have been able to produce a better version, free from the many mistakes found in this precious work.... As it is mentioned in its introduction, the author, the respected Rabbi Shmuel Horowitz, relied on the oral tradition passed on from R. Yitzchak and most of what is recorded herein was heard from him alone.'[26] This introduction reads:

> The first *Scroll of Secrets* was related during our Rebbe's journey from Ladazin to Breslav, and some soldiers, called Cossacks, passed by, upon which our rebbe commenced to tell us of Russia and what will come to

---

25 Ibid., 208. Weiss has discussed this point.

26 *Siach Sorfei Kodesh*, book 1, 6-7. R. Avraham Weitzhandler, the author of this work, told me that together with R. Levi Yitzchak Brand he carefully studied the entire book *Avneiha Barzel*. He claimed that the additions and corrections made by R. Brand are the sole source of the corrected version of *Avneiha Barzel* that appears in his *Siach Sorfei Kodesh*. These consultations between the two have been recorded (in Yiddish) and transcribed (also into Hebrew), but are not available to me at this time. It may be that we could find some differences between the original discussions which were conducted in Yiddish and the final Hebrew text which resulted from them as printed in *Siach Sorfei Kodesh*.

> pass in the future – the entire unfurling of the redemption. Seated with our Rebbe was his son-in-law, R. Yoske, together with R. Natan and R. Naftali. He commanded R. Natan and R. Naftali not to reveal this to anybody. Concerning R. Yoske, he said: I am responsible and his guarantor.[27] And so it was. Afterwards, when R. Natan engaged the rabbi, R. Yoske, in conversation, he saw that he knew nothing, only a story which he had heard, which our Rebbe had mentioned at the end, 'a tree with golden leaves'. The other two men from Teplik heard nothing at all.[28]

This version is in agreement with *Yemei Moharnat* that it was R. Nachman himself who decided upon the secret nature of the *Scroll.* However, it does not appear that the statement quoted here is R. Nachman's actual language. The word 'responsible' is not usually found either in R. Nachman's language or in that time period. Another difficulty with this improved-upon version of the story is that it is suspiciously similar to that which happened after R. Nachman told the tale known as 'The Tale of the Bread.'[29] In the booklet, *Hashmatot Mechayei Moharan* (*Deletions from The Life of Moharan)* the following is recorded:

> The copyist said: I heard that at the time he said you are guarantors one to another that nothing will be revealed, another was also present. They were worried lest he tell someone, for he was known to be somewhat loose-lipped. Although they thought this, they said nothing out of respect for our Rebbe. Our Rebbe answered – I am his guarantor. Afterwards they began to question this individual concerning what he

---

27 We also find similar language in the work *Toldot Moharnat* by R. Kramer: 'Our Rebbe warned R. Natan and R. Naftali not to divulge anything of what they heard and added, "The others will not say a thing – I will take care of this myself…"' (Rav Chaim Menachem Kramer, *Toldot Moharnat: Be'aish Uvmayim* (Jerusalem: 1996), 114.) It appears that this description is taken from *Siach Sorfei Kodesh.*

28 *Siach Sorfei Kodesh,* book 1, 230.

29 Regarding this work, see Mark, "*The Tale of the Bread – a Hidden Story of R. Nachman of Breslov.*"

> knew of the tale and he knew nothing. They understood that this is what our Rebbe had told them – I am his guarantor – he had caused him to know nothing of the entire story.[30]

In the 'Tale of the Bread' R. Nachman's pledge for this loose-lipped party fits well within the entire context. By so pledging himself, he removed the onus of responsibility for this chatterer which he had placed on the others who were present. However, regarding the *Scroll*, there was neither any mutual commitment nor any suspicion regarding R. Yoske's ability to keep from divulging what he knew. It may be then that the conclusion of one secret discussion was transposed upon another. R. Yitzchak Brand may not have known the exact language used by R. Nachman, but only a tradition which held that he himself had directed his followers not to reveal the content of the *Scroll*. This tradition, along with the need to reconcile the differences found in *Avneiha Barzel* and *Yemei Moharnat*, brought about the addition of the attributed quote even though the exact wording had not been previously mentioned.

From the clear language of R. Natan as found in *Yemei Moharnat*, and from what we learn from the other sources, we can conclude that R. Nachman himself ordered that the *Scroll* be kept secret. R. Natan, perhaps wanting to record the exact language of R. Nachman's instructions, turned to R. Yoske naturally assuming that he too was privy to the secret. However, it became clear that R. Yoske had absorbed nothing of the secret that had been spoken. The two men from Teplik had also apparently suffered a temporary hearing loss.

The Second Recitation

In the second telling of the *Scroll*'s contents we also find R. Nachman insisting that only R. Natan and R. Naftali hear his words and that they not be revealed to anyone else. In *Avneiha Barzel* we find the following:

---

30 *Hashmatot Mechayei Moharan*, (Jerusalem: 1893), 195.

> Afterwards he called them [R. Natan and R. Naftali] and opened the door to the study hall which was in our Rebbe's house. The Rabbi of Breslav was in the study-hall at the time and our Rebbe did not want him present when he told his story. Just as our Rebbe opened one door, the rabbi opened another and exited. Immediately, our Rebbe closed the door and began to tell them again the *Scroll of Secrets.*[31]

The Rabbi of Breslav was R. Aaron of Breslav who was one of the closest of R. Nachman's Chasidim. He was the subject of many compliments from his Rebbe. R. Nachman had also done much to win his appointment as town rabbi.[32] The secreting of the *Scroll* from him is surprising – he was not only a member of the inner circle of the court, but one of the two Chasidim to whom R. Nachman had chosen to reveal his secret story, 'The Tale of the Armor.'[33]

However, the secreting of the Scroll even from the inner circle is, in fact, in keeping with the Breslav tradition regarding the extraordinary status of the Scroll of which it was said that, 'only one individual in any generation need know of it.'[34] R. Natan did not mention it to anyone in his lifetime as R. Naftali was still living and he already knew its secret.[35]

This unique level of secrecy is reflected not only in the small number of individuals privy to the *Scroll*, but also in the manner in which the Scroll itself was written. Important information regarding its transcription is found

---

31 Chazan, *Avneiha Barzel*, section 32, 31.

32 R. Aaron was born in 1775 and drew close to R. Nachman while he was still in Medvedevkah. He died in 1845. For more on him, including extensive praise by R. Nachman, see, for example, *Siach Sorfei Kodesh,* book 2, 85 and Shternfeld, *Gidulei Hanachal,* 12. See also the comments of Mendel Piekarz in Weiss, *Studies in Bratslav Hasidism*, 209, fn. 33.

33 *Sichot Haran,* (Jerusalem: 1995), section one, 174-81. On the 'The Tale of the Armor' see Mark, "*Ma'aseh Mehashiryon (The Tale of the Armor) – from the Hidden Chambers of Breslav Censorship.*"

34 *Siach Sorfei Kodesh,* book 2, 83.

35 Ibid., 82-3.

in *Yemei Moharnat* in the publisher's introductory comments written according to documents found in the pouch belonging to R. Natan.[36]

> And then ... he revealed to us this secret written here which had never before been heard, etc. (That is the coming of the righteous redeemer mentioned above. And it was written only in a code – using acronyms and abbreviations. He had strictly warned us not to copy this pamphlet known as the *Scroll of Secrets* and certainly not to print it, despite its cryptic style. Even so it should not be revealed, etc).[37]

The *Scroll*, then, was encrypted in such a way as to ensure that even if it was revealed to an unauthorized individual, it would be difficult, if not impossible, to comprehend it without the aid of someone privy to its secrets. Despite this cautionary encoding, even with no additional key, it was still 'not be revealed.' This stringency includes not just a prohibition on revealing it to another or printing the *Scroll*, but also copying it by hand. As we noted above, the language, 'he commanded not to speak of it and to write it in code,'[38] implies that R. Nachman himself had decided upon the esoteric nature of the *Scroll* – including its cryptic style.[39]

We see, then, that the *Scroll* is, from amongst all of R. Nachman's oeuvre that survived in the hands of his court, the most restricted Breslav secret. There are other materials which R. Nachman decided to hide completely – such as his 'hidden' book or the 'burned' book which were kept from all.[40] There are other secret works like 'The Tale of the Bread,' also known as 'The Tale of Receiving the Torah,' or the 'Tale of the Armor,' which R. Nachman

---

36 See above notes 15 and 16.

37 Nemirov, *Yemei Moharnat*, section 1, 20.

38 Ibid.

39 See Weiss, *Studies in Bratslav Hasidism*, 201.

40 Excluding small excerpts which have survived in other published works. On the *Burned Book*, see Piekarz, *Studies in Bratslav Hasidism*, 63-4 and also Weiss, *Studies in Bratslav Hasidism*, 215-44.

commanded be transmitted to successive generations, but kept secret. His injunction was that 'it not be revealed to any stranger'[41] and that 'it not be revealed to any other than the inner circle.'[42] These works were in fact hidden not only from those not belonging to the Breslav Court, but also from the majority of Breslav Chasidim as well.[43] In these cases, we do not have an instance of complete and total withdrawal of the material, but rather its transformation into esoteric restricted text available only to a select few to whom its revelation was considered obligatory. The *Scroll of Secrets*, in accord with R. Nachman's directive, was to be encrypted and made in only one copy which could not be revealed even to those of the innermost court. Only a single individual in each generation was to even know of its existence in order to pass it on to the next one.

The Loss of the Scroll

The Breslav tradition tells that the restrictions placed upon the *Scroll* by R. Nachman worked so well that at a certain point it was lost and no one knew of its whereabouts. In *Yemei Moharnat*, after noting that the *Scroll* was in the pouch of writings kept by R. Nachman of Tscherin, the author added:

> After the untimely passing of R. Natan, the writings of the *Scroll* mentioned above were stolen and lost. To this day, no one knows of their whereabouts – Oh, how great the loss, etc.[44]

In 1969 Joseph Weiss wondered whether, 'this is yet another example of Breslav trickery – denying the existence of texts which were in fact well

---

41 See Mark, "*The Tale of the Bread – a Hidden Story of R. Nachman of Braslav*," 422.

42 See Mark, "*Ma'aseh Mehashiryon (The Tale of the Armor) – from the Hidden Chambers of Breslav Censorship.*"

43 See Weiss, *Studies in Bratslav Hasidism*, 191, fn. 7.

44 Nemirov, *Yemei Moharnat*, section 1, 21.

guarded by them?' Or perhaps the *Scroll* actually was lost forever? Weiss concluded that 'only time will tell.'[45]

Evidence Affirming the Scroll's Existence

In the same year that Weiss recorded his doubt, a Breslav Chasid, R. Natan Zvi Koenig, published his book, *Neveh Tzadikim* (*Oasis of the Righteous*), an annotated bibliography of Breslav literature. In his description of the *Scroll* he quotes R. Nachman of Tscherin regarding its loss. However, he adds:

> It is known to our friends that the brilliant Chasid, R. Avraham, son of R. Nachman of Tulchin the author of *Biur Halikutim*, knew what was written in the *Scroll*. It is possible that the *Scroll* itself was found afterwards or even earlier in the days of R. Nachman of Tulchin and he passed it on to his son. Also, R. Alter of Teplik[46], the son-in-law of R. Nachman of Tulchin and the brother-in-law of R. Avraham possessed these writings. They copied them in a special volume together with other corrections and additions to *Chayei Moharan* and other books from which material was missing. They wrote: 'A copy of the work known as 'The Scroll of Secrets' from the manuscript of our teacher R. Natan – letter for letter, which he heard from our holy Rebbe (the flowing fount of wisdom) containing the details of the coming of the redeemer (may he arrive speedily). I have copied this from a volume of *Chayei Moharan* which was in the possession of R. Naftali. In this volume were found the manuscripts of R. Natan.'[47]

---

45 Weiss, *Studies in Bratslav Hasidism*, 203. He originally published this in Weiss, "*R. Nachman of Breslav's Hidden Book of the Advent of the Messiah*." *Kirjath Sefer* 44 (1969).

46 His full name was R. Moshe Yehoshuah Bezshilianski. He was known as R. Alter. His father, R. Asher Zelig of Teplik, was a student of R. Natan. R. Alter himself was a student and the right-hand of R. Nachman of Tscherin. For more on him, see Shternfeld, *Gidulei Hanachal*, 13-4.

47 Koenig, *Neveh Tzadikim*, 78-9. See the comment of Piekarz in Weiss, *Studies in Bratslav Hasidism*, 203, fn. 22 and also Piekarz, *Studies in Bratslav Hasidism*, 78-9.

From Koenig's words here, it is clear that he possessed a copy of the *Scroll*. Thus he was able to quote the introduction of the manuscript's copyist. Further on he quoted a few additional lines. The question then, was why R. Nachman of Tscherin so mournfully reported the Scroll as lost ('Oh, how great the loss') when in fact the scroll was extant. Koenig needed to explain. He claimed that the Scroll was, in fact, lost for a time, but later recovered. This claim, however, Koenig raised only as a possibility ('perhaps') and mentioned no authoritative Breslav tradition. Therefore, we may want to raise other possible solutions to this question. For example, that of purposeful obfuscation mentioned by Weiss. Perhaps R. Nachman of Tscherin's words were actually meant to lower the interest level in the *Scroll* and to help hide its existence. This possibility gains credibility when we consider that even today copies of the *Scroll* can still in fact be found amongst Breslav Chasidim.

'In every generation, only one individual may know its secret'

A slightly different picture of the *Scroll's* transmission emerges from the description in *Siach Sorfei Kodesh.*

> Our tradition teaches that when our Teacher revealed the Scroll to R. Natan and R. Naftali, he warned them not to make it known – only one individual in each generation should know of it. Therefore, R. Natan told no one, as R. Naftali was still living at the time of his death. Afterwards, R. Naftali revealed it to R. Aaron of Lipvotsk[48] – a holy man whose birth was the result of R. Nachman's blessing.[49] He passed it on to R. Avraham

48 In other traditions it seems that R. Naftali gave the Scroll to R. Aaron. For example, in *Siach Sorfei Kodesh*: Once R. Aaron Lipvotski turned to R. Naftali and said to him: 'You have heard from our Master the *Scroll of Secrets*. Where does this matter stand?' R. Naftali answered him quite emphatically: 'At the least you must learn much from the Rebbe's book… He [R. Nachman] taught us, "When my book is accepted in the world it will be time to prepare for the messiah." Afterwards, at another time he gave him the *Scroll* (*Siach Sorfei Kodesh*, book 3, 83).

49 R. Aaron Lipvotski was a student of R. Naftali. For more on him see, Shternfeld, *Gidulei Hanachal*, 10-11 and Rav Avraham Chazan, *Yemei Hatlaot* (Jerusalem: 2000), 45.

> son of R. Nachman. Before his death, when he was already very ill, Tziril, the daughter of R. Aaron entered his chambers and pressed him to pass on the *Scroll*, for this was the tradition received from our Rebbe, that one individual in each generation should know of it. However, R. Avraham was already very ill and had lost his power of speech (it is not known whether he passed it on or to whom).[50]

In the manuscript known as *Sichot Me'anash* (*Discourses of the Inner Circle*) which contains copies of various manuscripts including the Scroll,[51] the same tradition is found in a slightly different version.

> R. Aaron Lipvotski was a student of R. Natan. In his old age he was blind. His daughter, Tziril, used to claim that she knew that her father knew of the *Scroll* and had taught it to R. Avraham son of R. Nachman. (R. Nachman himself knew of the *Scroll* even though R. Natan had not taught it to anyone. Assumedly, R. Aaron had learned of it from R. Naftali). At the time of R. Avraham son of Nachman's passing, Tziril came and berated him for not teaching the *Scroll* to anybody – for she had heard from her father that one individual in every generation needed to know of the *Scroll*. When he left this world, no one would know of it. But it was too late – for his power of speech was already gone.[52]

In this description of the *Scroll's* transmission, there is no mention of its having been lost, and naturally, none of its rediscovery. Until it reached R. Avraham son of Nachman, it was passed on successfully.

This tradition, though, raises a number of questions. First, why wasn't R. Nachman of Tscherin included in the list of those who knew of the Scroll? He himself claimed not only that he knew of the Scroll, but that he had it

---

50 *Siach Sorfei Kodesh*, book 2, 82-3. For a similar description, see Rav Natan Anshin, "Rav Avraham Ben Rav Nachman..." *Mebo'ei Hanachal* 4, no. 37 (1985).

51 For more on this manuscript, see below on the *Sichot Me'anash* manuscript.

52 *Sichot Me'anash*, section 35.

in his possession. It may be, though, that his own testimony concerning the fashion in which he happened to find the *Scroll* – in a pouch of manuscripts and that he did not learn of it directly from R. Natan – supplies the answer. He was not part of any chain of transmission – he found the *Scroll* coincidentally and passed it on to no one.

Another difficulty is the claim that R. Avraham son of R. Nachman was the one individual in his generation to know of the *Scroll.* We saw above that the manuscript in the possession of R. Natan Zvi Koenig from which he quoted in *Neveh Tzadikim* was in fact a copy of the *Scroll* made by R. Alter Tepliker. If so, R. Alter was also amongst those who knew of the *Scroll* – why wasn't he mentioned in any discussion of the chain of transmission? Additionally, this entire description ignores the fact that the *Scroll* does in fact still exist and has been in the hands of various Breslav Chasidim until today. These difficulties make the value of this dramatically colorful tradition of the *Scroll's* transmission history rather questionable. Later, I will return to this story and offer an explanation as to how it may in fact fit with the rest of the known details concerning the *Scroll's* history.

The Removal of the Scroll from the Ukraine

The book, *Against all Odds*, by Gedaliah Fleer,[53] describes the story of the pilgrimages made to R. Nachman's tomb in the years 1962-66, long before the fall of the Iron Curtain. In the midst of this tale, we find another chapter concerning the *Scroll* – how it was spirited out of the Ukraine and came into the hands of contemporary Breslav Chasidim. Fleer recounts how the Scroll came into his hands as part of a number of writings that he received from R. Yechiel Michel Dorfman.[54]

---

53 R. Gedaliah Fleer grew up in the United States, grew close to the world of Breslav Chasidism through his teacher, R. Zvi Rosenfeld. Today he lives in Jerusalem.

54 He was one of the few Breslav Chasidim who continued to make the pilgrimage to R. Nachman's grave on Rosh Hashana even under the Communist regime. Today he is considered to be the 'Elder of the Inner Circle' and heads the central Breslav yeshiva in Mea She'arim, Jerusalem – Ha'or Haneelam (Hidden Light).

R. Alter Tepliker at the entrance to R. Nachman's memorial
(The building was constructed by R. Nachman's second wife).

He presented me with a small handwritten book penned by Rav Alter Tepliker that included many Torah insights previously published in the book 'Kokhavey Or' as well as some information about Rebbe Nachman and his followers that had never been published. Rabbi Avraham Sternhartz[55] had given this book to Rav Michel before he left the Soviet Union. It was a very rare volume. 'This book is very dear to me,' Rav Michel said. 'But if I remain in Russia so few people will ever see it and in the end it will be lost. I am giving this book to you as a gift since you will be able to take it out of the country.'[56]

The determination to remove this rare book from the borders of the communist controlled territories stemmed from a fear that the harsh conditions under which the Jewish communities in the Eastern Bloc struggled

55 For more on him, see below in Appendix B, note 13.

56 Gedaliah Fleer, *Against All Odds* (Jerusalem Breslav Research Institute 2005), 102.

could lead to its loss. This fear held especially for the Ukraine. At that time, any Jewishly orientated activity was quite dangerous and the possibility of living a religious life was severely curtailed. R. Michel worried that his would be the last generation of Breslav Chasidim in the Soviet Union, thus ending the possibility of transmitting this important book onwards.[57] Fleer relates other details concerning the book as well.

> The small book that Rav Michel gave me to take out of Russia was a manuscript transcribed by Rav Alter Tepliker, may Hashem avenge his blood. It contained many insights which Rebbe Nachman had told his disciples Reb Nason and R. Naftali regarding what would happen in the end of days. Rebbe Nachman had instructed Reb Nason to record his words in a cryptic, abbreviated form without telling anyone what he had heard. In every generation, the Rebbe said, one chassid would possess this book and it should be passed from hand to hand. A part of this book *Megilas Setarim Katzar* (A Short Book of Secrets) was contained in the manuscript that Rav Michel gave me. When I came to Israel and showed the manuscript to Rav Hirsch Leib Lippel[58] he told me that it really belonged to him. He said that after Rav Alter had transcribed the book he left it with his son[59] and Rav Hirsch Leib had bought the book from him for fifty rubles. However when he was ready to leave Russia Rav Hirsch Leib was afraid to take the book with him so he left it with Rabbi Avraham Sternhartz. Rabbi Avraham in turn gave the manuscript to Rav Michel who had married his granddaughter. 'Rav Michel gave you this book so that it should reach me because it is mine,' Rav Hirsch Leib insisted. 'But don't be frightened.

---

57 Ibid., 100.

58 R. Hirsch Leib died in 1980. For more on him see Fleer, *Against All Odds*, *151-9

59 I am not certain which son is meant. R. Alter had three sons: R. Shmuel Shmelka (Shternfeld, *Gidulei Hanachal*, 14), R. David (Rav Mordechai Frank, "*Mevo*," in *Biur Halikutim*, ed. Rav Avraham Chazan (1993), 9.), and R. Eliezer, who lived in Tscherin (*Siach Sorfei Kodesh*, book 5, 216). It is most reasonable to assume that R. Eliezer is meant, as tradition holds that he inherited his father's writings (Frank, "*Mevo*," 10).

If it is in your possession it means that it was supposed to be in your possession. Just allow me to look at it.'[60]

This information enables us to reconstruct the circumstances of the *Scroll*'s history – or at least of one of its copies – from the days of R. Nachman himself until today. R. Nachman revealed the contents of the Scroll orally to R. Natan and R. Naftali. R. Natan recorded this on a scroll and left it in a pouch with other writings. R. Nachman of Tscherin, who was responsible for the writings of R. Natan after his death, and published many of them,[61] saw the Scroll and commented upon it in his commentary to *Yemei Moharnat*. R. Alter of Teplik, his faithful assistant who helped him copy many of the manuscripts,[62] also helped copy the *Scroll* found amongst R. Natan's writings. R. Alter was murdered in a pogrom that occurred in Teplik in 1919 and the copies that he made remained in his son's hands. R. Hirsch Leib bought these from the son, but upon leaving Russia for Israel was forced to leave them with R. Avraham Sternhartz. R. Avraham Sternhartz passed them on to R. Michel, who was married to his granddaughter and then they were given to Fleer who got them out of the Soviet Ukraine.[63]

After the Hebrew version of my book was published, I was lucky enough to view the manuscript itself. It is in the possession of R. Leibel Berger, a friend of Fleer's and his companion on some of his journeys to Uman. He eventually purchased it from Fleer. I am grateful that he allowed me both to see and to include a copy of it in this book.

---

60 Fleer, *Against All Odds*, 173.

61 For more on him, see Shternfeld, *Gidulei Hanachal*, 74 and Koenig, *Neveh Tzadkim*, 76, 138 and 44.

62 See Shternfeld, *Gidulei Hanachal*, 13-14.

63 For further discussion of these and other sources on the existence of the *Scroll* and its transmission history, see Appendix A.

Knowledge of the Scroll and Knowledge of its secret

Our attempt to reconstruct the history of the *Scroll's* transmission has still not enabled us to explain the story surrounding Tziril, R. Aaron of Lipvotsk's daughter, and how R. Aaron had taught it to R. Avraham son of R. Nachman Chazan. Earlier we mentioned that this story presents us with a number of inconsistencies regarding the fact that others, such as R. Nachman of Tscherin and R. Alter of Teplik, knew of the *Scroll*. (We will also see that according to some of the *Scroll's* manuscript versions R. Zalman of Medvedevka[64] not only knew of the Scroll, but had even copied it).[65]

In some of my discussions with Breslav Chasidim, the argument was raised that there is a real difference between knowing *of* the *Scroll*, and even knowing what is written in it, and actually understanding its secret meaning. The story concerning Tziril and the end of the chain of transmission, may only relate to knowledge of its esoteric message, not knowledge of its existence. Therefore, even if R. Nachman of Tscherin saw the *Scroll*, this does not mean that he understood its true meaning. In his youth, he had not considered himself to be a student of R. Natan and only after the latter's death did he come to accept that R. Natan had been the central conduit of R. Nachman's teachings.[66] It is not all that reasonable, then, to conclude that R. Natan would have chosen to reveal the secret of the *Scroll* to him. Rather, as we see from R. Nachman of Tscherin's comments in *Yemei Moharnat*, his discovery of the *Scroll* was merely a

64 See the end of the second section of the *Scroll*. R. Zalman Medvedevka was one of the outstanding students of R. Natan. R. Zalman was the son of R. Yeshayahu Shalom, who was the son of R. Yudel of Doshiv. All three served as rabbis in Mevedevka. The grandfather, R. Yudel, was one of R. Nachman's longtime students. He received from him the secret tale, 'Tale of the Bread'. (For more on this, see Mark, "*The Tale of the Bread – a Hidden Story of R. Nachman of Braslav*." 420, 423 and fn. 54 there). The father, R. Shalom, preserved an interesting vision of R. Nachman that is known from no other source. (I am currently preparing an article on this, '*Mivchan Haotiot*' (in preparation). See also, Shternfeld, *Gidulei Hanachal*, 29.

65 The Tziril narrative does not fit the transmission history as presented by R. Schik in his book *Pualat Tzadik*.

66 See Shternfeld, *Gidulei Hanachal*, 74.

coincidence. It was found in the pouch along with other writings. Even R. Alter of Teplik, who copied the *Scroll* and other manuscripts, may not have necessarily understood the true meaning of what he had copied.[67] Others who have encountered the *Scroll* may also have read the text, but not deciphered its meaning. Thus the *Scroll* may have remained hidden even after being discovered. Its true meaning was only known to a single individual in each generation. R. Naftali passed this secret to R. Aaron Lipvotzker; he to R. Avraham Chazan. But there the secret ended. So, according to these Breslav Chasidim, while many may know of the *Scroll's* existence, not a soul knows its secret.

This claim is supported by the cryptic nature of the *Scroll* itself. Only an abbreviated short-hand of the discourse given by R. Nachman on the coming of the redeemer was recorded. The singular individual, who knew the secret of the *Scroll*, knew not only how to decode its acronyms, but also the oral tradition of the complete discourse of which the *Scroll* is only a partial record. The last such person was R. Avraham Chazan.

3. MANUSCRIPTS

In my possession are photocopies of two manuscripts of the *Scroll*. The first, and more important, is that of R. Alter of Teplik. The second is known as *Sichot Me'anash*. It is a contemporary copy which included the copyist's name, but was purposely erased from the pamphlet. I have seen additional manuscripts which are themselves copies of these two.

---

67 In a converstation which I had with one of the central rabbis of the Breslav community, he claimed in no uncertain terms that, 'R. Alter is not trustworthy,' with the implication that his manuscript was not to be trusted. On the Shabbat after our conversation, he made the same point in a public sermon before hundreds of Breslav Chasidim. It appears that this a proactive move taken before the publication of this book, designed to ensure that it would not be uncritically received. I have no doubt that the Tepliker manuscript is complete trustworthy. There is no reason to doubt his testimony that he copied the Scroll from the writings of R. Natan. Among various Chasidim, all considered experts in Breslav manuscripts, with whom I discussed the matter, not one mentioned any reservations about R. Tepliker.

The Teplik Manuscript

The traditional provenance of this manuscript is that it was written by R. Moshe Yehoshua Bezshilansky, known as R. Alter of Teplik. This seems reasonable enough given some of the manuscript's details and can be proven through comparison to some letters written in the hand of R. Alter.[68] This manuscript is part of a longer work which includes copies of various other Breslav works. Aside from the Scroll, the most important work is *Sefer Hashmatot Mechayei Moharan*, a list of addenda to *Yemei Moharan*. This book is described by R. Natan Zvi Koenig in *Neveh Tzadikim*. He writes that it is 'a collection of missing parts of manuscripts which were collected by the Rav, the Chasid, R. Moshe Yehoshua known as R. Alter of Teplik containing oral traditions which were not recorded for a number of secret reasons which the Rebbe warned against revealing.'[69] (The manuscript is in all likelihood the source for the printed booklet, *Sefer Hashmatot Mechayei Moharan*, which was bound together with the work, *Yemei Hatlaot* (*Days of Hardships*) in 1833 by R. Shmuel Horowitz.[70] This work includes the secret 'Tale of the Armor' and 'Tale of the Bread.')

The *Sefer Hashmatot Mechayei Moharan* contains an introduction written by its copyist.

> This is a collection of additions to *Chayei Moharan* which were left out at the time of printing. Included here are both complete texts as well as ends of certain texts which were only partially printed: Notice is given that the pagination and the letters noted here regarding the printed text of *Chayei Moharan* refer to the first printing of the text in Lemberg in the year, 'this will console us from our deeds', 1876. Also contained here

68 See below in Appendix A.

69 Koenig, *Neveh Tzadikim*, 193-4.

70 Apparently when he was in Ukraine R. Shmuel Horowitz copied from this manuscript.

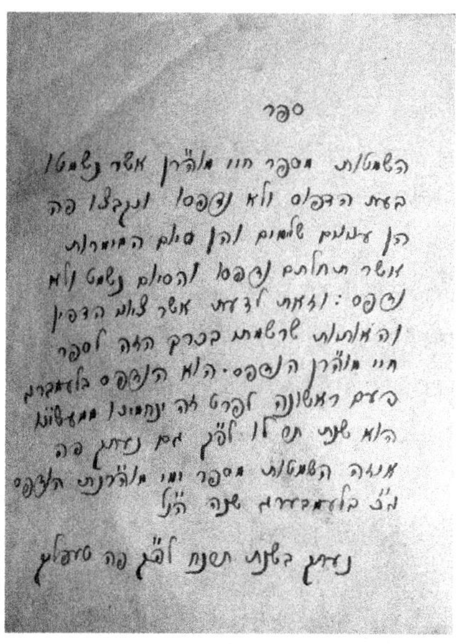

ספר

השמטות מספר חיי מוהר"ן אשר נשמטו
בעת הדפוס ולא נדפסו ונקבצו פה
הן ענינים שלמים והן סיום המאמרות
אשר תחלתם נדפסו והסיום נשמט ולא
נדפס: [illegible] לדעת אשר [illegible] הדפין
והוספות שרשמתי בכרך הזה לספר
חיי מוהר"ן הנדפס. הוא הנדפס בלעמברג
בפעם ראשונה [illegible] ממעשיות
הוא שנת תר"ן לפ"ק גם נדפס פה
איזה השמטות מספר ימי מוהרנ"ת הנדפס
ג"כ בלעמבערג שנה הנ"ל

נכתב בשנת תרנ"ח לפ"ק פה טעפליק

are additions from *Yemei Moharnat* which was printed in Lemberg in the same year. Written in 1898 in Teplik.[71]

These details accord with R. Alter's personal history. He had been the assistant of R. Nachman of Tscherin, who had published both *Chayei Moharan* and *Yemei Moharnat.* Additionally, he had spent much time copying and editing a variety of other manuscripts.[72] The year mentioned in the introduction, 1898, was four years after his death. Teplik, of course, was the home of R. Alter.

After *Sefer Hashmatot Mechayei Moharan,* the *Scroll* appears, also preceded by an introduction.

A copy of the work known as the *Scroll of Secrets* from the hand of our teacher,[73] R. Natan,[copied] letter for letter – that which he heard from

71 This introduction was printed in Koenig, *Neveh Tzadikim.*

72 For more on him, see Shternfeld, *Gidulei Hanachal*, 13-4 and Frank, "Mevo," 8-10.

73 On the way in which the text was transcribed using acronyms and abbreviations, see fn. 1 in the next chapter.

our Rebbe, the flowing fount of wisdom, concerning the coming of our righteous redeemer (he should come speedily in our day). I copied this from a volume of *Chayei Moharan* which had belonged to R. Naftali written by R. Natan himself.

The size, format and style of both manuscripts – *Sefer Hashmatot* and the *Scroll* – are the same and appear to have been written by the same individual. The one discrepancy between the two – that the *Scroll* is written in larger letters – can be explained by the fact that it is constituted of acronyms and as such needed to be copied more carefully in order to assure accuracy. Additionally, its greater importance may have thus been highlighted.[74]

For some reason R. Alter copied the text of the Scroll non-chronologically, first that part which was taught in 1809 and afterwards that from 1806. In the reproduction printed below, I have arranged the two sections chronologically. (For a comparison of this manuscript with those described in *Neveh Tzadikim*, *Pe'ulat Hatzadik* (*The Acts of the Righteous*), and *Against all Odds* see appendix 3, section 1.)

The Sichot Me'anash Manuscript

This manuscript is found in a lined hard-bound notebook. On the frontispiece of the notebook is written, 'Discourses of our Friends and in addition the Secret Scroll from the manuscript of R. Natan'. The name of the copyist and the patron of the copy for whom it was made were both recorded and purposely erased. The majority of the manuscript, it is noted, 'was copied from the manuscript and booklets belonging

74 This also appears to be the case regarding the transcription of the tale concerning R. Yosef Shlomo of Kondia, the author of the book, *Alim*. This tale was printed in Chazan, *Kochvai Or*, 29. This tale is not part of the Scroll. It was written on the back of the title page of the Scroll in crowded, tight script – similat to *Hashmatot Mechayei Moharan*, but unlike the *Scroll*. Weiss attempted to connect this tale with the *Scroll*, see Weiss, *Studies in Bratslav Hasidism*, 213.

to R. Nosson Liebermensch.'[75] However, it also contains, 'discourses copied from manuscripts belonging to R. Moshe Glidman and from those heard by R. Levy Yitzchak Brand.'[76] At the top of each page upon which the *Scroll* is copied appears, 'The Scroll of Secrets, copied from the manuscript of R. Nosson Liebermensch.' This version contains only the second of the original discourses – that delivered on Friday, Marcheshvan 8, 1809.

In the introduction to the *Scroll* we find only slight variations between it and the Teplik version aside from the mention that, 'I copied this from a volume of *Yemei Moharan* which had belonged to R. Naftali written by R. Natan himself.' This indicates that this version was copied from another copy, and not from the book which belonged to R. Naftali.

After the conclusion of the *Scroll* and some comments by the copyist concerning his sources, on the same line with no break, there appears another comment which opens, 'I heard from R. Avraham the son of R. Nachman of Tulchin who said...' Here we find the words of R. Nachman of Tulchin, recorded in a censored and abbreviated version in *Neveh Tzadikim,* in full.[77] From this we can infer that this manuscript and that which belonged to R. Zvi Koenig share a common source which differs from that of the Teplik manuscript.

In this version of the *Scroll,* many of the acronyms are written in full with no indication that this is not the original form. In one section the acronyms are left intact, but deciphered in parentheses. In another section, the full meaning of the acronyms is given in footnotes. At times, the copyist was doubtful as to the proper meaning of the acronym and noted this either with a question mark or the word, 'perhaps.' There is evidence of changes in opinion as to the meaning of certain acronyms, as we find that in some places a particular word

---

75 R. Nosson Liebermensch, one of the well-known *mashpi'im* (spiritual influencers) among Breslav today, was a member of the World Council of Chasidei Breslav.

76 He died in 1989.

77 See above in the text at note 47.

was written, erased and then written over with another word.[78] It appears that the decoding of the acronyms was the work of the copyist himself who had no oral or written tradition upon which he based his deciphering.

We can also infer from these corrections that the Liebermensch manuscript itself contained many undeciphered acronyms which the copyist attempted to unravel himself. However, the similarity between this manuscript and the Koenig manuscript raises the possibility that this copyist also worked from a manuscript in which a number of the abbreviations were in fact written out in full. Koenig mentions regarding his manuscript: 'many acronyms were deciphered.'[79] Others, however, needed to be decoded by the copyist himself.[80]

It is my opinion that many of the suggested solutions to the acronyms found in the *Sichot* manuscript are mistaken. That the decoding found therein was so faulty also strengthens the assumption that it was the work of the copyist himself.

---

78 For example, the acronym '*beit-beit*' was written out as *ben-beno* (the son of his son), yet afterwards he changed the letter *nun* of *ben* and added a *vav*. He also erased the second word *beno* and wrote above it *bechoro* – thus rendering the acronym as *beno-bechoro* (the son of his first-born). See Appendix C for more details.

79 Koenig, *Neveh Tzadikim*, 79.

80 It is important to note that R. Koenig was the brother-in-law of R. Liebermensch.

SECTION TWO

Deciphering the Tepliker Manuscript[1]

SECTION I

A copy of the work called the Scroll of Secrets From the hand of our teacher, our teacher, the rabbi, R. Natan, of blessed memory Letter for letter as heard by our teacher, the rabbi, R. Natan Of blessed memory, from the mouth of our leader, teacher and rabbi, the holy – the fount of flowing wisdom – the entire course of the coming of the righteous redeemer, may he come speedily in our day, amen. I copied this copy from a volume of the book *Chayei Moharan* which had been in the hands of R. Naftali, of blessed memory. This volume was in the handwriting of our teacher and rabbi, R. Natan, of blessed memory. The year 566[2] (with no thousands), on Sunday 5 Menachem [Av] … and more. After … At every half-year. And will study/teach the …. And at the beginning …. And he will send epistles to all of the wise-men and they will send him the sons of the kings and each one will write to his father until each one will give. Afterwards he will exchange with the Sultan and if it is too far then he will exchange it with another, and another with another. And he will go there with all Israel and then he will be the king of Israel, this will be after ten years.

---

1 Square brackets are additions added by the author or translator while round brackets are found in the original manuscript. See note 27 below.

2 The original reads 567, but this seems to be a mistake. The year 566 appears in *Yemei Moharnat*. Unfortunately, in both 5567 (1805-6) and 5566 (1806-7), the fifth of Av falls on a Sunday. This, then, cannot help determine the proper year.

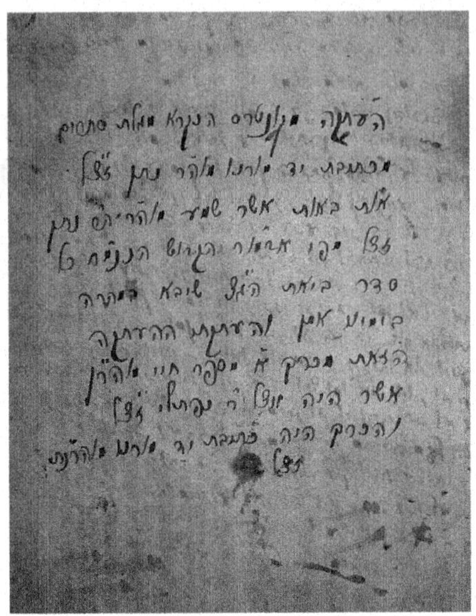

Afterwards he will travel to all the kings … and he will make for them customs similar to Israel's religion[3]
Also there will be prayers that the nations will pray. He will preach a learned[4]
sermon and there will be
… even those that do not understand much will see the elders
and start saying amen, amen.

---

3 The expression, *dat yisrael* (Israel's religion) appears in *Chayei Moharan* in the context of 'repairing' the nations of the world: 'I can return all of the world's nations to Blessed God and I could have brought them all to Israel's religion [*Chayei Moharan Im Hashmatot*, (Jerusalem: 2000), 264].

4 This is a translation of the term *chiluk* (distinction), which has a central place in the history of the 'pilpulistic' school of Torah scholarship. Its original meaning denoted the distinguishing between different concepts and cases, but eventually it came to be used as a term connoting a sermon based on this exacting intellectual style. For example, in the book, *Ben Porat Yosef*, a long piece of this nature is titled '*Chiluk* of the Author from His Days of Sharp Study in The Yeshiva' [Rav Yaakov Yosef of Polnoy, *Ben Porat Yosef* (New York: 1954), 183]. See also Aharon Wertheim, *Halachot Vehalichot BeChasidut* (1989), 234-5. The term, *chiluk*, saw continued use in later generations as well. For instance, a poster advertising a lecture by the Ilui of Rokov announced that the '*chiluk* will commence at …' [Ha'ilui of Rokov, *Kitvei Ha'ilui of Rokov: Mesridei Izvono Shel Echad Megdolei Yahadut Lita*, ed. Tzvi Kaplan (Jerusalem: 1963), 2]. For a discussion of this term see Chaim Zalman Demitrovsky, "Al Derech Hapilpul," in *Sefer Hayovel Lechvod Shalom Baron Lemelot Lo Shemonim Shana*, ed. Shaul Liberman (Jerusalem: 1975).

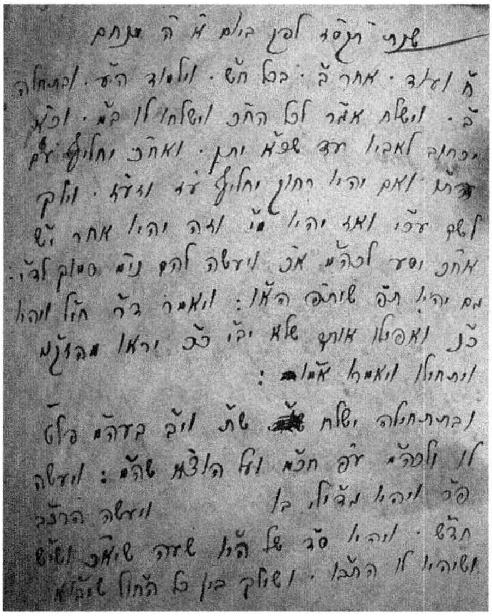

At the outset[5] he will send … and he will build in the king's city a palace
For him and for all the kings in accord with wisdom and with the expenditures of
the kings. He will make
an orchard and growing in it and he will make
new compounds.[6] The daily schedule will be an hour in which he will eat and will drink
and he will practice contemplative religious introspection. He will walk amongst all the sick that come
and quickly command each what he should take – each effective things
from the same orchard, from the new compounds. He will have a chair
carried by able men and he will walk a few steps
and they will lower the chair for him and he will sit. There will be a choir[7]
with musical instruments[8] and they will sing each time.
Every individual … today except [that/for] the nations

---

5 The Hebrew text here reads *uvattchila*, but should be *uvatchila*.

6 See below note 21.

7 The term used here, *kapela*, is from the Italian for choir – *capella*. R. Nachman used it frequently. See, for example, *Chayei Moharan Im Hashmatot*, 109, 72. Also, *Sefer Sipurei Ma'asiot Hamenukad*, (Jerusalem: 1985), 261.

8 The Hebrew, *clei shir*, is found frequently in R. Nachman's writings. See Rav Natan of Nemirov, *Sefer Likutei Moharan Hamenukad* (Jerusalem: 1994), section one, 237. *Chayei*

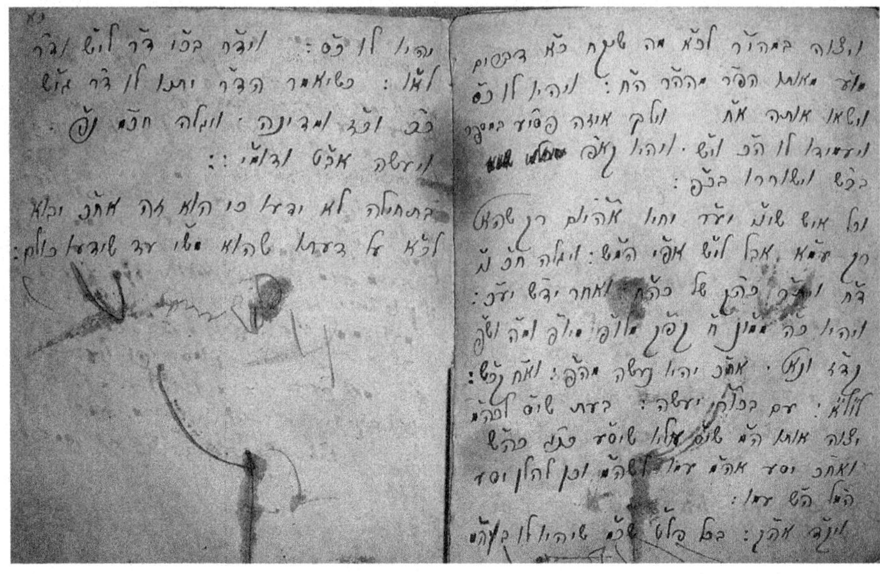

just … but for Israel even the messiah. And he will reveal great wisdom
new things … all the precedents[9] of all the wisdom
After[10] fourteen years ….
There will be five/twenty-five new appointees…
…Afterwards there will be made from the … and afterwards …
… with the youth he will do it. At the time that he will travel to all the kings
This king will command all the ministers to travel to him.
Afterwards this king will travel with him to the other kings and so
the second king will travel with him.
He will sanctify the holy land. In each palace of every king that will be in the king's city
there will be a chair. Each day he will preach a sermon to Israel and a sermon
to the nations. When he preaches this sermon they give him a sermon-gift[11]
silver vessels, gold vessels and lands. He will reveal wondrous wisdom

---

Moharan Im Hashmatot, Sipurim Chadashim, 109 *Sefer Sipurei Ma'asiot Hamenukad*, 19, 80.

9 'Each type of wisdom has its precedents and they are called servants to wisdom' (*Likutei Moharan Hamenukad*, section one, 64:6). Also see there 21:1; 25:1,6; 60:1.

10 The Hebrew script is not clear and perhaps it should read 'and after'.

11 The term, *drasha geshank*, is a gift given to the speaker by those who hear his sermon. It appears in the *Tale of the Seven Beggars*: 'I give you a present for the sermon, which is called a *drasha geshank*' (*Sefer Sipurei Ma'asiot*, 243).

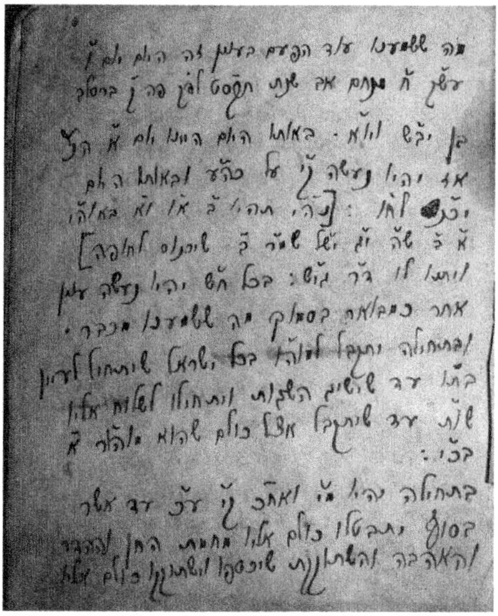

and will make precious stones and jewels.[12] At first they will not recognize that he is the one, afterwards each one will come to acknowledge that he is the messiah until all know [this].

SECTION II

That which we heard again about this matter today on Friday Sabbath eve, 8 Menachem Av 569 (with no thousands) here in the town of Breslav. Twelve years and one-day old. On this day, that is the day mentioned above, Then he will become emperor over the entire world and on that day he will enter under the wedding canopy. (… [She will] be[13] … [eleven]-and-a-day[14] on that day … … On that day when he will marry.) They will give him a sermon-gift. Every half-year something else will happen, as explained above as we have already heard. Initially he will be accepted as the halachic authority throughout Israel as he

---

12 The Yiddish term here is *domiten*. It appears in the 'Tale of the Fly and the Mouse' (*Sefer Sipurei Ma'asiot*, 67) as well as in the 'Tale of the Lame One' (ibid., 32).

13 The copyist apparently switched a *nun* for a *vav* here.

14 The copyist apparently switched *yud-alef* for *alef-vav*.

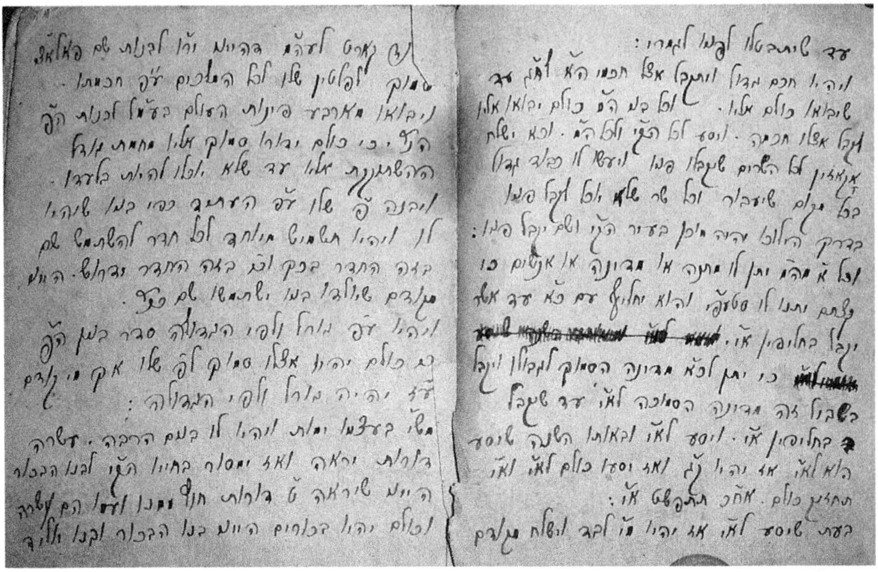

begins to scrutinize the Torah until he attains deep insights. They [will] begin to send him queries until it is accepted by all that he is the premier halachic authority. in all of Israel. Initially he will be king of Israel and afterwards emperor over all until finally all will surrender themselves to him due to the favor, glory, love and yearning that they will all feel towards him until they will completely nullify themselves before him. He will be great in wisdom and accepted by the wisemen of the nations as great in wisdom until all come to him. And all the sons of the kings all will come to him to receive wisdom from him. And he will travel to all the emperors and to all the kings. And each will send a royal command[15] to all the ministers that they shall receive him and honor him greatly in every place where he will pass. Any minister who cannot receive him on his journey's path will ready himself in the emperor's city and there he will receive him. Each of the kings will give him a present – or a country or a people

15 The Yiddish term used here is *okozin*. This term appears in the 'Tale of the King's Son': The king sent his command (called *okozin*) after him, and they brought it to the king' (*Sefer Sipurei Ma'asiot*, 55).

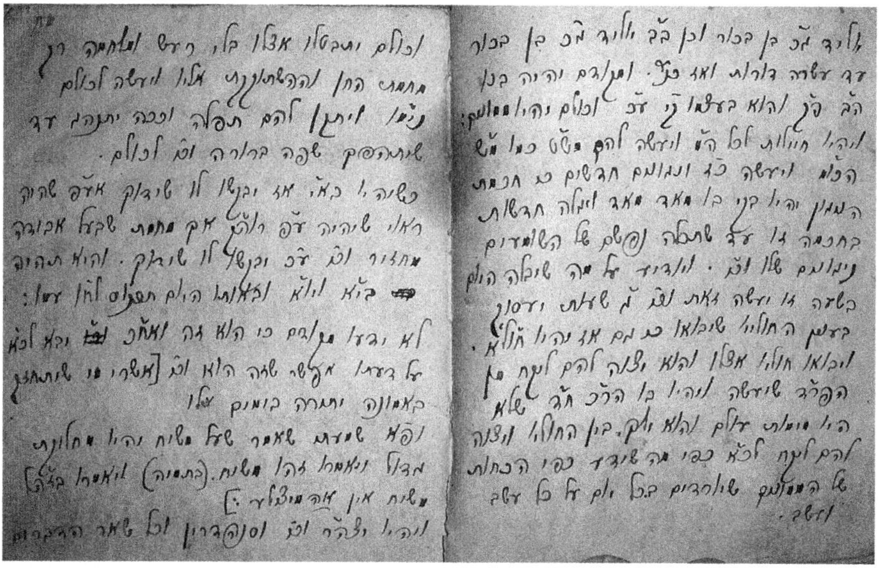

And some will give him a stipend[16] and he will exchange with each of them until he receives through barter the Land of Israel. That is, he will give to each the country near his border and receive for this a country closer to the Land of Israel until he receives through barter the Land of Israel. He will travel to the Land of Israel and in that year in which he travels To the Land of Israel then the ingathering of the exiles will occur and then all will travel to the Land of Israel and the Land of Israel will have room for all. Afterwards the Land of Israel will expand. At the time that he will travel to the Land of Israel he will be the only king of Israel and he will send ahead a map[17] to the capital city, that is Jerusalem, to build there palaces near his own palace for all the kings according to his wisdom. From the four corners of the world artisans will arrive to build these palaces mentioned above. Because everyone will live nearby him due to their great yearning for him such that they cannot be without him.

16 From the Yiddish *stipendiah*.

17 The Yiddish here is '*landkart*', which is used several times in *Sefer Sipurei Ma'asiot*. For example, in the 'Tale of the Master of Prayer' 'Afterwards all was enscribed on the same hand, for he would thus enscribe the place of each world in detail just as one writes on a *landkart* ....' (*Sefer Sipurei Ma'asiot*, 99).

He will build his palace in accord with the future, according to the children he will have. There will be a unique use for each room
this room will be used for such, etc. and in this room he will sermonize. That is,
before his children are born he will use them as mentioned above.
By lot and by high standing the building of the palaces will be ordered
for everyone will be near his palace but the absolute proximity,
this will be according to lot and high standing.
The messiah himself will die but he will have many children. Ten
generations will he see, and then will pass on, while still alive, the empire to his first-born son.
That is, he will see nine generations aside from himself – including himself, ten.
All will be first-born sons. That is, his first-born son and his son will
sire[18] also a first-born son and so too the son of his son will sire also a
first-born son
for ten generations and then as mentioned above. And before this,
his first-born son will be the viceroy[19] and he himself the emperor over all. And all will be appointed.

---

18 There is a transcription error here – the word *yolid* (sire) is repeated.

19 The Hebrew here is a two letter abbreviation *peh-kuf*, which I believe should be read as *palgei-kaisar* in light of this Talmudic source. The Talmud (TB Sanhedrin 98b) relates a discussion concerning the identity of the messiah. Rav states: 'In the future God will bring another David'. That is, the historical King David will not become the messiah, but rather

There will be a host of soldiers for every king and he will give them orders*
Like the order of the stars and planets.[20] And he will make new musical instruments and songs, for his genius
in song will be very great. He will innovate in this art such that the souls of those who hear
his songs will faint. And he will announce what he will do each day
at this hour such an activity, etc. For three hours he will treat the
sick that will come, as even then there will be illness.
The sick will come to him and he will instruct them to take from
The orchard which he will make containing the new compounds[21] the likes of which
have never been before. He will go among the sick and instruct

---

another will take his place. Rav Papa asks: '[Is is not written] "David my servant will rule them forever"?' Abayei answers: 'Like a Ceasar and a palgei (vice) Ceasar.' Another reading of the *peh-kuf* could be *printz-kaisar* or *pakid* (officer).

20 Behind this sentence lies the verse from Job: 'Do you know the order of heaven? Did you establish its rule over Earth?' (Job 38:33). This verse suggests that heavenly constellations influence the earth. The notion of such influence is found elsewhere in the Scroll – in the description of the messiah as the maker of medicinal compounds in accord with 'the powers of the appointed angels who daily visit each blade of grass.' See the following note.

21 R. Nachman mentioned the proper preparation of medicinal compounds in several of his discourses. For instance in the discourse, 'Ask R.Yosi,' he writes: 'All cures are compounds – that is one takes this drug and this herb in such and such an amount, another herb in such an amount, and one weighs several types. Each herb has its own particular potency. They are all combined and from this, one makes a [healing] compound (Nemirov, *Sefer Likutei Moharan Hamenukad*, section one, 57:8). The connection that R. Nachman makes between the various medicinal properties of each herb and the heavenly host's influence on each blade of grass is related to the order that an individual makes in his own world to correspond with the system of the Zodiac. The messiah arranges his own troops 'like the astrological system.' This is found in *Likutei Moharan* as well. 'When one reaches the verse [in the *Alaynu* prayer], "and the hosts of heaven prostrate themselves to You," it is fitting to pray for each and every thing. For all healing is through the powers of the constellations which are the heavenly hosts. Each gives strength to a particular drug and herb that belongs to it. From them the drugs and herbs receive their healing potency. When one requires healing, one combines several of these potencies from the constellations which give strength to each such that they combine. So one makes a healing compound' (*Likutei Moharan*, section one, 241). The source for this trope is found in an earlier midrash. 'Bar Sira said: "God has raised plants from the earth so that the doctor can heal wounds and prepare healing compounds." R. Simon said: "There is no plant which lacks a star in the heavens which strikes it, saying, 'Grow!' That is, 'Do you know the order of heaven? Did

each of them to take that which he knows according to the powers of the appointed angels who daily visit[22] each blade of grass. All will surrender themselves to him with neither war nor struggle in light of his beauty and their longing for him. He will fix for everyone practices and make for them prayer. Thus he will do until all turn to one clear tongue.[23] When he will be in the Land of Israel, they will search for a match for him even though it is proper that his match be made through divine knowledge. However, just as one who has lost an object [seeks] its return, etc.[24] therefore a match will be searched out for him. She will be eleven and one day, on that day, will enter under the wedding canopy with him. They will not know at first that he is the one. Afterwards, each will reach his own conclusion and will consider that it is possible that this is him etc. (Happy will be the strong of faith in those days. Once I heard that he said concerning the messiah there will be a mighty argument. And they will say, 'This is the messiah?!' They will say in these words, 'The messiah isn't a fancy hat!')[25] The evil inclination and the Sanhedrin and all those things that [once] were will be [again] but each thing will be much more pleasant than before. Each and every one according to his station will have his eyes opened in wisdom and will gain great new understanding, better than before – each in accord with his station. [Of] the days of the messiah there is much discussion in the Tractate Sanhedrin in

---

you establish its rule over Earth?'" ["*Breishit Rabbah*," ed. Theodor Bialik (Jerusalem: 1965), 78-9.]

22 See above note 20.

23 'For then I will turn the nations to one clear tongue that all should proclaim the name of God and worship Him together' (Zephaniah 3:9).

24 This follows the *gemara*: 'Why is it the way of man to pursue the woman and not of the woman to pursue the man? A parable – If one loses an object [Rashi: one of his ribs], who seeks whom? The one who lost something pursues that which he lost' (TB Kidushin 72b).

25 The term here is the Yiddish *mitzeleh* – an expensive hat worn by the rich. 'R. Nachman said: I saw that all of my followers will be poor – therefore I influenced the Holy One so that he should toss a *mitzeleh* among them' [*Siach Sorfei Kodesh*, vol. 1-5 (Jerusalem: 1994), book 2, 32]. His intention is that there should always be a wealthy member of the Breslav circle.

the chapter
'Portion' [-] how long they will be. There are opinions that it will only last forty years
And there are other opinions concerning this.) See there.
His traveling wardrobe, what his attire will be, what will be his name.
Before the messiah will arrive, the grandchild/ren of the Baal Shem Tov will come before all the kings
And master their written and spoken language.
(The general rule: Despite what has transgressed during
the near 2000 year exile, we expect that he will arrive any day.
Even if he should tarry, we await him [for] he will surely come and not be late.
Even though all the ends [of days] have come and gone, he will certainly come and be beautiful
and very pleasant. Happy is he who merits this – may he strengthen his faith then.
Regarding his being a halachic authority mentioned above, it seems that he said that
he will be three years old and then he will be accepted as the authoritative teacher in all of Israel.
Also, the text is missing what he discussed: that he may be poor[26] at one time.
Many other matters were forgotten, may the Blessed One grant us to see [him]
speedily soon in our day.
He said that regarding this matter everyone knows a bit, but he
knows everything.)

Thus says the copyist – these things in round parentheses[27]
I did not find in the manuscript of R. Natan, may his memory be a blessing.
I only copied that which I saw in the copy of the rabbi and righteous teacher
R. Zalman of Medvedevkah, may his memory be a blessing which was written in his
hand.[28]

---

26 This follows the famous description of the messiah in Zachariah: '… behold, your king will arrive, righteous and victorious, riding a donkey' (9:9). This description has echoed throughout Jewish tradition.

27 See note 1 above.

28 From this it is obvious that R. Alter had seen both the manuscript written by R. Natan as well as that of R. Zalman of Medvedevkah which contained the text in parenthesis.

SECTION THREE

CHAPTER ONE

The Messiah as a Breslavian Tzadik: Made in the Image of R. Nachman

The *Scroll of Secrets* is a small vessel containing much. It contains a wide variety of messianic themes, along with R. Nachman's relation to them. Some of these are emphasized in the *Scroll*, others merely hinted at. What follows in this chapter is a preliminary examination of the *Scroll*: an attempt to sketch its main concerns before a closer investigation of some of the many issues that it raises.

I want to begin by discussing the principal concept upon which the *Scroll* rests: the description of the messiah as a *tzadik* made in the image of R. Nachman himself. Understanding this point is essential to understanding both the *Scroll* and R. Nachman's own quite self-conscious conception of himself. My discussion here will be limited to those aspects of this messianism which were given voice in the *Scroll* itself and not to the many other messianic topics found throughout Breslav literature.

1. THE NATURE OF THE SCROLL

The *Scroll* is a depiction of the messianic age, and of the messiah himself, as a utopian fulfillment of the entire range of Breslav values. While these values are described in the *Scroll* in a much abbreviated form, careful reading of its contents reveals that it holds within, in a concentrated form, the very DNA out of which Breslav thought is made. The *Scroll* presents us with the process through which this messianic utopia comes into being – created through the conduct of its central figure – the messiah. While this description does not encompass the *Scroll*'s entire meaning, it does allow us to interpret a large portion of its contents.

Before turning to the messianic trope in the *Scroll* itself, however, I would like to devote some time to exploring the foundations of messianic thought in the Breslav oeuvre which point to the coming of the messiah as a fulfillment of those very values out of which R. Nachman spun Breslav Chasidism. The messiah is envisioned as the very embodiment of the Breslav *tzadik* – who is, of course, the reflection of R. Nachman himself. So first, it is worthwhile to examine the idea of R. Nachman himself qua messiah.

2. ON THE MESSIAH AS A BRESLAVIAN TZADIK AND ON R. NACHMAN'S ROLE IN THE MESSIANIC PROCESS1

> He said: Anything of benefit that the messiah will bring to Israel so too can I. The only difference is that the messiah will decide, proclaim and it will come to pass, whereas I ... (he stopped and said no more). Another version: But I cannot yet finish.[2]

This definitive statement implies that there is no difference in either spiritual powers or beneficence between R. Nachman and the messiah – excepting

1 For a clear description, see Hillel Tzeitlen, *Al Gvul Shnei Olamot* (Tel Aviv: 1997), 318-21 and 26-63. For more on Breslav messianism, see Mendel Piekarz, *Studies in Bratslav Hasidism*, expanded ed. (Jerusalem: 1996), 56-82; Arthur Green, *Tormented Master* (New York: Schocken, 1987), 182-220; Yehuda Liebes, "*Hatikun Haclali Shel R. Nachman Mebreslav Veyachaso Leshabta'ut*," in *On Sabbateanism and its Kabbalah* (Jerusalem: 1995); Joseph Dan, *Apocalypse Then and Now* (Israel: 2000), 253-63 and 309-12.

2 *Chayei Moharan Hamenukad*, (Jerusalem: 1995), 266 (26). In *Chayei Moharan Im Hashmatot* (Jerusalem: 2000) another version, which does not appear in earlier editions, is found: 'There is a version like this: With me there is still choice, but with the messiah there will be no choice' (271). This version is not found in any of the manuscripts with which I am familiar. It may be in fact a word for word copy (including 'there is a version') from an edition published by R. Eliezer Schick which included a number of additions, including this one. See *Chayei Moharan Hamenukad*, 601-2

the ability to enforce his will upon his followers.[3] This ability is not negligible and, in fact, is one of the outstanding messianic characteristics described by Maimonides. 'If a king of the lineage of David should arise… and compel all to follow and support the Torah … then he is the presumptive messiah.'[4]

A well-known oral-tradition among Breslav Chasidim preserves this same aphorism in Yiddish: 'The messiah will be obeyed, but they do not want to obey me.'[5] This version sharpens the implications of the message – if only the world would listen to him, there would be no difference between R. Nachman and the messiah. In other words, if obeyed – R. Nachman would be the messiah.[6]

This same spirit pervades the text found in the additions to the 1928 edition of *Chayei Moharan* but missing from later editions.[7]

I heard in his name that he would learn Torah with all seven shepherds. (The copyist says: See the epistle of the Baal Shem Tov which explains

3 Perhaps this even includes the possibility of influencing God as the the Talmud states: 'The righteous man proclaims and God carries out [his will] (*TB Moed Katan* 16b).

4 Maimonides MT Hilchot Melachim 11:4. My emphasis.

5 I heard this tradition from R. Avraham Weitzhandler (see above page *, fn.26) in the name of R. Levi Yitzchak Brand. It fits well with the text found in *Siach Sorfei Kodesh*: 'They said regarding … what our Rebbe claimed – that there is no difference between him and the messiah etc., "We have already merited to come to know and draw close to our Rebbe and his works – to taste the aura of his holiness. At least we will obey any command or order of his" (*Siach Sorfei Kodesh,* vol. 4, 30).'

6 This is reminiscent of R. Chaim Vital's claim that he was the Josephian messiah of his time. He related a prophecy in his *Book of Visions* concerning himself: 'Undoubtedly if all of Israel would obey him [R. Vital], redemption would come in his day [Rav Chaim Vital, *Sefer Hachizionot,* Eshkoli ed. (Jerusalem: 1954), 15].

7 The book, *Chayei Moharan,* written by R. Natan, was published by R. Nachman of Tscherin. Parts of the book, such as those including the 'Tale of the Armor' and the 'Tale of the Bread,' as well as pieces of various sentences, were censored. This was done in order to prevent the publication of those things which R. Nachman wanted concealed, as well as to supress various portions that R. Nachman of Tscherin deemed inappropriate for general consumption. Some of the manuscript versions of *Chayei Moharan* retained these deleted sections and several were added to later printed editions.

that the messiah will learn Torah with all seven shepherds.)[8] It is already noted several times in our Rebbe's works that he had in him the potential to be the messiah – if only the generation had been worthy.[9]

R. Nachman could have been messiah, but the generation that closed its ears to him was not worthy. The idea of a 'potential' messiah is certainly not new. It has a long tradition. This designation of potentiality has been affixed to various dynasties of tzadikim in different generations, to the preeminent tzadik in a given generation and, at times, even to each and every tzadik.[10] The words of S. Y. Agnon are noteworthy in this context:

> We are told in the tales of the righteous that each one considered himself to be the messiah. When one would receive a blessing to merit the coming of the messiah [in his time], he would not answer 'amen – so be it,' but rather, 'together with all of Israel' showing that he understood that he would be the messiah if only his generation would be worthy.[11]

---

8 'Then I entered the hall of the messiah where he studies Torah with all of the sages and righteous, also with the seven shepherds "*Shibchei Habesht* (Manuscript)," (1992), 235.

9 *Hashmatot Mechayei Moharan*, (Jerusalem: 1893), 39. This last sentence does not appear, however, in *Chayei Moharan Im Hashmatot*, (Jerusalem: 2000). Neither is it found in the Tepliker manuscript -Rav Alter Tepliker, "*Hashmatot Mechayei Moharan*," (1898). However, it does appear in a manuscript copied by R. Yitzchak Meir Korman: "Sefer Chayei Moharan (Manuscript)," in *Machon Schocken* 14282, 8. From the copyist's introduction we learn that it was copied from a manuscript written by R. Nachman of Tscherin and that 'only to the members of the inner circle of the tzadik … was the rest of the work *Chayei Moharan* entrusted. He told them not to reveal any of it to any others. All this was the wish of our holy Rebbe.' For more on this manuscript, see Zvi Mark, " *Ma'aseh Mehashiryon (The Tale of the Armor) – from the Hidden Chambers of Breslav Censorship*," *Zion* 70, no. 2 (2005): 194-5. On Korman himself, see there pp. 212-5.

10 This is connected to the concept of the tzadik as an individual redeemer. See Dan, *Apocalypse Then and Now*, 253-63, 309-12; Rivka Shatz Uffenheimer, *Chasidism as Mysticism* (Jerusalem: 1988), 168-77; Moshe Idel, *Messianic Mystics* (New Haven: 1998), 212-47.

11 Shmuel Yosef Agnon, *Elu Ve'elu* (Tel Aviv: 1997), 352. On the Chasidic sources drawn upon for this story, see Elchanan Shilo, "*The Use and Literary Function of Kabbalah in the Works of S. Y. Agnon*" (Bar Ilan, 2005), 77-9. For further sources on this subject, see Rav Yisachar David Kloizner, *Meshiach Bekol Dor*, pages 76-78. For other expressions regarding the

In several of his sermons, R. Nachman relates to the subject of 'potential' messiah as part of a larger discussion of the implications of such a determination.[12] But here, his statement is not theoretical, but rather comes to emphasize his own unique personal standing and his exceptional status. R. Nachman declared himself not only 'potential messiah' at present – but as the messiah in fact – if only his words would be heard and he obeyed.

As we will see below, his statement that 'the generation is not worthy' should not be interpreted as an expression of despair. R. Nachman did not abandon his aspirations to move from potential to actual. He believed that he would one day, 'learn Torah with all seven shepherds.' His claim was that even though he was not obeyed at present, in time he eventually would be heeded, thus ushering in the messianic era. His confidence that one day he would be able to 'finish' his project was expressed more than once. Certainly over the years we find distinct changes in his thought as to when this would occur, but it seems that he never abandoned the fundamental belief that in the end he would indeed complete his task.

At first, R. Nachman believed that this would all happen in his own lifetime.

> He said: Haven't my eyes already grown weary – yet I wait each day hoping that at any moment God will allow me to see you as real servants of the Lord – according to my true will. I hope with God's help that this will come to pass. Not only those of my inner circle, but even anyone who has grown close to them, even one who has barely touched them – he will certainly become a truly good man. Not just good, but even a great tzadik… He also said: then I will finish – and I will.[13]

---

messianic potential of a given generation's tzadikim, see David Asaf, *The Regal Way: the Life and Times of R. Israel of Ruzhin* (Jerusalem: 1997), 348-55.

12 See for example the discourse, 'Speak to the Priests,' Rav Natan of Nemirov, *Sefer Likutei Moharan Hamenukad* (Jerusalem: 1994), 2; the discourse 'When One Studies' (ibid., 118). On this theme see Green, *Master*, 190-97.

13 *Chayei Moharan Im Hashmatot*, 300.

But R. Nachman's hopes were dashed. His disciples who disappointed,[14] the bitter struggles and denunciations,[15] the discovery that his illness was to be terminal[16] – all these made him realize that he would not reach his goal in his own lifetime.

> Once I asked him what would become of all those things of which we had spoken? That which we heard from his holy mouth as to how he would live long and fulfill his desires, etc. He answered: 'Did you hear what he said? Even for me this is difficult.' Despite this, he said: 'I haven't finished? I have already finished and I will finish!'[17]

The details of R. Nachman's desires are hidden behind the 'etc.' in this quote. However, we already know that the fulfillment of his wishes was that which separated him from the messiah. So, we may infer that what he truly wanted was to tear down this partition and become the very one who would grant the Children of Israel all that was promised by the messianic age.

R. Natan's question shows that, more than once, he heard optimistic words from R. Nachman regarding his ability to fulfill his wishes. In *Chayei Moharan* we see evidence of this: 'When I will be old like R. Baruch of

---

14 'He once said … didn't I think that you would all be *tzadikim* – great *tzadikim* with such intellegence that for many generations there was no intellegence like this. But now they have broken us like shattered pottery' (Ibid., 250). 'Once our Rebbe complained: "Even though you are good men, I didn't want only this. I meant that I would have men who would howl all night long like animals in the forest"' (*Siach Sorfei Kodesh*, vol. 1-5 (Jerusalem: 1994), 31.

15 For sources on the opposition to R. Nachman, see Zvi Mark, " *Why Did R. Moses Zvi of Savran Persecute R. Nathan of Nemirov and Breslav Chasidim?*," *Zion* 69, no. 4 (2004): 487 fn.1.

16 'When the cough [tuberculosis] came upon him, immediately, even from the first cough, he knew that he was going to die and began to speak of his passing – even though … he lived for more than another three years. Even so, already in the summer of 1807 when he grew ill, he began to to speak of his passing' (*Chayei Moharan Im Hashmatot*, 193).

17 Ibid., 260.

Mezibush, I will surely sit in a house of silver and gold'.[18] The optimism here reflects both on attaining old age and on recognition and honor as well.

Sometime later, however, R. Natan came to realize that his Master's optimism had been exchanged for a more sober appreciation that he would never grow old. Those hopes he had pinned on his mature years were gone. He had no answer to his disciple's query – even for R. Nachman himself this realization was 'difficult.' But in the same breath, he claimed that he had in fact finished. He had already accomplished that which he set out to do and his deeds would lead to the fulfillment of his desires.

Merely six months before his death this subject would again be raised.

> Also when we traveled to Uman together, he spoke to me concerning [the idea] that God always completes.... At first when we grew close to him, he had contemplated finishing his task of repair at once, as we had discussed several times. Afterwards, due to our great sins and the sins of the generation, as well as the great attacks of the Evil One which brought the controversy which hounded him, the world became confused and he could not accomplish in his life-time that which he had intended. Despite all this, though, he said that he had finished and that he would finish (as mentioned above). For after he arrived from Lemberg, he began on this path and spoke of these things – that his light would never be extinguished. And I heard in his name that he had said, 'My flame will burn until the messiah comes.' Speedily in our day, amen.[19]

The fire that R. Natan found in Breslav, and that he prayed for nights on end should 'burn in his heart,'[20] was the flame that would ignite the

18 Tepliker, "*Hashmatot Mechayei Moharan,*" 16 in the photocopied pages. The same sentiment (in slightly different language) appears in *Chayei Moharan Im Hashmatot*, 297.

19 *Chayei Moharan Im Hashmatot*, 260.

20 'He would go out of the town of Breslav to the nearby river Bik and would yell the entire night... "Master of the World – here a fire is burning ... let such a fire burn in my heart"' (*Siach Sorfei Kodesh*, 31).

coming of the messiah – of whom it is written, 'his candle will never be extinguished.'[21] The words of R. Nachman, 'but I cannot yet finish,' must be read with an emphasis on the 'yet.' R. Nachman was speaking only of the present – but was confident that the still glowing embers which he had kindled would in the end burst into flames and finish what he had begun. These embers were his words of Torah – especially those that he taught after returning from Lemberg. It was his expressive force – poured into them – that would keep them lit forever.

Understanding this latter point is essential if we are to understand the role of R. Nachman, as he himself understood it, in the entire messianic process. After his hopes of actually ushering in the messianic age in his own day failed, he realized that his work would be done, not through direct leadership of a court as is usual for a tzadik, but rather through his words: his discourses and his words of Torah which would long survive him. These would finish the work that he had begun until the arrival of the righteous redeemer.

It was this understanding that influenced his disciples after his death. His statement, 'My flame will burn until the messiah comes' was heard not merely as a prophecy, but as an injunction which called upon them to act.

> He then mentioned that there were many great men who had done what they could, repaired all that they were able to, but whose works had then ended. His meaning was that the enlightenment that they had effected in their students – having brought a few closer to God – had ended. But we need to ensure that this will never occur. Students will teach others, then these yet others and so on forever. This is what I heard – that our inner circle must influence others – their friends and students. Everyone must do something in order to enlighten his fellow, then he others, as well. For every tree has branches, and these branches spread out into other

---

21 'Gladden us Lord, our God, with Eliyahu the prophet Your servant and with the reign of the House of David your messiah, may he come speedily and gladden our hearts…for in Your Holy Name have You sworn to him that his candle will never be extinguished' (The Blessing after the reading of the Haftorah).

> branches, and so forth. That which he said is already recorded in another place– 'My flame will burn forever, never will it be extinguished.' As he said in Yiddish, 'My flame will burn until the messiah comes.'[22]

This method of proselytizing depends upon each and every of R. Nachman's disciples. Each is called upon to bring others into the fold one by one – every man his friend, each teacher his student – until they too walk the path of the Rebbe. Additionally, though, R. Nachman developed another strategy, also useful posthumously. I refer to his devotion to the preparation of his book which would come to be called *Likutei Moharan*. This work would come to play a central role in spreading the Breslav message.

Even a mere two weeks before his passing – fighting his fever-racked frame, barely able to breathe – he discussed his own death with his followers and stressed his belief that he would indeed complete his mission.

> In Uman, before the last Rosh Hashanah, he talked to his followers about his death…they moaned, 'What will we do? Who will help us?' He answered that they must stick together and then they will be good men – not just good, but even tzadikim – great men. 'For God will surely help to fulfill my will, as He has done up until now. With His help, I have finished, and I will surely finish just as I wanted.'[23]

R. Nachman did not doubt that, 'In the future the entire world will be Breslav Chasidim.'[24] The connection between the acceptance of R. Nachman (through his teachings) and the future messianic age is evident in R. Naftali's words regarding the *Scroll*.

> Once R. Aaron Lipvotski turned to R. Naftali and said to him: 'You have heard from our Master the *Scroll of Secrets*. Where does this matter

---

22 *Chayei Moharan Im Hashmatot*, 54.

23 Ibid., 241.

24 Ibid., 309.

stand?' R. Naftali answered him quite emphatically: 'At the least you must learn much from the Rebbe's book... He [R. Nachman] taught us, "When my book is accepted in the world it will be time to prepare for the messiah." Afterwards, at a later time he gave him the *Scroll*.[25]

Before delving into the theme of the messiah as depicted in the *Scroll of Secrets*, one must learn the 'Rebbe's book.' Not only is it impossible to understand the *Scroll* without solid grounding in *Likutei Moharan*, but the learning itself and the book's general acceptance is one of the very signs of the coming redemption. R. Naftali's answer was not an evasion, but rather a practical answer to the question of where the whole matter of the messiah stands. For in actuality, the messianic process is dependent upon the level of acceptance of R. Nachman's work in the world.[26]

3. ON THE DEPICTION OF THE MESSIAH IN THE SCROLL: MADE IN THE IMAGE OF R. NACHMAN

They will not know at first that he is the one. Afterwards, each will reach his

---

25 *Siach Sorfei Kodesh*, vol. 3, 83. Similarly in *Chayei Moharan:* 'It was heard from his holy mouth that he said that the publication of his holy book, *Likutei Moharan*, was the beginning of the redemption.... He said that one who learns from his holy books is the beginning of redemption' [*Chayei Moharan*, (Jerusalem: 1983), 314-19]. In another section we find the following addition by the copyist: Says the copyist – Regarding the dimming of the great and wonderous light of our Rebbe ... May it be Your will that the truth be revealed and his holiness be made known throughout the world. Then the redemption will come speedily in our day, amen' (Ibid., 344-45).

26 This is a clear continuation of the messianic conception of the Baal Shem Tov as found in the epistle he sent to R. Gershon, his brother-in-law. In it he describes how his soul rose up to the Hall of the Messiah where he asked the messiah, 'When will you come?' The answer: 'When your springs overflow.' Regarding the connection between this 'overflow' and the coming of the messiah in Breslav thought, as well as its connection to the phenomenon of Chasidic messianism, see Idel, *Messianic Mystics*, 212-47.

own conclusion and will consider that it is possible that this is him etc.[27]

They will not know at first that he is the one. Afterwards, each will reach his
own conclusion and will consider that it is possible that this is him etc. (Happy
will be the strong of faith in those days.
Once I heard that he said concerning the messiah there will be a mighty argument. And they will say, 'This is the messiah?!' They will say in these words, 'The messiah isn't a fancy hat!')[28]

The question of the messiah's actual identity has always been one of the central messianic concerns. False messiahs and shattered messianic hopes only served to sharpen the interest in discovering how to separate the messianic wheat from its disappointing chaff. Different theories developed in order to accomplish this difficult task. Maimonides differentiated between an individual who could be considered a 'presumptive messiah' on account of his ability to 'learn Torah and observe the commandments as his ancestor David did – both the Written and Oral Torah; compel all of Israel to follow [the Torah] and to support it; and to wage God's battles.'[29] Even so, it may be that this presumption could prove, in the end, unfounded.

Others have presented specific individuals as actual messiahs and some have even insisted that death itself cannot for certain rule out the identification of the departed as the actual messiah.[30] This last option has often found expression in the character of the Josephian messiah, who is killed before the promised redemption actually arrives, but is still nonetheless considered a true messiah.

---

27 First section line 75.

28 Second section line 78.

29 Maimonides MT Hilchot Melachim 11:4.

30 Ibid., 14:4.

The prophet Isaiah already discussed the identification of the messiah as one who has been, 'smote by God with sickness,'[31] thus making his discovery as the messiah, not surprisingly, difficult to accept: 'Who believed our news? Upon whom was God's hand revealed?'[32] This prophecy turned the problematic identification of the messiah and questions concerning its accuracy into an integral part of the messianic character. Paradoxically, then, doubtful authenticity becomes a prerequisite for certain identification of the messiah.

This motif also appears in the works of R. Chaim Vital. He describes a stage in which the messiah, 'himself will know that he is the One ... but others will not recognize him'. Only after a period of uncertainty and doubt will 'he be completely revealed and recognized by all of Israel who will gather around him.'[33]

The *Scroll* develops this very idea. Without a doubt, in the minds of the Breslav Chasidim who read the *Scroll*, the quizzical call, 'This is the messiah?!' becomes one of the actual affirmative signs regarding his true identity. It seems, then, that the lack of general acknowledgment which was a part of R. Nachman's life history – accompanied by the hints and explicit declarations concerning his unique status by his followers – all added to the messianic proportions of his persona.

An important text which was censored out of *Chayei Moharan* details an interesting discussion between R. Nachman and R. Natan.

> It is possible that this is the meaning: The scion of David will arrive only unobserved. That is, it will not be evident that he is the messiah. Actually, he has already come, here he is, etc. He agreed with me and added

---

31 Isaiah 53:4.

32 Ibid., 53:1.

33 Rav Chaim Vital, "*Arba'ah Meot Shekel Kesef*," (New York: 1995), 241. For more on this source, see Gershom Scholem, *Shabbetai Zevi and the Shabbetaian Movement during his Lifetime*, 2 vols. (Tel Aviv: 1984), 42 and fn. 1. R. Chaim Vital connects the recognition of the messiah with the description in the Zohar of the messiah's vanishing in a cloud, similar to Moses' retreat on Mt. Sinai for forty days (ibid.).

that so it is written, 'His leader will be from among them.'[34] Afterwards he grew excited and said, 'This is what [the Talmudic Sage] Rav Nachman said in Tractate Sanhedrin, "[Rav Nachman said]: if he [the messiah] is among the living, it is me" as it says, "… [Israel's] leader will be from among them,"[35] speedily in our day.'[36]

R. Natan interprets the aphorism, 'the scion of David will arrive only unobserved,'[37] as describing not only the messiah's unannounced entrance,

---

34 Jeremiah 30:21.

35 TB Sanhedrin 98b.

36 *Chayei Moharan Im Hashmatot*, 276. The same text is found in Tepliker, "*Hashmatot Mechayei Moharan*," 14 and in *Hashmatot Mechayei Moharan - Typed Manuscript*, 5. It is worth noting that from the different manuscripts it seems that this text was relocated in the wrong place. In the manuscripts 'before paragraph 33 missing' appears, while the copyist's introduction notes that the references are keyed to the Lemberg edition of 1876 in which the paragraphs are numbered differently. Placed according to the Lemberg numbering, the passage fits more logically. The section preceeding it deals with the personal-familial connection of R. Nachman to the messiah; the section following also discusses the messiah. The former reads: 'He said, "What God will do with me, I don't know. But I have influenced Him so that the righteous redeemer will come from my offspring." This he said in public and warned [us] to honor and respect his children for they are very precious trees and will produce wonderously good fruits. He also said that his children were from the world of *atzilut* (emanation). The latter reads: 'The world believes that when the messiah arrives mortality will cease. This is incorrect - even the messiah himself will die. This he said in public.'

The Korman manuscript has a slightly different version. 'It is possible that the meaning of what our Sages said, "The scion of David will arrive only unobserved." That is, he will be in the world, but they will not know that he is already etc. Here he is, etc. He agreed with me and said that so it is written, "His leader will be from among them." Afterwards he grew excited and said, 'This is what [the Talmudic sage] Rav Nachman said: if he [the messiah] is among the living, it is me" as it says, "… [Israel's] leader will be from among them"' (Rav Yitzchak Meir Korman of Lublin, "Sefer Chayei Moharan (Manuscript)", 8.

37 The expression, 'The scion of David will arrive only unobserved' occurs in another place in *Chayei Moharan*, as well (*Chayei Moharan Im Hashmatot*, 425). I have not found this exact expression in the Talmud, midrashic literature or the Zohar. It seems to be a combination of two Talmudic expressions: 'Three come unobserved - the messiah, a found object and a scorpion' (TB Sanhedrin 97a) together with a series of expressions which begin, 'The scion of David does not arrive rather than…' (ibid. and elsewhere). This Breslav version is found in other of R. Natan's works as well: Rav Natan of Nemirov, *Likutei Halachot* (Jerusalem:

but also the fact that even afterwards he will not be acknowledged. The lack of attention paid to the messiah becomes one of the very conditions necessary for his arrival.

The conclusion of the sentence in the above text which begins, 'Actually,' which has been replaced by the 'etc.' may be reconstructed with the help of other parallel texts concerning this same conversation. The copyist added:

> This was spoken by our teacher, R. Natan to our Rebbe after he had taught the discourse, 'Da Sheyaish Hevdelim bein Hatorot' [Know That There Are Differences Between the Torahs] (found in *Likutei Moharan* II 28). Our teacher, R. Natan, full of heartfelt emotion upon hearing the awesome holy words, to the point that they burned in his heart like a flame, could not be still and he raised his voice before all the assembled and spoke. 'It is possible that this is the meaning…'[38]

What so excited R. Natan? Perhaps the messiah's presence was not just presented as a theoretical possibility, as his word's 'here he is' – indubitably directed at R. Nachman – indicate. In the course of the continued discussion, 'he agreed with me'[39] – that is R. Nachman agreed

---

1984), vol. 2, 188. It also appears in the work of R. Menachem Nachum of Chernobyl: Rav Menachem Nachum of Chernobyl, *Me'or Eneyim* (Jerusalem: 1999), 34, as well in the Ben Ish Chai: Rav Yosef Chaim ben Eliyahu, *Ben Ish Chai* (Jerusalem: 1986), Hilchot Rosh Hashanah,34.

38 *Chayei Moharan Im Hashmatot*, 276 The same text is found in Tepliker, "*Hashmatot Mechayei Moharan*," 14 and in *Hashmatot Mechayei Moharan – Typed Manuscript* 5.

39 This interpretation of R. Natan's words is supported by R. Avraham, the son of R. Nachman Chazan, whose own report of this event fills in some details. 'Now as the matter is known regarding that which our Rebbe said while revealing the discourse in Likutei Moharan II 28 when R. Natan, out of his great emotion at the merit in comprehending the awesome depths of his holy words which burned in him like a flame so that he could not contain himself, stated before those assembled: "It is possible that this is the meaning…." I heard from my father a clearer interpretation in these words: "They will say, 'messiah, messiah,' and finally – there he is." Our Rebbe opened his [R. Natan's] eyes and showed him that [the Talmudic sage] Rav Nachman also said so…. (I seem to recall that my father said that R. Nachman ended, "then I am he.")

with R. Natan's estimation that he was in fact the messiah. This he, in fact, reinforced by pointing out the source from Sanhedrin – a statement by the eponymous Talmudic Sage, Rav Nachman, that if the messiah is amongst the living, it is he. Thus, our R. Nachman more than hinted (just as the earlier Rav Nachman had done) that he may very well be the messiah.

The parallel between this description of the tzadik-messiah, who, though unnoticed is already present, and that found in the *Scroll* is striking. The *Scroll* notes that, 'at first they will not recognize that he is the one,' (section I:45) only later noticing that the messiah is in their midst. The phrase, 'concerning the messiah there will be a mighty argument' (section II: 75-76) is also a quite apt description of the controversy that dogged R. Nachman throughout his career as a Chasidic leader.[40]

We find here a clear statement of R. Nachman's messianic identity confirmed by the Rebbe himself. However, the case is not as simple as it may seem. R. Nachman had, in fact, admitted only to R. Natan's, 'It is possible…' – that he was possibly the messiah, but never affirmed more than that possibility. His answer, recalling the words of the Talmudic Sage, Rav Nachman, also serve to highlight this as a possibility rather than a certainty. The Talmudic text in question mentions Rav Nachman as one among a long list of possible messianic candidates – both living and dead at the time. This

---

See *Chayei Moharan*, 6. It seems, then, from what he [R. Natan] said that these words were directed at our Rebbe himself (Rav Avraham Chazan, *Kochvei Or* [Jerusalem: 1983], 122-3). See also, with minor changes ibid., 101-2. Even though some may think that Chazan's readings nearly always run to hyper-messianism (see Piekarz, *Studies in Bratslav Hasidism*, 137-9, 49-50) here we are dealing less with interpretation and more with some additional information brought by his father which reinforces the indentification between R. Nachman and the messiah.

40 Chazan describes at great length the controversy which surrounded R. Nachman regarding his messianic standing and the meaning of such verses as 'Who would believe our news' (Isaiah 53:1) which we discussed earlier. R. Avraham Chazan, *Sichot Vesipurim (Printed with Kochvei or)* (Jerusalem: 1983). He claims rather straightforwardly that 'regarding these problems which encompassed him, anyone who investigates them will see that all that our Rebbe suffered – all the conflict and trouble – in the future when the truth will be revealed everyone will say to his fellow: "Who would believe our news, etc."' (ibid., 125-6).

sage's claim that if the messiah is indeed among the living it is him, despite not having been crowned King of Israel nor building the Temple, is, in context of the entire passage, better understood as meaning that he is as good a choice as anyone else for the role. The passage continues to give possible names of the messiah and we find that the list is in fact comprised of various sages' names, each offered by their respective students.[41] The answer, then, given by R. Nachman does not mean that he was about to commence the construction of the Temple and reinstate the Divine Service therein, but rather only that he did not deny that he understood himself as standing in the long line of rabbis, sages and leaders who in accord with ancient tradition, may merit ushering in the messianic age. The actual meaning of 'being the messiah,' however, needs further explication.

The Messianic Horizon: Repairing the Nations

The *Scroll* describes the messiah as devoting a good portion of his time to the nations of the world. After first establishing his reputation among the Jews, he is recognized by the gentiles. From this point on most of his energies are directed towards the general, non-Jewish populace. His daily schedule includes sermons for them; he teaches them new wisdom and new songs; and he spends time healing them with his stock of newly created medicines. Two areas in which his concern for the nations is especially noticeable are liturgy and religious custom.

---

41 What is the name of the messiah? The students of R. Shilo said, 'Shilo is his name, as it says, "until he reaches Shilo."' The students of R. Yanai said, 'Yinon is his name, as it says, "his name will stand before the sun forever, eternal (*yinon*) is his name."' The students of R. Chanina said, 'Chanina is his name, as it says, "I will not grant you pardon (*chanina*)"'. There are those who say Menachem son of Hezekiah is his name, as it says, "succor (*menachem*) is far from me, restore my soul." The rabbis said, 'Chivrah (leper) of the house of Rabi is his name, as it says, "our sickness he bore, our wounds he suffered; yet we thought him sick, wounded by God and suffering." R. Nachman said, 'If he is among the living, [he is] like me, as it says, "[Israel's] leader will be from among them and her ruler from her midst will come." Rav said, 'if he is among the living, [he is] like Rebbi, the holy; if among the deceased, [he is] like Daniel the beloved' (TB Sanhedrin 98b).

> Afterwards he will travel to all the kings ... and he will make for them customs similar to Israel's religion.[42]

> He will fix for everyone practices and make for them prayer. Thus he will do until
> all[43] turn to one clear tongue. [44]

These more universal messianic activities were already part of R. Nachman's thought. He had included them among the benefits that he himself was prepared to bestow.

> When he traveled to Novorich, sitting in the wagon,[45] he said: 'It is in my power to bring the entire world to true penitence – not only the simple people, but even the great and righteous. Even the righteous need to repent. Regarding the holy Jewish people, there is no question – but I can even bring all of the world's nations closer to God, may He be blessed. I could have brought them close to the religion of Israel, but it is enough that a servant be like his master.'[46]

> He said: 'The entire world needs me. There is no question that you do, for you yourselves know how [much] you need me. But even all the righteous need me, for they also must truly repent. And also the nations of the world need me. But – it is enough that a servant be like his master.'[47]

---

42 Section I, line 18.

43 For then I will turn the nations to one clear tongue that all should proclaim the name of God and worship Him together (Zephaniah 3:9).

44 Section II, line 68.

45 Rav Nachman was in Novorich during Purim 1807.

46 *Chayei Moharan Im Hashmatot*, 264.

47 Ibid., 264.

The world needs R. Nachman – it has much to learn from him. 'Our Rebbe said: "Kings and emperors can send their children to me to learn manners."'[48] R. Nachman failed to realize this dream and no princes arrived at his door ready for instruction. However, the messiah, as described in the *Scroll*, will garner universal recognition – the entire world beating a path to his door to learn from him. 'They will send him the sons of the kings;'[49] 'And all the sons of the kings all will come to him to receive wisdom from him.'[50] They can learn from him not just proper behavior – table manners and courtesy– but rather something much deeper and meaningful. All of the nations will be led to practice something very 'similar to Israel's religion.'[51]

'But it is enough that a servant be like his master'

What does this phrase mean in the above story's context? How does it explain R. Nachman's reaction to his failure? This expression appears in the Talmud and midrashic literature in a variety of contexts.[52] Here its meaning can be best understood by comparing its use here to other sources and relating to the concrete circumstances in which R. Nachman uttered it.

The gemara in Tractate Brachot (58b) relates the following: 'R. Yochanan said: From the day that the Temple was destroyed it was decreed that the houses of the righteous will be destroyed. …They said to him: It is enough that a servant be like his master.' Rashi's gloss *ad loc* reads: 'For the Temple

48 This phrase appears in Yiddish in *Siach Sorfei Kodesh*, vol 3, 34

49 Section I, line 13.

50 Section II, line 19.

51 Both Green and Tzeitlin have pointed out that R. Nachman's ambitions for 'repairing the world' went well beyond the confines of the Jewish people and were directed at the entire world. This is especially clear in those of his Tales which focus on 'repairing the world' as they are not based in a Jewish context. See Green, *Master*, 91 and the sources he cites on 219 fn. 42.

52 TB Brachot 58b; Breishit Rabba 49b; Shemot Rabba 42, 5; Tanchuma, Chayei Sarah, chapter 4. This expression is found throughout the homiletic, kabalistic and Chasidic literature.

was destroyed, the house of the Holy One, blessed be He.' This decree was understood by the author of the *Tikunei HaZohar* as describing the fate of the righteous whose fortune was exile from their homes and who are neither able nor allowed to rest in peace and quiet.[53]

> Also, 'so will a man wander from his place'[54] (who is this?) this is Moshe ... Also, 'so will a man wander from his place' whosoever is a righteous man will leave the place of the divine presence and wander as it says, 'and the dove found no rest.'[55] Thus our Sages established at the time that the Temple was destroyed: it was decreed that the homes of the righteous be destroyed so that each would wander from his place, for it is enough that a servant be like his master...Thus the masters of the Torah walk hunched-over.[56]

R. Avraham Azoulay, in his work, *Chesed Le'Avraham*, discusses the 'matter of the righteous' contemplative introspection on the roads and in the wilds and discovers additional meaning in their wanderings which echo the custom of 'divorce' practiced by the kabbalists of Tzfat.[57]

> We need to understand the matter of the divorce of the righteous like R. Shimon and his fellows, the majority of whose teachings were taught while traveling on the roads. Without a doubt this was not coincidental. Rather, it was by design that all of their deliberations on the Torah were held while traveling on the roads. After the temple was destroyed, the divine presence was divorced from the Hall of the King and could no longer dwell together with Him in solitude. She then left and [still]

53 As the bird wanders from her nest, so man wanders from his place (Parables 27:8).

54 Genesis 8:9.

55 *Tikunei Zohar*, trans. Rav Yehudah Edrei (Jerusalem: 1998), 4.

56 Ibid.

57 On this custom see, Moshe Hallamish, *Introduction to the Kabbalah* (Jerusalem: 1991), 71-2.

> wanders from here to there, from place to place as is mentioned in the *Tikkunim*. There they said, 'It is enough that a servant be like his master' as it was decreed that the houses of the righteous will be destroyed. ... However, the righteous, who are the masters of the tradition, have the strength to go from place to place, here to there. Therefore, the kabalists, R. Shimon and his followers would study the wisdom of the kabala while restlessly moving from place to place, divorced from their homes so as to be a vehicle of the exiled Royalty. Through their wanderings and divorce, they would merit Her presence and She would rest upon them.[58]

These sources become even more meaningful given the time and place that R. Nachman brought up his claim that, 'it is enough ....' This was in Adar 1807 while traveling to Novorich.[59] However, this Ukrainian town was not his final destination. Rather, it was the first of many stops over the course of a long and mysterious period of self-imposed wandering. 'Afterwards, he traveled to Novorich and then he was in Bazoslav and Duvno, Brod and other places where he disguised himself and hid undiscovered.'[60] In a letter sent by R. Nachman to his followers in the midst of this journey he told them of his dramatic decision to abandon Breslav – apparently for good.

> I announce to all of our friends that due to the extent of the troubles and trials that have ensnared me, I am terminating my stay in Breslav. And now I will wander from tent to tent,[61] not settling, but merely dwelling ... God is righteous and I am at fault! My deeds have brought these pains, the death of the precious children – discord and accusers upon me. Despite all this, though, I know as well that all my efforts

58 Rav Avraham Azoulay, *Chesed Le'avraham* (Vilna: 1917), 4:28.

59 *Chayei Moharan Im Hashmatot*, 169.

60 Ibid.,190-1.

61 This echoes the verse from Samuel II which describes the wanderings of the Shechinah: 'I have not settled in a house...I have wandered in tent and tabernacle' (7:6).

> spent saving you from the jaws of the 'Filthy One,' have caused him to fix his eyes upon me and to gnash his teeth at me.[62]

'It is enough…,' in this context is connected to the decree of exile pronounced upon the righteous banishing him from the tranquility of home. This decree is realized here through the trials and tribulations which had befallen R. Nachman, leading him to leave Breslav and take to the road. While he took personal responsibility for his troubles – 'my deeds have brought these pains,' – he was also convinced that his spiritual efforts aroused the 'Filthy One' against him – preventing him from continuing this work which began with his own followers, but was meant to reach even to 'all the nations of the entire world.' While he had once thought that he would one day sit in 'a house of gold and silver'[63] in his old age, using his unique spiritual powers to benefit the entire world, he came to realize that 'it is enough that a servant be like his master'. The destruction of the Temple and the Exile brought the very same fate to the tzadik. His own house would be destroyed and he would wander far from home, prevented from actualizing his dream of bringing the world closer to God. After half-a-year of roving the Ukraine,[64] he changed plans and returned to settle in Breslav.[65] The troubles, persecutions and accusations, however, did not cease and would follow him until his last day on earth.

The Place of Prayer in the Messianic Process

The *Scroll* does not give many details regarding the customs that the messiah intends to establish for the gentiles. Aside from asserting that they will be similar to the religion of Israel, neither their express content nor general

---

62 *Chayei Moharan Im Hashmatot*, 195-6.

63 Tepliker, "*Hashmatot Mechayei Moharan*," 16 in the added pagination.

64 See *Chayei Moharan Im Hashmatot*, 187.

65 For more on R. Nachman's travels and on the causes for his change in plans, see Green, *Master*, 227-33.

nature are actually described. Against this general silence, the prayer mentioned in both of the *Scroll*'s sections as one of the central aspects of the messiah's mission to the gentiles resonates all the more loudly. 'He will fix for everyone practices and make for them prayer. Thus he will do until all turn to one clear tongue.'[66] Whether the 'thus he will do' corresponds to both his legislative and liturgical activities or only to the latter, in any case, the special place of prayer in the messianic revolution predicted by the prophet Zephania is echoed here by R. Nachman: 'For then I will turn the nations – for all to call the name of God in a clear tongue and worship him with united effort.'[67]

'All That He Does Is Tied To Prayer'[68]

The messiah, as he appears in the *Scroll*, is both a vivid reflection of R. Nachman himself as well as the actualization of the Breslav religious value system which saw prayer as its very keystone. The Breslav *tzadik*, modeled after R. Nachman, is more than anything a 'master of prayer.' While prayer is one of the cornerstones of every Jew's life, and especially that of the *tzadik*, it also plays a critical role in the messianic process.

R. Nachman testified that prayer was the most important aspect of his life's work. The exceptional importance which he attached to prayer, both in his own life and in his work with his followers, influenced his life profoundly.

> I heard in his name regarding the conflicts in which others ensnared him, that as our Sages have said: "'men have exalted the petty'[69] – these are exalted things which men have disdained. What are they? Prayer."[70]

66 Section II, line 68.

67 Zephaniah 3:9.

68 Nemirov, *Sefer Likutei Moharan Hamenukad*, 93.

69 Psalms 12:19.

70 TB Brachot 6b.

> Therefore, since all that he did was tied to prayer – he spoke to his followers about it: warning them to pray much, introspect much, talk much with the Creator, as is explained in his holy books (and more than this, he exhorted us without end regarding prayer and introspection) – it was for this reason that others so disdained, disparaged and fought him. All that he did was tied to prayer – that very exalted thing which men have disdained – understand this.[71]

Prayer stands at the pinnacle of R. Nachman's world: he devoted all of his efforts to its refinement. The disdain of prayer brought with it the disdain of R. Nachman – so identified with prayer that its disparagement was his own.[72] R. Nachman felt that this was the reason, or at least one of them, for the troubles and conflicts that hounded him his entire life.

Solitary religious introspection (*hitbodedut*)[73] appears in this source and many others as intimately connected to prayer. *Hitbodedut*, one of the central identifying characteristics of Breslav Chasidism,[74] was the framework

---

71 Nemirov, *Sefer Likutei Moharan Hamenukad*, 93.

72 For sources on the conflicts surrounding R. Nachman see Mark, " *Why Did R. Moses Zvi of Savran Persecute R. Nathan of Nemirov and Breslav Chasidim?*," 487, fn. 1.

73 On *hitbodedut*, see Moshe Idel, "*Hitbodedut*: On Solitude in Jewish Mysticism," *Enisamkeit, Archaeologie der Literarischen Kommunikation* VI (2000). On the meaning of the term and its various connotations in philosophy and kabalah, see Moshe Idel, " *Hitbodedut as Concentration in Jewish Philosophy*," Jerusalem *Studies in Jewish Thought* 7 (1988); Moshe Idel, " *Hitbodedut qua Concentration in Ecstatic Kabbalah*," *Da'at* 14 (1985); Sarah Klein-Breslavi, " *Prophecy, Clairvoyance and Dreams and the Concept of 'Hitbodedut' in Gersonides' Thought*," *Da'at* 39 (1997). As a religious practice, *hitbodedut* appeared at the start of the Chasidic movement, both as a social practice (*Tzva'at Haribash*, (Brooklyn: 1996), 26) and as a meditative practice (ibid., 2b). See also *Keter Shem Tov*, (Brooklyn: 1987), 42. See also Ze'ev Gries, *Conduct Literature (Regimen Vitae). Its History and Place in the Life of Beshtian Chasidism* (Jerusalem: 1989), 222-4.

74 In *Sichot Haran*, (Jerusalem: 1995), 148-9 the difference between the Breslav Chasidim and others in terms of the practice of *hitbodedut* is defined. R. Natan is quoted as claiming that, 'Whoever wants a taste of our Rebbe, who is the hidden light, should practice much *hitbodedut*' (R. Avraham Chazan, *Avneiha Barzel* (Jerusalem: 1983), 69). Even today it appears that 'It is around this very practice that the real Breslav Chasid's world revolves' (Meor Hanachal Monthly 23 [Elul 1993], 5).

developed by R. Nachman to allow the creation of a meta-liturgical individual prayer experience for his followers. This, he felt, was of the utmost importance in any religious work and saw it as a critical ingredient for anyone seeking union with God.[75] It is not surprising, then, that the *Scroll* describes a fixed time for this practice[76] as part of the messiah's daily schedule. In fact it need be as regular as his meal times: 'The order of the day will be an hour in which he will eat and will drink and he has [time] for *hitbodedut*.'[77] The messiah not only fixes prayers for the nations of world, but *hitbodedut* will occupy a central place in his own private life, as well.

The Master of Prayer and the Messianic Process

In several places R. Nachman describes prayer as an essential element of the messianic revolution and as one of the main interests of its leader. In the tale, 'The Master of Prayer,'[78] a fellowship formed around such a master is described as 'involved only with these things: prayer, song and praise of God.'[79] For each member that joins this group (which is not described as Jewish), the master would 'fix prayers.'[80] After a lengthy process led by the master, accompanied by his insistent attempts to convince any who would

---

75 '*Hitbodedut* is the greatest and highest of all practices' (Nemirov, *Sefer Likutei Moharan Hamenukad*, 25). See also there 95-101;*Sichot Haran*, 111, 48-52; *Chayei Moharan*, 292-6. The pamphlet by Rav Alter Tepliker, *Hishtapchut Hanefesh* (Jerusalem: 1904) is dedicated just to this practice. See Green, *Master*, 145-8. For more on the mystical side of this practice, see Zvi Mark, *Mysticism and Madness In the Work of R. Nachman of Breslav* (Jerusalem: 2003), 232-56, esp. 35-8.

76 'Therefore it is imperative to command them that they should practice "hitbodedut" for some time' (Nemirov, *Sefer Likutei Moharan Hamenukad*, 96.

77 Section I, 27.

78 *Sefer Sipurei Ma'asiot Hamenukad*, (Jerusalem: 1985), Tale 12. For an interpretation of this story as a tale of redemption, see Rabbi Adin Steinsaltz, *Six Stories of Rabbi Nachman of Breslav* (Jerusalem: 1995), 132-53; David G. Roskies, "The Master of Prayer: Nachman of Breslav," in *A Bridge of Longing: The Lost Art of Yiddish Storytelling* (Cambridge, MA: 1995).

79 *Sefer Sipurei Ma'asiot*, Tale 12, 175.

80 Ibid., 219.

listen of the paramount importance of prayer for the individual, and indeed for the world, the story ends with the repair of humanity as a whole. 'The whole world returned to God – involving themselves only in Torah, prayer, penitence and good deeds. Amen – may this be His will.'[81] The clear symmetry between this tale's master and R. Nachman has been noted in both traditional interpretations of his work, as well as in the scholarly literature.[82]

An example of the former is found in *Siach Sorfei Kodesh*. 'Some of his close circle said to R. Natan: You are the most qualified to be the Master of Prayer (mentioned in the *Tales*, number 12). R. Natan said to them: The Master of Prayer is our Master'.[83] Even for the inner circle of Chasidim it was difficult to see R. Nachman as the 'master of prayer' – he already died without redeeming the entire world. This left R. Natan as the most likely candidate. He, however, answered them that R. Nachman, despite not having finished what he set out to do, had left behind the still burning embers of the flame which he had ignited. This would eventually draw all back to God, Torah and prayer.

The Messiah's Main Weapon is Prayer[84]

> All will surrender themselves to him with neither war nor struggle in light of his beauty and their longing for him. He will fix for everyone practices and make for them prayer. Thus he will do until all turn to one clear tongue.[85]

The *Scroll* describes the coming of the messiah – the arrival of the righteous redeemer – as a peaceful revolution: no noise, no war, no bloodshed.

---

81 Ibid., 233.

82 'R. Natan said to them, "The Master of Prayer is our Rebbe"' (*Siach Sorfei Kodesh*, vol. 2, 136 See also Piekarz, *Studies in Bratslav Hasidism*, 20.

83 *Siach Sorfei Kodesh*, vol. 2, 136

84 'Speak to the Priests,' in Nemirov, *Sefer Likutei Moharan Hamenukad.*

85 Section II.

It is a revolution of language – of a renewed crying out to God. This radical change is engendered with neither force nor its threat. It occurs because of the messiah's grace and the masses' yearning for him. In stark contrast to Maimonides' position in the *Mishneh Torah* which clearly stipulates that actual fighting of God's wars is a precondition for presumptive messianic status,[86] the *Scroll*'s messiah is anything but a warrior. His true power lies in his ability to awaken a longing to draw close to him in his followers as he creates new customs and prayers, 'until all turn to one clear tongue'. (Below I will return to the nature of the world in messianic times.) Here, however, I want to draw attention to the fact that the unique characteristics of the *Scroll*'s messiah are not unique to the *Scroll*, but are found in *Likutei Moharan* as well. The special connection of the messiah to prayer is also characteristic of R. Nachman himself.

In the discourse, 'Emor el Hakohanim' (Speak to the Priests of Israel), [87] this is made quite clear.

> The weaponry of the messiah is prayer, which is identified with the nose, as it is written, 'I will stop-up my honor for your sake'[88] – from this stems the main of his life-force. All the battles that he will wage and all of his conquests stem from this, as it is written, 'he will nose out [the truth] using the fear of God.'[89] This is the aspect of the nose and this is his main weaponry, as it is written, 'with my sword and my bow.'[90] As Rashi interprets [sword and bow], 'prayer and supplication,' as it is written, 'Not

---

86 Maimonides, MT Hilchot Melachim 11:4.

87 'Speak to the Priests,' in Nemirov, *Sefer Likutei Moharan Hamenukad.* This discourse was actually written by R. Nachman himself. It was related in Zlotipol in 1801 or 1802. See Rav Avraham Kochav-Lev, *Tovot Zichronot (Bound with Yerach Eitanim)* (Bnei Brak: 1978), 103.

88 Isaiah 48:9. [The biblical Hebrew idiom for anger, *cheri af* or patience, *'erech api'im*, both use the word *af*—nose. This verse describes God's patience using this term and another for nose, *chotem* (as a verb), which describes His forebearance. This is rendered as *stop-up* to keep the homiletic connection to nose in the passage. *NM, translator*]

89 Ibid., 11:3.

90 Genesis 48:2.

> upon my bow shall I depend .... God we have praised...'[91] – like, 'I will stop-up my honor for your sake.' [The Hebrew word for praise and honor here are the same: *tehila*.]

The messianic arsenal, his sword and bow, is actually composed only of prayer and supplication. His battles are waged with the power of prayer. From it emanates his very life-force. Some may want to dull the point of R. Nachman's innovative reading here by suggesting that the messiah's fights are won through the power of prayer, but actual physical battle is not supplanted. However, the *Scroll* teaches us that the messianic revolution is born 'with neither war nor struggle.' The might and strength of the messiah is measured not in military divisions, but stems directly from his being a master of prayer able to stir deep longing in his followers. Through the lens of the *Scroll*, we see clearly that R. Nachman's words in the above discourse are meant to be read quite plainly: the weaponry of the messiah is really prayer. The messiah will not gird his loins in physical battle, but will engage in prayer – not war. His conquests will all stem from the power of his prayer.[92]

Further in this discourse R. Nachman explains that aside from the messiah's prayers those of each and every individual will play a role in the redemptionary process, as well.

> There are those of our people, the children of Israel, who mistakenly believe (heaven forbid) that all prayers are for naught. But the truth is that all prayer is kept, supported and raised aloft by the *tzadikim* of every generation as it is written, 'and Moses raised the tabernacle.'[93] They raise each and every board to its proper place and slowly build

---

91 Psalms 44:9.

92 'Speak to the Priests,' in Nemirov, *Sefer Likutei Moharan Hamenukad* was related in Zlotipol in 1801 or 1802. It may be that by 1806, when the Scroll was first related, R. Nachman had changed his mind. However, as the interpretation that we have suggested for the former accords with the attitiude expressed in the Scroll, there is no real reason to see any change here.

93 Exodus 40:18.

the Divine Presence until it reaches its full height. Then the messiah arrives, that is Moses, and completes the work, raising it in its entirety.

All prayers, not just those of the tzadik, are essential parts of the whole out of which the Divine presence is constituted. The messiah's role is to gather together the generation's prayers bit by bit and stitch them together into the whole cloth out of which the fullness of the Divine is woven. For this reason, 'all prayer must be brought to the Moses-messiah-like-one who will raise the tabernacle.' [94] This is not merely a description of the far off future, but also of a conceivably contemporary process. This can occur when the 'generation's tzadik – the Moses-like-one' (on condition that all the prayers are brought to him) 'shines and lights prayer,'[95] bringing them all together and raising the tabernacle which houses the Divine presence.

We may assume that these last remarks of R. Nachman concerning the 'Moses-like' tzadik reflect upon himself. This is not only because of R. Nachman's general self-reflective intent when discussing the generation's tzadik (something well understood both in traditional and scholarly commentary[96]), but also because of the special identification which R. Nachman felt towards prayer. He was devoted to prayer while the rest of the world disdained it. R. Nachman was the tzadik who relentlessly sought to uncover the shining face of prayer and reveal its splendor; he was the one who set it above all else.

The Moses-messiah-like-one's role in elevating prayer is expressed in another discourse '*Tehomot*' (Depths).[97] Here both the esthetic quality of prayer as well as its proper place in the Upper Worlds of the cosmos is discussed.

---

94 Nemirov, *Sefer Likutei Moharan Hamenukad*. For an investigation of the theme of the rebuilding as an expression of redemption in kabalah and Chasidism, see Idel, *Messianic Mystics*, 221-7.

95 Nemirov, *Sefer Likutei Moharan Hamenukad*.

96 See, for example, Joseph Weiss, *Studies in Bratslav Hasidism* (Jerusalem: 1995), 152; Piekarz, *Studies in Bratslav Hasidism*, 10; Green, *Master*, 31.

97 Rav Natan of Nemirov, *Likutei Tefilot Hamenukad* (Jerusalem: 1989), 9:4. This discourse was written by R. Nachman himself and related in 1803. See also, *Chayei Moharan Im Hashmatot*, 67.

> Every individual must connect his prayer to that of the generation's *tzadik*. The *tzadik* knows how to align the gates [of prayer] and elevate each prayer to its proper gateway, for every tzadik is akin to the Moses-messiah, as they said, 'Moses, you spoke correctly'[98] and it is written, '"until he reaches Shiloh"[99] – that is Moses'.[100] The messiah is the whole of all prayer. For this reason the messiah 'smells and judges,'[101] for prayers are connected to the nose, as it is written, "I will stop-up my honor for you.'[102]

Here R. Nachman identifies the Moses-messiah-like-one with the tzadik of each generation. There is no doubt that he viewed himself as the tzadik of his own generation, but he also points out that 'every tzadik is akin to the Moses-messiah.' This measurably tones down what may have been an absolute identity between himself and the ultimative builder of the tabernacle of prayer.

Further in this discourse, R. Nachman makes the same connection between battle and prayer that we saw earlier in 'Emor el Hakohanim.' "The sword is akin to prayer, as it is written, 'with my sword and bow'... for all the prayers are akin to swords in the hands of the messiah."[103] We find more support for the claim that R. Nachman saw himself as the messianic gatherer of prayers described in this discourse in his use of the verse used previously to describe his devotion to that which others had disdained: 'The wicked encircle us, while men have exalted the petty.'[104]

---

98 This is an expression used in the yeshiva world to compliment scholars, even those not named Moses. See TB Shabbat 101b.

99 Genesis 49:1.

100 Zohar, Genesis 25b.

101 TB 93b. This is based on the verses from Isaiah 11:3-4: He will be scented by the fear of God and will not judge by what his eyes see nor reproach by what his ears hear.

102 Isaiah 48:9.

103 Nemirov, *Likutei Tefilot Hamenukad*, 9:4.

104 Psalms 12:9 – quoted in the third paragraph of this discourse.

He suffers from his exaltation of prayer – held in contempt by others.[105]

Then Will Sing Moses the Messiah

> And he will make new musical instruments and songs, for his genius in song will be very great. He will innovate in this art such that the souls of those who hear his songs will faint.[106]

Music and song hold a special place in the messianic age. The messiah, no matter where he goes, is constantly surrounded by song. 'And he will have a chair carried by able men and he will walk a few steps and they will lower the chair for him and he will sit. There will be a choir with musical instruments and they will sing each time.' However, the messiah will be more than an interested audiophile. He himself will be a great innovator[107] in the musical realm, 'for his genius in song will be very great.'[108] This is so regarding both the fashioning of new musical instruments as well as the creation of new melodies. It may be that his musical innovation is not limited to these concrete realms, however – it may include more general areas of the art as well. Regardless, his songs will be noteworthy for the dramatic effect which they will have upon those who hear them, such that, 'their very souls will faint.'[109]

The *Scroll* reveals a hitherto unknown facet of the messiah which reflects upon the messianic age at large. The messiah is a music lover; he makes certain that he is constantly surrounded by song. The messiah's travels are part of

---

105 In other discourses R. Nachman claims that the Moses-messiah-like aspect of tzadikim can be manifested not only through prayer, but also through Torah scholarship and other disciplines. See, for example, Nemirov, *Likutei Tefilot Hamenukad*, 118.

106 Section II, line 57.

107 Ibid.

108 Ibid. A similar sentiment is found in *Siach Sorfei Kodesh*, vol. 3, 38: He said, 'The messiah will reveal a new path in music.'

109 Section II, line 58.

an intensive musical awakening throughout the world. He walks only a 'few steps' between each of his accompanying choir's musical numbers. He himself is a musical genius, reaching the very hearts of his listeners with his innovative art. Not a soul can remain unmoved by his compositions. The messiah conquers the world, first and foremost, by conquering the hearts of his followers with prayer, wisdom and the power of never-before-heard song.[110]

Here too, though, we find that the image of the singing messiah as the ultimate actualization of the tzadik found in the *Scroll* is not new. Rather, it too is part of the exoteric Breslav literature which depicts the tzadik as a reflection of R. Nachman himself.

The Tzadik's Song

In the discourse, 'Bo el Paroh' (Come to Pharaoh), R. Nachman discusses the kabalistic concepts of contraction and empty space. In this context he relates to the subject of music and its connection to the messianic age. The concept of 'empty space' is a fundamental part of R. Nachman's theology and much has been written about it in the scholarly literature.[111] In order to better understand the background and context of the role that R. Nachman prescribes for music and song I will briefly sketch here the stream of thought which he presents in this discourse.[112]

Empty space and contraction are Lurianic concepts which pertain to processes which preceded the creation of the world. Before any being was formed, God's totality filled the entirety of all space – leaving no room for

---

110 This description of the messiah can be seen as an expansion of the Talmudic comment that Hezekiah's failure to become the messiah was due to his failure to sing (TB Sanhedrin 94a). R. Nachman's messiah is intent on correcting this fault. I hope to write on the connection between song, messianism and R. Nachman's two *Tikunim* in a forthcoming work.

111 Hillel Tzeitlen, *Rav Nachman Mebreslav: Chaiyav Vetorato* (Warsaw: 1910), 14; Weiss, *Studies in Bratslav Hasidism*, 87-95 and 109-49, esp. 21-41; Green, *Master*, 311-18; Shaul Magid, "Through the Void: The Absence of God in R. Nachman of Breslav's *Likuttei Moharan*," *Harvard Theological Review* 88 (1995).

112 Mark, *Mysticism and Madness In the Work of R. Nachman of Bresav*, 257-80.

anything but Him. When he decided to create the world, He contracted himself creating a space empty of His light. In this empty space He created the world. It is the very fact that our existence is located in a space devoid of Divine knowledge and speech, claims R. Nachman, which precipitates heretical doubt and questioning. These problems are unanswerable. Therefore, both the tzadik and the ordinary believer need to remain silent in the face of this void. However, there is an essential difference between the tzadik's silence and that of the ordinary individual. Whereas the ordinary person is called upon to faithfully ignore these problems and move beyond them, one of the tzadik's tasks is to wrestle with the heretical beliefs which stem from this emptiness so that he may elevate the souls trapped within. Silence is not the final step for the tzadik, but only a temporary measure which prepares the way for the decisive stage – song. 'Know that through song, the tzadik, Moses-like, raises the souls from the heresy of the empty space into which they have fallen.'[113] The empty space is void of words, not melody; the silence therein is lack of speech, not song.

The instrument through which the Moses-like tzadik is called upon to engage the heretical is music. R. Nachman explains, 'Every single type of wisdom has its own special melody... from its own song stems each type of wisdom.'[114] These types of wisdom are arranged hierarchically; so too their melodies. At the pinnacle of the hierarchy is that which lies beyond the grasp of the human intellect.

> It is impossible to know or comprehend the wisdom which resides in the Endless Light, for the Endless Light is the Holy One Himself. His wisdom is impossible to comprehend, so there we find only faith – we believe in Him.... Faith was its own unique song and melody. Just as we see regarding even the false beliefs of the nations, each belief has its own melody which they sing and use in their houses of worship – so too in

113 R. Natan of Nemirov, *Likutei Tefilot Hamenukad*, 64:5.

114 Ibid.

> the holy, each belief has a unique song and melody. The unique song of faith, which corresponds to that belief which lies above all types of wisdom and beliefs – that is, the belief in the Endless Light Itself which surrounds all worlds, as we mentioned above – that song also lies above all the other songs and melodies in the world which belong to the other types of wisdom and belief.[115]

Only through this song of faith can the tzadik raise up those who have fallen into the heretical empty space which admits of no penitence by way of ordinary speech or knowledge.[116] This melody which belongs to the Moses-like tzadik, claims R. Nachman, is akin to the World-to-Come. This is the song of the messianic age.

> In the future he will convert all the nations to one clear language so all may call in the name of God,[117] and all will believe in Him, and then [the prophecy will be fulfilled] 'Come sing from the peak of Mount Faith.'[118] From the peak of faith specifically: that is from the highest type of belief, as mentioned above, the pinnacle of all faith. And 'sing', specifically: that is the melody and song which belongs to this belief.[119]

Similar to that which we saw in the *Scroll*, the song of faith will be actualized in full only in the messianic age – as part of the messianic revolution which will sweep the entire world. However, it is important to note that this does not necessarily mean that this song cannot be sung already today. The Moses-like tzadik can already hear the music which echoes from within the world-to-come, even before the age of the messiah has begun.

---

115 Ibid.

116 For further explanation see Mark, *Mysticism and Madness In the Work of R. Nachman of Breslav*, 266-70.

117 Following Tzephaniah 3:9.

118 Song of Songs 4:8.

119 Nemirov, *Likutei Tefilot Hamenukad*, 64:5.

> Nobody beside the generation's tzadik is deserving of this song of highest faith, for he is akin to Moses, who alone has reached this level of faith.... This is 'Then will sing Moses'[120] of which our Sages said, '*sung* is not used, rather *will sing*, from this we know of the raising of the dead from the Torah'[121] – for in the future Moses will also sing. All song, whether of this world or the next, belongs only to Moses, who is connected to silence, as he merited the song which belongs to the highest faith, wherein is contained all song, for all song emanates from it.[122]

The generation's tzadik, then, despite being only Moses-like and not having risen from the dead himself, can already ascend to the heights from which Moses himself will sing in the World-to-Come. Therefore, it is incumbent upon this tzadik, who has reached these heights and attained the messianic melody of faith, to use it as it will be used in the future today: to rescue those who have fallen into heresy and disbelief.

> Therefore, by means of the tzadik's melody, who himself is akin to Moses, he elevates and rescues all those souls which have fallen into the heresy of the empty space. This song is akin to the pinnacle of faith; that is the faith which is above all, for through song and this faith all heresy is dissolved – as all songs are diffused within this song, which is above them all.[123]

We see, then, that also regarding the place of music, the messiah depicted in the *Scroll* is similar to the one painted by R. Nachman in his exoteric works. The *Scroll* describes a future wherein the messiah actualizes the principle 'through song and this faith all heresy is dissolved' and develops a picture of that future where the importance of song is made manifest in

---

120 Exodus, 16:1.

121 TB Sanhedrin 91b.

122 R. Natan of Nemirov, *Likutei Tefilot Hamenukad*, 64:5.

123 Ibid.

the messianic revolution. In his other works, R. Nachman emphasizes that the song of the future, to be sung by Moses, is also available to the contemporary tzadik, who is Moses-like.

The Song that R. Nachman will Sing

In an unpublished fragment found in the manuscript of *Chayei Moharan*, R. Nachman describes the song that he will sing in the future.

> He said: I will sing the song in the future that will be the World-to-Come of all the tzadikim and Chasidim.[124]

The manuscript's copyist connected this statement to the discourse 'Bo el Paro.'[125] It is difficult to ignore the connection between the future song of the Moses-messiah who 'is above everything'[126] and R. Nachman's statement regarding his own song. R. Nachman's song will itself not only represent the highest attainable understanding, but will be the very World-to-Come for the righteous. There is not only a connection between singers and songs, but a near equivalency between the two.

As we saw above, the future song of faith is already extant in the hands of the generation's tzadik. So too, the irresistible melody which R. Nachman will eventually sing already exists.

> He said: 'The world has tasted nothing yet. If they would hear just one of my teachings together with its melody and dance, they would all submit completely. The entire world, even the animals and plants – everything

124 *Chayei Moharan Im Hashmatot*, 272. A similar sentence is found there at page 312 as well as in other manuscripts.

125 Ibid. The copyist refers to 'Blow the Shofar,' related on Rosh Hashana of 1810. We will return to this discourse below.

126 R. Natan of Nemirov, *Likutei Tefilot Hamenukad*, 64:5.

> – all would submit completely. Their very souls would faint from the sheer wondrous ecstasy.'[127]

Just as R. Nachman explained that each type and level of wisdom has its own melody, so too, each of his own teachings has its own special melody and dance. Only one who has heard them all together has really experienced something of R. Nachman.[128] The claim that anyone who would hear one of his teachings with its complete choreography would undergo such a radical experience that his 'very soul would faint' is, of course, parallel to the description of the power of the messiah's melody found in the *Scroll* which also causes souls to faint.[129]

Further on in the text, R. Natan extols the power of R. Nachman's melody, defining it as, 'the pleasure of pleasures which has no equal.'[130] Afterwards he details two distinct stages in the melody's influence on those who hear it. The first stage contains neither understanding nor action, but only longing and yearning. 'Those standing nearby do not know what to do, their souls faint and they feel a wondrous longing stemming from sheer force of delight.' Afterwards, this longing leads to action, albeit action which stems not from any cerebral understanding, but rather which occurs almost of its own volition.

> Also, each person who is closer, his movements happen of their own accord, as he senses that mentioned above. Whoever is closer to the melody and dance understands more and performs the melody's movements automatically due to his great pleasure.... Likewise, the closer one is to the holy, that is – the closer to the teaching, the song and the dance

127 *Chayei Moharan Im Hashmatot*, 310.

128 On dance in R. Nachman's thought see Michael Fishbane, "*The Mystery of Dance according to Rabbi Nachman of Breslav*," in *Within Chasidic Circles*, ed. Emanuel Etkes (Jerusalem: 1990); Paul B. Fenton, "*Sacred Dance in Jewish Spirituality: Chasidic Dance*," *Da'at* 45 (2000).

129 Section II, line 58.

130 See above, note 127.

– the more the movements occur on their own owing to the holiness. All this I heard myself.[131]

The influence of R. Nachman's holy melody is 'automatic.' The song sweeps away its listener causing him to dance the melody as if enchanted. These descriptions match the *Scroll*'s depiction of the messiah's authority as well. In the second section, the messiah is envisioned as a powerful charismatic who draws others to his side not by dint of arms or through any intellectual persuasion. No religious debates take place and no Kulturkampf is needed to herald the messianic revolution. The messiah's strength lies in his own personal charisma and appeal, his skill in the arts of healing and, especially music, which he uses to create new irresistible songs.

'...such that the souls of those who hear his songs will faint, etc';[132]

'Because everyone will live nearby him due to their great yearning for him such that they cannot be without him;'[133]

'Initially he will be king of Israel and afterwards emperor over all until finally all will surrender themselves to him due to the favor, glory, love and yearning that they will all feel towards him until they will completely nullify themselves before him;'[134]

'All will surrender themselves to him with neither war nor struggle in light of his beauty and their longing for him.'[135]

Yearning, attraction, love – these are the feelings that are characteristic of the connection to the messiah. The strength of this connection reaches complete dependence – 'they cannot be without him' and even beyond

131 Ibid.

132 Section II, line 58.

133 Ibid., line 40.

134 Ibid., line 13.

135 Ibid., line 67.

– to complete surrender. These emotions are remarkably similar to those that R. Nachman mentioned in describing his own potential influence on the world – if they would only listen. 'If they would hear just one of my discourses together with its melody and dance, they would all submit completely. The entire world, even the animals and plants – everything – all would submit completely. Their very souls would faint from the sheer wondrous ecstasy.'[136]

R. Nachman likened his own ability to influence the world to that which a master musician can have upon his audience. As we saw above, when R. Nachman traveled to Novorich he claimed that if not for the interference of the 'Stinking One,' he would be able to affect the entire world for good. Just as 'it is enough that the servant be like his master', he too was fated to wander and suffer leaving his potential unfulfilled. However, despite this, his departure on this journey was cause for great optimism and even joy.

> Before he set out on this journey, he clapped his hands with joy and said, 'Today is the beginning of something new.' Then he said, 'We are like musicians who play and the audience dances. To someone who can't hear the music this spectacle is absurd. Why are they running about? When I return from my trip, I'll be able to play and you will be able to dance.' After this he traveled to Novorich....[137]

R. Natan's words seem odd. Even before this journey, R. Nachman played and his followers danced. What was meant to change after his return? It may be that behind this episode lies the well-known parable told by R. Nachman's grand-father, the Baal Shem Tov, about the musician and the deaf man. This is the tale as told by R. Nachman's uncle, R. Ephraim of Sedelikav:

> I heard this parable from my father while traveling: There once was a musician who played his instruments with such beauty and sweetness

136 *Chayei Moharan Im Hashmatot*, 310-12.

137 Ibid., 190.

> that those who heard him could not contain themselves. The sweet delight [of the music] would start them dancing with unbelievable zest. The closer anybody was to an instrument, the nearer he would draw to hear the instrument and the greater his joy would be and the more he would dance. Once, a deaf man who could hear nothing of the beautiful music, but only saw the people dancing, thought them crazy. He said to himself, 'What are they doing?' If he had been wise, he would have known that it was because of their great delight in the music and he too would have danced there. The moral is obvious.[138]

After reading this parable we can understand that R. Nachman's hoped that after his return even the audience that wondered why his followers ran after him so, would themselves hear the music or at least understand why his followers were dancing. The musical imagery used in this parable is utilized in the *Scroll* to describe the power of the messiah's influence as well as by R. Nachman to explain his own effect on his world. '...Whoever is closer to the melody and dance understands more and performs the melody's movements automatically due to his great pleasure.... Likewise, the closer one is to the holy, that is – the closer to the teaching, the song and the dance – the more the movements occur on their own owing to the holiness.....[139] Here too we see that the descriptions of the messiah and the messianic age in the *Scroll* are in fact quite clear reflections of R. Nachman's own persona as presented elsewhere.

The Messiah as Doctor

> ...and he will make new compounds. The daily schedule will be an hour in which he will eat and will drink and he will practice contemplative religious introspection. He will walk amongst all the sick that

---

138 Rav Efraim of Sedlikolov, *Degel Machaneh Efraim* (Jerusalem: 1994), 101.

139 *Chayei Moharan Im Hashmatot*, 311.

come and quickly command each what he should take – each effective things from the same orchard, from the new compounds.[140]

And he will announce what he will do each day – at this hour such an activity, etc. For three hours he will treat the sick that will come, as even then there will be illness. The sick will come to him and he will instruct them to take from the orchard which he will make containing the new compounds the likes of which have never been before. He will go among the sick and instruct each of them to take that which he knows according to the powers of the appointed angels which daily visit each blade of grass.[141]

Just as in the field of music, so too in the field of medicine the messiah will innovate on several levels. He plants a unique orchard containing new medicinal agents. He is also able to prepare new compounds never before seen, thanks to his knowledge of the heavenly spheres above and their agents.

The understanding that the potency of these compounds is dependent upon a process which begins with heavenly agents, moves through flora and ends in the compounds that the doctor makes from them, appears in a number of R. Nachman's works. Thus for example, he explains the secret of medicine in his discourse, 'Beshaah' (At the Time).

All medicine works through the cosmic forces, which are the heavenly hosts. Each one gives potency to a particular drug or plant which belongs to it, and from which each of the drugs or plants receives its medicinal power. When one needs healing, one combines several of the astral forces which are found each in one of several plants. By combining them all, one makes a medical compound.[142]

140 Section I, line 25.

141 Section II,

142 Nemirov, *Sefer Likutei Moharan Hamenukad*, 231.

A more detailed explanation of this theory is found in the discourse 'Sha'alu Talmidav' (His Students Asked),[143] in which the connection between medicine and messiah is also explained. This discourse opens with a quote from Tractate Sanhedrin: 'His students asked R. Yossi ben Kisma, 'When will the son of David arrive….' He said to them, 'When this gate will collapse and be rebuilt, collapse and be rebuilt and collapse. And it will not be rebuilt until the son of David arrives.'[144] After this quote, R. Nachman begins by describing the chain of being which opens with the word of God and ends with medicinal compounds.

> Know, for each and every word that leaves the holy one's mouth an angel is created...[145] Each of these angels is responsible for a specific thing, even the trees and the plants have their own angels, as our Sages said: There is no plant below that lacks an angel above.[146] Every angle receives his life-force from that word and acts upon that for which he is responsible – that is, the plant or other thing.... So all healing is dependent upon the Torah, in the sense, '[My words] are a remedy to all flesh.'[147] For the Torah gives strength to the angels, the angels act upon plants, and the plants heal through the power of the Torah.[148]

In an addendum to this discourse printed as an afterword, it is made clear that 'all healing results from mixtures.'[149] It is also emphasized that healing power is not found in the medicinal herbs themselves but rather, 'the essence of all healing comes through the compounding of [plants] – the creation of one new power which receives its potency from all those herbs

---

143 Ibid., 67. This was also written by R. Nachman himself.

144 TB Sanhedrin 98a.

145 TB Chagigah 14a.

146 Breishit Rabbah, 10.

147 Parables 4:22.

148 R. Natan of Nemirov, *Sefer Likutei Moharan Hamenukad*, 67:1.

149 Ibid., in additions.

which are combined. From this power of combination are illnesses healed.'[150] The knowledge of compounds is the expertise of the 'master physician, but the non-expert – even if he would take the herbs which have healing properties, they will have no affect, for he does not know how to combine them.'[151] Because the herbs and herbal compounds receive their potency from their ministering angels and these from the word of God found in the Torah, ultimately the power to heal depends upon the Torah.

The process of combining and creating new healing compounds which requires expert knowledge finds its parallel in the study of Torah itself.

> So too the Torah, which is the remedy for everything, as it is written, 'a remedy to all flesh,' only the generation's sages really understand it, for only they received the thirteen hermeneutic principles. It is impossible to know anything from the Torah itself, only from the generation's sages who interpret it, for the Torah is sparce in one place and rich in another.[152] It is the sages who harvest and combine the Torah and interpret from place to place using the thirteen principles. They remove, add and interpret (TB Baba Batra 111b) – even if in the Torah it is written thus, they remove a letter or a word and position it in other place. In this way they interpret it as they know, as has been entrusted to them.[153]

The parallel that R. Nachman finds between the Torah and the art of healing is not understood as a mere analogy. Rather it is an actual amalgamation which carries real medical consequences.

> Therefore if one insults a Torah sage, one finds no remedy for his injury. For the essence of healing potency that one receives from the

---

150 Ibid.

151 Ibid.

152 TY Rosh Hashana 17a.

153 R. Natan of Nemirov, *Sefer Likutei Moharan Hamenukad*, ibid.

Torah cannot be received except through the sages of one's generation. To them was interpretation entrusted and [only] they know how to combine the letters of the Torah (as explained above), which is the essence of the potency of all healing – for all herbs receive their potency from the Torah – and the essential potency of healing resides in their compounding (as mentioned above). Therefore, essentially, all depends upon the generation's sages. They know how to interpret the Torah and combine its letters [through which] all the herbal compounds receive their potency – through the Torah. Faith in the sages, then, is vital. One must honor and greatly respect them .... Therefore one must believe in the sages, abandon his own reason and knowledge and only rely upon them – for to them the Torah was entrusted for interpretation.[154]

The ability of a Torah interpretation to influence a medicinal compound depends upon the trust of the ill patient in the sage and his interpretations. Even if a sage prepares a new compound, if he does not acquire the trust of the patient there can be 'no remedy for his injury.' These ideas are developed in the body of the discourse alongside new claims concerning the ability of fasts and eating on the Sabbath to alleviate pain and rid one of enemies. At the conclusion of this discourse, R. Nachman returns to the curious text with which he opened, 'when will the son of David arrive.' Unfortunately, the text has been censored: that which he related orally regarding the intimate connection between healing and the coming of the messiah, he later decided to excise from the written record.

Here is the text with a comment from R. Natan following:

Regarding what they asked R. Yossi ben Kisma, when will the son of David arrive.... The main point is that [the gate] will fall three times and cannot be repaired [the third time] until the son of David arrives. For the gate of Aram is like the gate to the Evil Side, when it falls time after time, according

154 Ibid.

to that which I discussed above*, then the son of David will come and build the gates of holiness. That is, when there is no faith in our sages, and they are not heeded, as in 'they ensnare the critic in the [city-] gate,'[155] this causes incurable illness, as in 'they arrived at the gates of death.'[156] However, when they have faith, then the gates of holiness open for them.[157]

*[Here our Master, skipped several words which were written in his own language, in his holy hand, and when he gave me this discourse to copy, erased several words from his holy handwriting, so that I would not copy them. I saw that this was his clear intention, as was his want several times in different discourses. He would be especially careful when he gave a manuscript for copying to erase several of the words that were critical to the matter and to skip over the middle, for he did not want these things to be discovered. One who carefully examines these places can discern that something from the body of the matter is missing, and this can be noticed here as well. He wrote 'when it falls… according to that which I discussed above,' – but this is not his usual language. All this was carefully and clearly written, but he intentionally skipped this part – all his words were well measured as to what to reveal and what not to reveal. He was careful not to speak or write even one extra word in accord with his great wisdom … if it was not necessary to reveal this. …and so it was in several of the discourses that he gave to be copied, but these are old matters.][158]

It is difficult to know what exactly R. Nachman had written and why he excised it. However, other extant materials which are directly related to our subject offer us some clues. The coming of the son of David is tied to faith in sages, a faith which requires the abandonment of one's 'reason and knowledge' – a veritable blind faith. This faith, though, delivers one from

155 Isaiah 29:21.

156 Psalms 37:18.

157 R. Natan of Nemirov, *Sefer Likutei Moharan Hamenukad*, 67:8.

158 Ibid.

enemies and also from death which stems from incurable disease.[159] Only this absolute faith in the abilities of the sages to create new Torah interpretations, despite the appearance that they conflict with what is explicitly written therein, allows for these 'compounds' to work their healing magic and 'then the son of David will arrive.'

We see that the connection between medicinal herbal compounds and messianic times is already found in this discourse. However, there is no direct linkage between the messiah himself and this healing activity here. In the *Scroll*, this identification is made explicitly: the messiah himself is the innovative healer who will create new, never before known healing compounds and will personally distribute them to the myriad sick who beat a path to his door. According to the *Scroll*, this medical role is a standard part of the messiah's day.

However, as we saw in other spheres, also regarding the art of healing, it is only the messiah himself who is endowed with ultimate healing power. R. Nachman evaluated his own abilities as not falling far from these.

> (This belongs to the *Alef-Bet* [*Sefer HaMidot*] and the matter of healing which is written in another place) He said that he had in his *Alef-Bet*, under R for remedies, written all the remedies and there was no illness in the world for which the remedy was not there written. However, he did not want to transcribe it and so burned it.[160]

R. Nachman possessed the knowledge and skill to cure all of the world's illnesses, but decided to forsake his unique skill and destroy the medical records. This is similar to the hiding of the medical book by Hezekiah the king as described in the Talmud. According to legend, he possessed a book of cures which he hid away and the Sages blessed him for this.[161] Hezekiah, who according to the Talmud was destined to become the messiah but lost his op-

---

159 Ibid.

160 *Chayei Moharan Im Hashmatot*, 06.

161 TB 10b.

portunity by failing to praise God in song (and according to some, in fact did become the messiah and actualized all the messianic prophecies)[162] possessed outstanding medical knowledge which could cure all illness. He too, however, decided to forsake this ability and hid his famed book away.[163]

The similar decision by R. Nachman to burn his own list of cures strengthens the parallel between him and the biblical king/potential messiah, yet also underscores the realization that the messianic age had still not arrived. Like Hezekiah, R. Nachman could have been the messiah, but upon realizing that he would not attain this status and that the messianic age would have to wait for another, he destroyed his own book of cures.

Faith in Sages and the Coming of the Son of David

From the language in the discourse, 'Sha'alu Talmidav' (His Students Asked), it is not clear whether absolute faith in the sages is what leads to the messianic age or if the arrival of the messiah is what heralds this change in belief and its resultant benefits. It may be, though, that the two are actually cotemporaneous in nature – part of one spiritual process.

At the beginning of this section we quoted R. Nachman's assertion that the only difference between himself and the actual messiah was the matter of obedience: the messiah would be obeyed, but R. Nachman was not. We also noted how R. Nachman saw himself as a potential messiah denied the chance to fulfill his destiny by those who made trouble for him. I would like to suggest that these two notions taken together can help advance a thesis as to why he censored the section of his discourse that dealt with the personal, and perhaps even actual,[164] connection between healing, faith

162 TB Sanhedrin 94a.

163 R. Nachman develops this idea in 'Teku Memshala', R. Natan of Nemirov, *Sefer Likutei Moharan Hamenukad*, section 2, 1.

164 We have no evidence regarding the exact date that 'Sha'alu Talmidav' was first related. The discourse preceeding it was related in 1805; that following on Rosh Hashana 1805. Even though the discourses are not arranged in a strict chronological fashion, we may assume that this discourse was related between these two dates. If this is the case, it was related before

and messianism. The linkage of blind faith[165] to messianic times perhaps intimated that it was just the stubborn refusal to accept his, R. Nachman's, word with complete faith that prevented him from actualizing his potential. If only he had been believed, he would have been able to open the gates to the holy before the entire world and release the healing potential found in the unique combination of Torah and flora for all.[166]

Messianic Appeal

> Initially he will be king of Israel and afterwards emperor over all until
> finally all will surrender themselves to him due to the favor, glory,
> love and yearning that they will all feel towards him
> until they will completely nullify themselves before him.[167]
> All will surrender themselves to him with neither war nor struggle in
> light of his beauty and their longing for him.[168]

The importance of beauty and grace is a subject that occupied R. Nachman from his first recorded discourse in *Likutei Moharan* – '*Ashrei Temimei Derech*' (Happy are Those who Agree on the Path), until his last – '*Breishit*' (In the Beginning), told to his followers in his last year on Earth.[169] In the former, R. Nachman describes the Torah as 'a beautiful doe, which beautifies all those who study it (TB Eruvin 52b).' Beauty plays an important role in the relationship between Israel and her heavenly Father for with the help of the

---

R. Nachman's despairing of the hasty arrival of the messiah after the death of his son in the summer of 1806.

165 Ibid.

166 The use of healing herbs, described here and in other discourses, contradicts the ideal of healing through prayer alone which also finds expression in R. Nachman's writings. This matter requires attention.

167 Section II, line 13.

168 Ibid., line 67.

169 This discourse was related in the fall of 1809.

grace that it bestows, 'all prayers and supplications are answered.' It is also an important aspect of the place that Israel holds among the nations, 'for now, due to our many sins, the grace and importance of Israel has fallen, for now these are found among them [the nations],' but with the help of the Torah, 'the grace and importance of Israel will rise before all that matter, both physically and spiritually.' While R. Nachman describes how Jacob merited this grace which he then passed on to his son Joseph, in general he uses the concept to relate to the entire nation of Israel as a whole.

In the *Scroll*, however, there is no discussion of the Jewish people as the possessors of grace – rather grace and beauty are two of the main attributes of the charismatic messiah. His very physical loveliness draws his followers to him and is part of what allows him to lead them. The *Scroll*, then, depicts the messiah as the conduit of Israel's grace which raises its status among the nations.

In the discourse, 'Teku Beshofar' (Sound the Shofar), which was recited on the New Year in 1808 and chosen as the opening text for *Likutei Moharan II*, R. Nachman again raises the subject of beauty and grace as part of the messianic modus operandi. Here the messiah is described as possessing the power to heal others to such a degree that all doctors and medicines are rendered superfluous.[170] The messiah does not just pray; rather he becomes the conduit for all prayer.

> Because of this he is called the *meshiach* (messiah), for he takes all *siach* (prayer) from the fields, that is all of the fragrances that waft up from prayer. This is connected to the nose, as in, 'I will stop-up my honor,' etc. The messiah receives these prayers, as we say 'the spirit of our noses, God's anointed,' as mentioned above.[171] This is connected to finding favor, as in, 'And Esther found favor in the eyes of all who saw her'[172] – 'to

---

170 See above note 166.

171 See note 101 above.

172 The Book of Esther 2:15.

> each and everyone she appeared as his own nationality.'[173] For the master of prayer is akin to the word of God, which is the uppermost source from which all forces and all of the heavenly hosts receive [their life-force]. Therefore, to all of the heavenly hosts and ministers who receive from him, he appears as one of them – of the same nationality: that is he finds favor in his eyes. To each one it seems that he deals with him alone, for all receive from him.[174]

The messiah, the master of prayer, is also a part of the persona of Esther, who saved the Jewish people with her ability to find favor in the eyes of others. This virtue, explains R. Nachman, following the Talmud, is the ability to relate to each individual in such a way that each feels a special connection – as if Esther was of his own people and relating only to him. The favor that the master of prayer can find in the eyes of others functions on both the cosmic and on the national/personal level.

In the discourse 'Breishit' (II 67), grace is described as a parallel to beauty, splendor and majesty. Beauty and grace are the attributes of the Joseph-like messiah, who 'is the grace and beauty of the entire world.' The beauty of the tzadik is not merely an external physical description, but rather 'the true tzadik, who is Joseph-like, is the splendor and beauty of the entire world.' Not only does the tzadik himself gain from his grace, but all who are drawn to him become part of his aura of beauty and can benefit from all that it offers.

An additional short sermon on the subject of beauty is preserved in *Sichot Haran* (R. Natan's Discourses). Here too, R. Nachman ties the notion of beauty to Joseph and claims that it was his beauty which granted him the power of dreaming prophetic dreams and dream interpretation.[175]

---

173 TB Megillah 13a.

174 R. Natan of Nemirov, *Sefer Likutei Moharan Hamenukad*, section II, 1:12-3.

175 *Sichot Haran*, 302-3.

'You found favor in the eyes of everyone, for your prayer's power was second to none':[176] R. Nachman the Beautiful

Throughout the Breslav literature we find many references to R. Nachman's physical beauty: 'He possessed all sorts of the world's beauty. He was full of the world's wondrous love and respect.'[177]; 'When a holy word would leave his lips, it was a most holy, awesome, beautiful truth.'[178]; 'He would often converse with us with great joy and wondrous, awesome beauty.'[179]; 'The wondrously sweet and holy words which he spoke in purity, respect, fear and trembling were simply indescribable – for he possessed all of the world's beauty which would delicately leave a mark upon any who heard him – even when he was speaking of everyday things.'[180]

R. Natan even breathlessly described the amazingly beautiful visage of R. Nachman's corpse.

> I returned and entered his room and found him already dead on the floor.... His face was uncovered, slightly smiling – how awesome his visage was! He appeared as he did when alive – just as when he was immersed in thought pacing in his house to and fro – blessed with all the world's beauty. He still had this same awesome grace and wondrous beauty when he lay on the floor. It is indescribable except to one who saw him when he was alive walking to and fro.[181]

---

176 *Shir Yedidut Hamenukad,* (Jerusalem: 1981). This was written in honor of R. Nachman, and 'was found in the pouch of one of his disciples' (68). This poem was also printed in *Chayei Moharan*, II, 4 In another poem we find, 'a thread of mercy and true favor lit upon his beautiful face' (13).

177 *Chayei Moharan Im Hashmatot*, 262.

178 Ibid., 207:23.

179 *Sichot Haran*, 199.

180 Ibid., 262. Note the following description of R. Nachman: Once R. Natan said, 'Our Rebbe had a true holy beauty. I have no such beauty, but thank God, I lack false beauty' (*Siach Sorfei Kodesh*, vol 2, 179).

181 Rav Natan of Nemirov, *Yemei Moharnat* (Jerusalem: 1982), 94.

The conclusion of the book *Chayei Moharan* is also devoted to R. Nachman's exceptional beauty. It gathers together several motifs connected to this attribute, R. Nachman and the messiah.

> This I found in the manuscript of *Chayei Moharan* written by R. Natan in the following language:
> Who can describe the great majesty of the holy speech which left the mouth of our Master in holiness, purity, clarity and the utmost lucidity? Even physically, the greatest beauty in the world rested on his holy words, which shocked even the simple folk as they would long to hear his words from his mouth. Everyone who would converse with him was drawn to him and grew attached to him with great longing. Even the wicked of the community in Uman were all quite attached to him and were awakened just enough that they began to feel the pangs of repentance – something that had never entered their hearts before. They themselves related that they had already given up on themselves, they were certain that they would never return to the fold, as they were so distant from any thought of penitence, as was well-known to any who knew them. But, his holy words touched them, bringing them to thoughts of penitence – despite his never having discussed with them either repentance or other spiritual matters. On the contrary, he only spoke to them of the mundane and ordinary. Despite this, they were drawn to the holy by his speech alone such that they were very close to becoming his followers. If not for the fact that time was not on his side and the 'prosecutor' gained the upper hand so that he departed still midstream, they surely would have repented and returned to God.[182]

This text opens with praise of R. Nachman's speech even on the physical level: it was possible to discern in his words the 'greatest beauty in the world'. Further on the power of this beauty is described. It was capable of enchanting even the simple folk and arousing in them great longing: 'Everyone who

182 *Chayei Moharan Im Hashmatot*, 470-1.

would converse with him was drawn to him and grew attached to him with great longing'. Both the content and the language found in this text are very similar to that found in the *Scroll*. Regarding the enormous influence of the messiah's beauty: '... all will surrender themselves to him due to the favor, glory, love and yearning that they will all feel towards him until they will completely nullify themselves before him.'[183] 'All will surrender themselves to him with neither war nor struggle in light of his beauty and their longing for him.'[184]

The force of his beauty and grace is exemplified through the interesting relationship that R. Nachman had with the 'wicked' of Uman – the *maskilim* of the Jewish community.[185] R. Nachman succeeded in drawing them to the holy without recourse to disputation, preaching or words of Torah,[186] but rather simply through discussions of 'the mundane and ordinary'. The force of these plain words lay in their inherent charm and holiness which drew his listeners closer to repentance. Even though it would be no insult to R. Nachman to suggest that his success in drawing the alienated nearer was due to his sharp intellect, R. Natan insists that it was only his grace and charm which effected this change in those who were in contact with him. It appears that behind this description lies the identification of the Rebbe with the Joseph-like tzadik – the master of both prayer and beauty. The story of R. Nachman's effect on the townsfolk of Uman is but one example of what he could have accomplished if his work had not been so unfortunately

183 Section II, line 13

184 Ibid., line 67.

185 On the relationship between R. Nachman and Uman's non-religious community, see Green, *Master*, 250-66. On R. Nachman's own thoughts on them see also, Shmuel Finer, " *Sola fide! The Polemic of Rabbi Nathan of Nemirov Against Atheism and Haskala*," *Jerusalem Studies In Jewish Thought* 15 (1999).

186 R. Nachman of Tscherin also stressed that in his dealings with this community, R. Nachman chose not 'the path of confrontation and chastisement, but despite this some of them were drawn to our Rebbe and surrendered to him until they whole-heartedly proclaimed that if he had not died so quickly after his arrival in Uman they would have repented' (Rav Nachman of Tscherin, *Parparot Lechachma* (Jerusalem: 1983), 110).

interrupted. R. Natan's claim that 'they surely would have repented and returned to God'[187] may also be a hint that the Rebbe's work there was but one stage in an ever expanding plan to widen his circle of influence which would have reached well beyond his own group of disciples and followers.

The rest of this text affirms that this is indeed the case. It suggests that the untimely death of the Rebbe was a mere delay in the spread of his word and influence: both are tied directly to the messianic age.

> No matter what we may tell about him it is an affront to his actual extraordinary stature. Despite all the days [that have passed], it is still impossible to describe but a small fraction of his greatness and holiness – his wisdom and his renowned learning, and his mighty holiness – silence is the highest praise.[188] Only with his [the messiah's] arrival in Shiloh[189] will they know and respect our great holy Rebbe – for then when our righteous messiah, of his own lineage, arrives, then it will be often told how he influenced God so that the righteous redeemer would be the fruit of his own loins.[190] May it be Your will that he arrive speedily in our day. Amen.[191]

The tension between speech and silence is noticeable in R. Natan's words. On the one hand, he realizes that less is often more – singing the praises of the Rebbe may actually have a deleterious effect leading to mockery and conflict. Therefore, silence may be best. On the other hand, R. Nachman himself was

---

187 *Chayei Moharan Im Hashmatot*, 471.

188 Rashi in TB Megillah 18a writes: The best of medicines is silence, to lessen one's speech, as it is written 'To You silence is praise' (Psalms 65:2).

189 Genesis 49:10.

190 See note 36 above. He said, "What God will do with me, I don't know. But I have influenced Him so that the righteous redeemer will come from my offspring." This he said in public and warned [us] to honor and respect his children for they are very precious trees and will produce wonderously good fruits. He also said that his children were from the world of *atzilut* (emanation). The latter reads: 'The world believes that when the messiah arrives mortality will cease. This is incorrect – even the messiah himself will die. This he said in public.' This notion is connected to R. Nachman's contention that 'his family has descended from King David, as all know' (254 5).

191 Ibid., 471.

not afraid to tell others that the messiah would be of his own lineage. During the actual messianic age, all would eventually come to know this. This would not only remedy past injury, but will become part of the messianic experience itself – an often told tale during messianic times. The relationship between R. Nachman and the messiah expresses more than the biological – it is an expression of spiritual continuity between the two. All this dovetails well with the R. Nachmanesque picture of the messiah that is presented in the *Scroll* and in *Likutei Moharan*. This is the messiah who will be obeyed and will be able to conclude all that which R. Nachman himself began.

R. Shmuel Horowitz, in the introduction to his book, *Tzion Mitzuyenet* (A Well Appointed Tomb), a panegyric on the pilgrimage to R. Nachman's tomb, offers a brief description of the traditional Breslav understanding of the connection between the Rebbe and the messiah.

> Our Rebbe is the fundamental root of the messiah's soul. It is known that the messiah will repair the world with the remedies of our Rebbe – that is by using the advice and remedies which are brought in his holy books. In *Chayei Moharan* it is noted that 'all that the messiah will do to benefit Israel I can also do, but the only difference is that the messiah will decree and it will come to pass, but I have still not finished.' Also the messiah will tie himself to a tzadik who has already died just like, 'and Moses took the bones of Joseph with him,'[192] etc.[193]

We should note that R. Horowitz does not claim that R. Nachman's soul stems from that of the messiah, but rather the opposite. It is R. Nachman who is the very source and root of the messiah. The messiah comes to complete that which R. Nachman himself began. The spiritual path of the messiah is the continuation of that devised by R. Nachman, set in motion through his example and detailed in his books. Although the Rebbe failed to

192 Exodus 13:19.

193 Rav Shmuel Horowitz, *Tzion Hamitzuyenet* (Jerusalem: 1990), 3-5.

complete his mission,[194] the messiah will succeed. The messiah's connection to the Rebbe is consciously made as he will 'tie himself to a tzadik who has already died just like, 'and Moses took the bones of Joseph with him.'

The Messiah, Hungarian Wine and R. Nachman

> He told a parable: 'Once a great merchant was on a journey and he had with him some special Hungarian vintage. One day his servant and the wagon driver said to him, "Aren't we also on this journey together with you and your wine – we are also forced to endure the hardships of travel – let us taste a bit of your wine." He gave them to taste this wonderful wine. Some days later, the servant happened to be in a small village together with a group of drinkers. They were drinking wine that they all greatly praised and claimed that it was of a special Hungarian vintage. The servant asked for a taste. After he tasted it, he said, "I know that this in not Hungarian wine at all." The others scolded him and pushed him away. "I know this is not Hungarian wine – I was once with a great merchant, etc." But they paid him no attention.'
> He said: 'In the future when the messiah comes, they will know what kind of wine they receive. Others can be fooled and they will give them old wine and tell them that it is from the great vintage. Only our circle will know the difference, for we have once tasted the real thing, etc.'[195]

The messiah will not deal in the theoretical, but with fact that people can taste for themselves. Once someone has tasted the real thing, he cannot be fooled by cheap imitations. 'The world has barely tasted me,' R. Nachman claimed. [196] But for those of his followers who had, the taste of messianic

194 A similar sentiment was expressed by R. Yitzchak Breiter, one of the more important Breslav Chasids in pre-war Warsaw. 'Know that the innovation of R. Nachman, the flowing fount, the source of wisdom, was not found in the world, but he prepared the vessels for the righteous messiah and the messiah will use them to repair the world' (Yitzchak Breiter, *She'arit Yitzchak* (Jerusalem: 1990), 74. I will discuss this analogy below.

195 *Chayei Moharan Im Hashmatot*, 267-8.

196 Ibid., 310.

times would stay with them forever and they would never be deceived by false prophets or sentiments.

> R. Nachman mentioned the Hungarian wine again.
> Of three things I have convinced God: … You will not suffer [even] published falsehoods, for you have already tasted from the Hungarian wine.[197]
> The tzadik of Breslav is the real thing. His Chasidim have had a taste of the messiah, not a cheap imitation. [198]
> Hillel Zeitlin was correct when he wrote: 'The tzadik, if he is a real tzadik – a tzadik for the generations – is not merely a conduit to the messiah, but an icon of, or more correctly, a prior instance of the messiah himself.'[199]
> 'Messiah-like' is a misnomer when applied to R. Nachman, for he possessed not merely some potential messianic quality which remained, in the end, unfulfilled. Rather, he was the messiah actualized; more simply R. Nachman was the messiah, and whoever accepted him merited redemption.[200] This is the meaning of what he once said: 'My messiah has already arrived.' That is, from his point of view, there is no more waiting for the messiah – he had already come.[201]

---

197 Chazan, *Avneiha Barzel*, 428-9.

198 On the tzadik who represents future achievement in the present, see Mark, *Mysticism and Madness In the Work of R. Nachman of Breslav*, 269.

199 Tzeitlen, *Al Gvul Shnei Olomot*, 327.

200 For a slightly different description of R. Nachman's attitude, see Joseph Dan, *The Modern Jewish Messianism* (Tel Aviv: 1999), 179-88; Dan, *Apocalypse Then and Now*, 253-63, 309-11.

201 *Siach Sorfei Kodesh*, vol.2 , 181 For an investigation of the tzadik as 'a reflection of the redemption', see Shatz Uffenheimer, *Chasidism as Mysticism*, 174-5.

CHAPTER TWO
The Messiah as Baby and Child in the Scroll

One of the more unusual details concerning the *Scroll*'s messiah is his youth.

> Twelve years and one-day old. On this day, that is the day mentioned above,
> Then he will become emperor over the entire world and on that day he will enter under the wedding canopy. (… [She will] be[1]… [eleven]-and-a-day[2] on that day… On that day when he will marry.) They will give him a sermon-gift.[3]

Already at the tender age of 12 the messiah is crowned emperor of the world – on the same day upon which he marries. Further on in the *Scroll* we learn that this is not the first of his public roles. Before his coronation, he has already been chosen for other public duties as well.

> Initially he will be accepted as the halachic authority throughout Israel as he

---

1 It seems that the copyist mistakenly switched a *vav* with a *nun*.

2 Again a mistaken switch of *yud-alef* with *alef-vav*.

3 Section II, line 6. This is also his wedding present. We should note that in the first section there is no mention of the messiah's age, marriage or his finding a suitable mate. All these matters are only discussed in the second section. It may be that the 'ten years' mentioned refer to the passage of this period of time since the messiah's birth or since some other stage in the messianic process.

> begins to scrutinize the Torah until he attains deep insights. They [will] begin to send him queries until it is accepted by all that he is the premier halachic authority in all of Israel. Initially he will be king of Israel and afterwards emperor over all until finally all will surrender themselves to him due to the favor, glory,
> love and yearning that they will all feel towards him until they will completely nullify themselves before him.[4]

If these two sections of the *Scroll* are in fact arranged chronologically, and it does seem logical that they are, we see that first the messiah becomes the halachic authority for all of Israel, then king of Israel, and after this, ruler of the entire world. There is also another reference to his marriage and the age of his bride.

> When he will be in the Land of Israel, they will search for a match for him even though it is proper that his match be made through divine knowledge. However, just as one who has lost an object [seeks] its return, etc. therefore a match will be searched out for him. She will be eleven and one day, on that day, will enter under the wedding canopy with him.[5]

The oddest fact concerning his age is found at the end of the *Scroll.*

> Regarding his being a halachic authority mentioned above, it seems that he said that he will be three years old and then he will be accepted as the authoritative teacher in all of Israel.[6]

---

4 Section II, line 9.

5 Ibid., line 71.

6 Ibid., line 96.

This sentence appears in square brackets in the Scroll, meaning that it was originally found only in the manuscript belonging to R. Zalman, but not in that of R. Natan.[7]

The language here, 'it seems that,' indicates that this sentence is the result of some speculation or unclear memory of what exactly was said. Perhaps this is the reason for its exclusion from R. Natan's text. However, be that as it may, the fact that the messiah is crowned emperor at 12 years of age, having already become the halachic authority and king of Israel by then, does indicate that in any event, he certainly must be a child prodigy.

1. THE CHILD-MESSIAH[8]

As we saw in the previous chapter, many of the messianic motifs in the *Scroll* can be found in R. Nachman's exoteric writings as well. However, this is not the case regarding his depiction of the messiah as a child. Almost nothing in R. Nachman's works relates to this aspect of the future world ruler. But – it does seem to be connected to R. Nachman's own biography, if not his literary output. This is noteworthy especially when we take into account the year in which he first related the contents of the *Scroll* – 1806.

Both Green and Piekarz point out that this year generated a tremendous amount of messianic anticipation in R. Nachman's circle. However, this only lasted until Shavuot of that same year, when the excitement all but vanished: hope was replaced by disappointment after the tragic death

---

7 Thus says the copyist – these things in round parentheses I did not find in the manuscript of R. Natan, may his memory be a blessing. I only copied that which I saw in the copy of the rabbi and righteous teacher R. Zalman of Medvedevkah, may his memory be a blessing, which was written in his hand.

8 On the child redeemer motif, see Carl Gustav Jung, "The Psychology of the Child Archetype," in *Essays on a Science of Mythology: The Myth of the Divine Child and Mysteries of Eleusis*, ed. C. G. Jung & Caroly Kerenyi (Princeton: 1969); David Ruderman "Three Contemporary Perceptions of a Polish Wunderkind of the Seventeenth Century," *AJS Review* 4 (1979); Gershom Scholem, "*Al Mekorotav Shel 'Ma'aseh Rabi Gadiel Hatinok' Besifrut Hakabbalah*," In *Explications and Implications*, Tel Aviv, 1975.

of R. Nachman's son, Shlomo Efraim, following the holiday.[9] R. Nachman's own words concerning his son, first printed in *Siach Sorfei Kodesh* in 1994, show the reversal in messianic mood quite clearly.

> When R. Yudel came to the celebration of the *brit* of R. Shlomo Efraim, son of our Master, dressed in new clothing, our Rebbe turned to him in joy and said: 'In these clothes you will yet greet the messiah.' When the child died, he said: 'The messiah will certainly not come for another 100 years.' R. Yudel asked him: 'Didn't you say that I would greet the messiah in these clothes?' He answered: 'Yes, I said that then, but today I say differently.'[10]

These dashed hopes have received a good deal of attention in the literature, so I will concentrate on those aspects that bear most directly upon the information found in the *Scroll*.

Green has shown that even though R. Nachman considered himself to be a Moses-like *tzadik* who could contain within himself seeds of both the Joseph-like and David-like messiah, his primary identification was with the Joseph-like messiah.[11] R. Nachman held out great hopes for his son and in his death saw not only a personal tragedy, but one on a national and even global scale. 'He said: What do you know of the great global trauma which resulted from the child's passing?'[12] The actual scale of this trauma in R. Nachman's eyes can be seen in a number of his statements.

---

9 See Mendel Piekarz, *Studies in Bratslav Hasidism*, expanded ed. (Jerusalem: 1996), 56-82; Arthur Green, *Tormented Master* (New York: Schocken, 1987), 186-220. While there are some details over which I disagree with Green, for the most part I agree with his general description. Regarding the connection of the Tikunim to the messianic fervor, see Zvi Mark, " *The Formulation of R. Nachman of Breslav's 'Tikkun ha-kelali,' the 'Tikkun for Nocturnal Pollution,' and Pilgrimage to the tomb of R. Nachman, and Their Relationship to Messianism,*" *Da'at* 56 (2005).

10 *Siach Sorfei Kodesh*, vol. 1-5 (Jerusalem: 1994), vol. 2, 36; Rav Chaim Menachem Kramer, *Toldot Moharnat: Be'aish Uvmayim* (Jerusalem: 1996), 112.

11 Green, *Master*, 187-98.

12 Rav Natan of Nemirov, *Yemei Moharnat* (Jerusalem: 1982), section one, 19.

To put these passages in their proper context, we must recall that R. Nachman had proclaimed that he had 'influenced God so that the righteous redeemer would be the fruit of his own loins.' This dramatic statement, even though it had the potential to sow not a small amount of tension and controversy throughout the Jewish world, was not censored and was published several times in different Breslav works – often with the phrase 'he said this in public' attached, perhaps given as an explanation for its publication.[13] In *Chayei Moharan* we find: 'If only the world had merited that a descendant of our Master had remained as a successor, the world would have already been healed and repaired completely.'[14] This is the hope that the child Shlomo Efraim had been.

It appears that this hope – for the complete repair of the world – is the expectation of the future messianic age. As such, we may suggest that the great tragedy of the child's death was connected to this very hope: that this boy himself, the progeny of the Master, was to be the actual messiah (or at the least play a pivotal role in his arrival). This is made even more explicit in other Breslav writings.

In *Chayei Moharan* R. Natan hints at something that R. Nachman had expressed after his son's death.

> Then in the summer of 1806, in the month of Sivan, his son, the child Shlomo Efraim died. It has already been noted in another place the matter of this dear holy child, that which our Master spoke of as being already prepared, etc[15]

What was 'already prepared'? The ellipsis of the 'etc.' ending the quote is R. Natan's own self-censorship. However, in the bundle of his writings in which the *Scroll* was discovered by R. Nachman of Tscherin we find this missing information.

---

13 *Chayei Moharan Im Hashmatot*, (Jerusalem: 2000), 267 and see 471.

14 Ibid., 403.

15 Ibid., 185.

> I found written there in this language: The year 5566, Sunday Menachem-Av – we heard from his holy mouth the entire sequence of the coming of the righteous redeemer (speedily in our day). He said that all was already prepared. He should arrive in a few years time and he knew in which year and month and day he would come. Now, though, he certainly won't come at this time. It was understandable from his words that this delay was due to the death of his young son, Shlomo Efraim.
> Earlier, he had discussed with me close to the time of the child's death this same matter, that all was already prepared that he arrive in so many years, etc. and he knew in which month, etc., but now he certainly would not come.
> I also found written… Then during the journey he divulged to us the secret written herein – things never before heard, etc. (That is, the entire sequence of the coming of the righteous redeemer mentioned above. This was written there only in hints by way of acronyms and abbreviations. He warned not to copy this booklet called the Scroll of Secrets and certainly not to print it, even though it was only written in hints – this too should not be revealed, etc.)
> He concluded: Much has been forgotten and never transcribed for the telling of all this took two hours and he prohibited us from discussing the matter and ordered us to write it in code. Immediately the majority was forgotten for it was not transcribed immediately.[16]

Although R. Nachman had twice mentioned to R. Natan that he knew when the messiah was to arrive, in only 'a few years time,' nonetheless the death of his son rendered all his calculations moot. After this tragedy the long awaited event was no longer expected.

The first conversation was held soon after the child's death; the second two months hence. Then 'the entire sequence' of the messiah's arrival was revealed. The delay in his arrival - once only a few years away - was then linked to the death of his son.

---

16 *Yemei Moharnat*, section one, 20.

In *Yemei Moharnat* R. Natan describes the birth of the child, Shlomo Efraim.

> In the year 1805, close to the beginning of the month of Nisan, his son was born, etc. Shlomo Efraim.... What would have been if only this child had lived is impossible to describe. The little that is written [about this] is only hinted at.[17]

Here it appears that R. Natan acknowledges that more about the child's interrupted destiny is found elsewhere. Concerning this, Joseph Weiss has written, 'We may surmise that what is referred to as being only "hinted at" is in fact the *Scroll* ....'[18] The *Scroll* is often described as being written only in 'hints,'[19] just as that concerning the dead son.[20] All this complements what we find in the testimony of R. Nachman of Tscherin in *Chayei Moharan*.

> I once heard from R. Natan an incredible tale concerning this [the son's death] which would make the hair of any who heard it stand on end. It is impossible to even hint at describing it.[21]

The description of this indescribable tale seems close to the prohibition on detailing the contents of the *Scroll* – which also needed to be transmitted only through hints.[22] This similarity may strengthen the hypothesis that this tale and the *Scroll*'s content are in fact one and the same. The incredible tale told in the *Scroll* reveals the depth of loss which attended the child's

---

17 Ibid., 11.

18 Joseph Weiss, *Studies in Bratslav Hasidi*sm (Jerusalem: 1995), 197. See also, Piekarz, *Studies in Bratslav Hasidism*, 78-9.

19 *Yemei Moharnat*, section one, 20.

20 Ibid., 11.

21 *Chayei Moharan Im Hashmatot*, 460.

22 *Yemei Moharnat*, section one, 20.

death. For if only he had lived, 'the world would have already been healed and repaired completely.'[23]

Now that the actual contents of the *Scroll* have come to light it seems that Weiss' hypothesis is conclusive. We should add that despite the fact that only in the second section of the *Scroll* (which was told in 1809 several years after the death of R. Nachman's child) is the matter of the messiah as a child discussed, there is a quite reasonable explanation for this. The first section of the *Scroll*, based on the first telling soon after the son's death, is admittedly missing much of what was described – 'the majority was forgotten for it was not transcribed immediately.'[24] The second section also mentions that it records 'that which we heard of this matter at another time.'[25] It may very well be that the this entire matter was spoken of in the first telling, but only transcribed after the second.[26]

If we accept this conclusion – and it seems that we have little reason not to – then we can understand that the story told in the *Scroll* is the story of the infant Shlomo Efraim who perished before he fulfilled his messianic destiny. At the same time, the Scroll depicts not only what could have been, but also what will be – once the redeemer does arrive.

2. MORE ON THE CHILD MESSIAH – PERSONA AND IMAGE BOTH LIVING AND DEAD[27]

As we have seen, lying behind the depiction of the messiah as child was the actual infant Shlomo Efraim. However, it is worth noting that throughout the Bible, Talmudic and kabalistic literature also lie a variety of mes-

---

23 *Chayei Moharan Im Hashmatot*, 460.

24 *Yemei Moharnat*, section one, 20.

25 Ibid.

26 See note 4 above.

27 On this motif in the works of Agnon, see Elchanan Shilo, "*The Use and Literary Function of Kabbalah in the Works of S. Y. Agnon*" (Bar Ilan, 1995), 120-4.

sianic visions which can help us better understand the one created by R. Nachman.

Isaiah prophesied:

> A child will be born to us, a son given us – leadership placed upon his shoulders. And he will be called Pele Yoetz, of the warrior Aviad Sar Shalom. His mission and his peace will never end – strengthening the throne of David and his kingdom, abetting it with justice and righteousness for ever.[28]

This prophecy of a newborn child who comes to establish the throne of David was understood by the Sages as referring to Hezekiah the king. He was to have been God's chosen, but because he 'did not sing [God's praises],' his chance was missed and this prophecy's actualization would have to wait for the future.[29] We need not understand that this prophecy foretells that the child will actually reign as king while still a child. Rather, from the time of his birth, he is destined to become the king – but this destiny rests upon his shoulders from birth. The imagery of the child messiah, then, remains.

Another image of a new-born king is found in the second chapter of Psalms where we find a description of the king as God's anointed.[30] The king in the psalm tells us, 'God told me, "You are my son, today I have fathered you."'[31] This verse was interpreted in the Talmud as describing the future messiah.[32] This same exegesis was also used by R. Nachman in his discourses.[33] Although the birth mentioned is symbolic – meant to express the coronation

---

28 Isaiah 9:5-6.

29 TB 94a.

30 Psalms 2:2.

31 Ibid., verse 7.

32 The Sages taught: The messiah son of David, may he speedily appear in our day – God says to him, 'Ask of Me anything and I will grant you it,' as it says, '... I have sired you today, ask of Me and I will give you the nations as a possession' (TB Sukkah 52).

33 Rav Natan of Nemirov, *Sefer Likutei Moharan Hamenukad* (Jerusalem: 1994), 61.

of the king as an experience of rebirth in which the king is reaffirmed as one of God's own - the imagery of infancy is, however, reinforced.

In both the Jerusalem Talmud and in Midrash Rabba we find the tale of Menachem son of Hezekiah who was born on the day that the Temple was destroyed and was named messiah. This infant was plucked from his mother's arms by the wind and disappeared with no trace.[34] The reader of this tale is left wondering whether the infant was snatched up to the heavens still alive – some day perhaps to return. His name is reminiscent of the king who missed his chance at becoming the messiah.[35] Here, then, is another example of the messiah-as-infant motif.

The Book of Kings relates the story of Aviah the son of Jeroboam son of Nabat. Aviah grew sick, and came, together with his mother, to the prophet Achiya so that he would pray for his recovery.[36] Achiya, however, decreed that the child would die and after his death he was eulogized by 'all of Israel…for some good thing for God, the God of Israel, was found in him.'[37] The biblical text does not tell us what this 'good thing' was. The Talmud, however, relates that Aviah had defied the instructions of his idol worshipping father to ensure that his subjects would not make the pilgrimage to Jerusalem, but rather worship the golden calf that he had built. Not only did Aviah not comply with his father the king, but he himself journeyed to Jerusalem.[38] The Zohar identifies his 'good thing' with the messiah.

> The messiah comes from the tribe of Efraim, from the lineage of Jeroboam son of Nabat, the son of Aviah who died in his father's lifetime. On that same day on which he died, a son was born to him…. [It is] from this son of Aviah [that] the messiah will come. This is what is written,

---

34 TY Brachot 5b; "*Eicha Raba*," ed. Shalom Buber (Vilna: 1899), 45.

35 TB Sanhedrin 45b. See also, Jacob Neusner, *A Life of Rabban Yohanan Ben Zakkai* (Leiden: 1962), 173, fn. 2.

36 Kings I 14:12.

37 Ibid., verse 13.

38 TB Moed Katan 28b.

> 'some good thing for God, the God of Israel, was found in him.' This is the messiah who is a good thing for God.[39]

The good found in the dead Aviah was the messianic potential within him – the Josephian (father of Efraim) messiah.[40] The way in which he was eulogized is reminiscent of that described in the Book of Zechariah, 'the [entire] land eulogized him.'[41] The Talmud interprets this as referring to the 'Josephian messiah who was killed.'[42]

There is another messianic tradition based on the story from the Book of Kings which tells of the prophet Elijah's resurrection of the widow's son.[43] Concerning this child, a midrash states, 'he was the Josephian messiah.'[44] The analogy between this miraculously resurrected child and the Josephian messiah is strengthened even more when we take into account the tradition that foretells of this messiah's own future resurrection after death.[45]

---

39 "*Zohar Chadash*," (Chamad, 1991), Parshat Balak, 549-50.

40 On the connection between Aviah and Jeroboam son of Nabat, his father, to the Josephian messiah, see Yehudah Liebes, "*Jonah as the Messiah ben Joseph*," in *Studies in Jewish Mysticism Philosophy and Ethical Literature,* edited by J. Dan and J. Hacker (Jerusalem: 1986), 286-8. For more Talmudic and later sources on the Josephian messiah and his death, see Joseph Heinemann, "*The Messiah of Ephraim and the Premature Exodus of Ephraim*," *Tarbiz* 40 (1971).

41 Zechariah 12:12.

42 TB 52a.

43 Kings I 17.

44 *Seder Eliyahu Rabbah Veseder Eliyahu Zuta*, Meir Ish Shalom ed. (Jerusalem: 1969), 97-8. This midrash is frequently quoted. See for example, TB Baba Metziah 114a-b, Tosphot ad loc.;Rav Chaim Vital, *Sha'ar Hagilgulim* (New York: 1995).

45 Green wrote that the hope that the Josephian messiah would rise from the dead was, 'a new element... (Green, *Master*, 196). It appears that this is true regarding pre-Christian era Jewish sources. See Rudolf Bultman, *Theology of the New Testament*, vol. I (New York: 1951), 31; Geza Vermes, *Jesus the Jew* (Philadelphia: 1981), 38; Israel Knohl, *The Messiah Before Jesus* (Jerusalem: 2000), 62 regarding the Qumran community. However, it should be noted that in later sources and in the Chasidic tradition, we do find such beliefs regarding the Josephian messiah. *The Book of Zerubavel* describes that Menachem son of Amiel

R. Yitzchak Luriah[46] claimed that the 'Josephian messiah is called a youth,' basing himself upon the verse describing the biblical Joseph - 'he was a youth.'[47] From the context of this claim, it seems that youth here is meant to describe character and not only age. However, it does not exclude the possibility that the young age of the messiah is also meant. The depiction of the youthful messiah in the *Scroll*, which seems to be an integral part of his identity, may have found its source here.

David Tamar has gathered a number of sources which provide evidence that both R. Yitzchak Luriah and R. Chaim Vital saw themselves as the Josephian messiahs of their respective generations (we will return to this below).[48] The tradition regarding two of R. Vital's sons, who were blessed with extraordinary messianic abilities from infancy, is also pertinent to the entire messianic infant trope. In his *Book of Visions*, R. Vital speaks of his sons while relating a particular dream that he had dreamt.

> A man came to me and gave me a jewel that sparkled like the sun. He told me: 'At first they gave you a lit candle, but it lacked oil and was extinguished, but now we are giving you this jewel, which needs no oil

---

(the Davidian messiah), together with Elijah, will bring Nechemiah son of Chushiel (the Josephian messiah) back to life (Yehudah Even-Shmuel, ed., *Midrashei Geulah* (Tel Aviv: 1954), 83). In the *Zohar* we find, 'Another messiah, son of Joseph … who will die until … he arises' (*Sefer Hazohar*, Reuven Margolit ed. (Jerusalem: 1984), III, 203b). R. Chaim Vital wrote, 'After he is killed … his body will remain intact 40 days until the Davidian messiah revives him' (Rav Chaim Vital, *Etz Hada'at Tov* (Jerusalem: 1991), I, 59b). In *Megaleh Amukot* it is written that, 'in the future when the Josephian messiah is killed, through prayer he will return and live (*Megaleh Amukot Al Hatorah*, 72a). So too we find in the book *Shnei Luchot Habrit*: 'The Josephian messiah will be killed and return to life' (Rav Yeshayahu Horowitz, *Shnei Luchot Habrit* (Jerusalem: 1975), Tractace Pesachim, 18a). Aside from these sources, the *Zohar* describes how the messiah will vanish for a certain period. For example, 'the messiah will be put away for 12 months' (*Sefer Hazohar, Margolit*, II, 7b). It may be that this disappearance and return lies at the root of the development of the idea of the messiah's death and rebirth.

46 Rav Chaim Vital, *Sefer Halikutim* (New York: 1995), 356.

47 Genesis 37b.

48 See David Tamar, " *Luria and Vital as Messiah Ben Jos*eph," *Sefunot* 7 (1963).

> and will never go out.' I awakened. Afterwards, in the month of Kislev, a son was born to me and I named him Nechemiah after the tomb of this righteous man and also after the village. I understood that the candle which had gone out was my son Joseph, mentioned above … who spoke prophesies but who died at the age of one-and-a-half this past Elul; the jewel is Nechemiah. Because of my sins, he also passed away when 13 years-old. He too spoke prophecies, and saw visions when he was four. In my humble opinion he was a reincarnation of my teacher [R. Yitzchak Luriah].[49]

It seems that these remarkable children, both with messianic names,[50] were reincarnations of the Josephian messiah - they contained the soul of R. Yitzchak Luriah who was himself a Josephian messiah. R. Luriah's own death, at the age of 38, was understood by his students as the death of the messiah as a 'youth.' In the book *Emek Hamelech* (Valley of the King) concerning R. Luriah we find:

> The verse: 'The spirit of our nostrils, the messiah of God, has been trapped by their corruption, of whom we said we will live in shadow among the nations' I apply to him. Also, 'The crown of our heads has fallen' which [in Hebrew] is the acronym y.o.u.t.h, applies to him as due to our many sins he died in his youth.[51]

---

49 Rav Chaim Vital, *Sefer Hachizionot*, Eshkoli ed. (Jerusalem: 1954), 59. On the reincarnation of R. Yitzchak Luria as his son Yosef, see there p. 49. David Tamar has already written on the connection between this story and that of the infant Nechemiah who spoke of redemption and the messiah. He felt that this connection may have been responsible for R. Vital's naming of his own son Nechemiah. See Tamar, "*Ha'ari Veharechav Kemeshiach Ben Yosef*," 175, fn. 28.

50 Nechemiah is the name of the Josephian messiah in the Book of Zerubavel. See note 46 above. On the messianic context of this name, see Gershom Scholem, "*A Document by the Disciples of Isaac Luria Israel Sarug – Disciple of Luria*," *Zion* 5, no. 2 (1940): 141.

51 *Emek Hamelech*, (Amsterdam: 1648), third introduction, chapter six, 13a. See also Tamar, " *Luria and Vital as Messiah Ben Jose*ph," 172.

We should also recall that R. Nachman himself died at the same age of 38,[52] allowing his followers to find in him yet another messianic aspect: the Josephian messiah who dies as a mere youth.[53]

3. THE BOOK MEGALEH AMUKOT AND THE DEVELOPMENT OF MESSIANIC FERVOR IN BRESLAV TOWARDS 1806

The kabalistic work *Megaleh Amukot Al Hatorah* (Revealer of Deep Secrets on the Torah), written by R. Natan Nettah Shapiro and first published in 1795, contains some of the deeper roots of the messianic child motif. Green has already noted the influence of this mystic upon R. Nachman, and has shown how another one of his books (also named *Megaleh Amukot)* which carried a dedication to R. Nachman in one of its discourses, influenced R. Nachman's understanding of the tzadik. For R. Nachman, the Josephian messiah was a wanderer through the ages manifesting himself in each generation's tzadik while attempting to repair the damage wrought by Jeroboam son of Nabat. Additionally, he understood that the Moses-like messiah contains within himself both the Josephian and Davidian messiahs.[54]

Aside from R. Nachman's connection to R. Shapiro, Green also speculated that the messianic fervor in Breslav which reached a crescendo in 1806 was tied to the fact that this year (rendered in Hebrew as the letters whose sum is 566) was numerically equivalent to the numerical value of 'messiah son of Joseph.' Although he never claimed that this calculation was mentioned in the Breslav literature, nor in that which preceded R. Nachman,[55]

---

52 *Chayei Moharan Im Hashmatot*, 137.

53 I will discuss the identification of R. Nachman with the Josephian messiah below.

54 Green, *Master*, 192-4, 113 fn. 76. See also Yehudah Liebes, "*Hatikun Haclali Shel R. Nachman Mebreslav Veyiahaso Leshabta'ut*," in *On Sabbateanism and its Kabbalah* (Jerusalem: 1995), 431 fn. 7, 40 fn. 90.

55 Green notes that R. Yitzchak Yehuda Saparin of Kumarana wrote in his mystical diary, *Megilat Setarim* (published in 1944), that the year of his birth, 1806 numerically equivilent

Green felt that, 'It seems inconceivable that Nachman ... whose works are so filled with numerological calculations, should not have noticed this fact.'[56]

Green's assumption is strengthened by the fact that this numerical comparison is in fact found in R. Shapiro's *Megaleh Amukot Al Hatorah*. Additionally, there is an entire section of *Megaleh Amukot* devoted to this subject. It is reasonable to believe that R. Nachman was well acquainted with these discussions and as such they may have played an important role in fanning the messianic flames which swept Breslav at the time.

In the examination of the texts from *Megaleh Amukot Al Hatorah* which follows, it is not my intention to uncover their author's original intent, but rather to seek to understand how they may have influenced R. Nachman's messianic views.

> The Holy One showed Moses 1000 week-days, [57] and also the two messiahs add up to 1000 - the Josephian messiah is 'an infant who suckles from his mother's breast' which equals 566[58] and the [name of the] future Davidian messiah will be spelled fully [with an additional yud] as it is spelled in Chronicles[59]... so that this equals 434,[60] which together with the Josephian messiah's 566 yields 1000.[61] This is the secret of '1000 to Solomon'[62] which hints at the two messiahs which the Holy One had shown to Moses... As it is written 'our oxen [in Hebrew 'thousands'] are laden'[63] – they correspond to the two messiahs whose secret is 1000 and

---

to 'Josephian messiah' was additional proof of his messianic mission (Green, *Master*, 216 fn. 30).

56 Ibid., 195.

57 *Sefer Hazohar, Margolit*, II 227b.

58 In Hebrew both *tinok* (infant) and *meshiach ben yosef* are equivilent to 566, the year 1806.

59 In the Book of Chronicles David is written with an extra 'yud' adding another 10.

60 Meshiach ben David=434.

61 566+434=1000.

62 Song of Songs 8:12.

63 Psalms 144:14.

who suffer [similar to the Hebrew word 'laden'] for Israel as it is written, 'he bore our illness'[64] [and] when they mate together,[65] 'then there is no breach' – their offspring are worth 1000 [measures of] silver.[66]

We see here a number of themes that R. Nachman may have picked up and developed in his depiction of the messiah. First is the description of the messiah as 'an infant who suckles from his mother's breast.' This may very well have been the background for R. Nachman's vision of the messiah's actual functioning as such at an early age. It may have led to his hopes that his own son, Shlomo Efraim, could himself become, even while still an infant, the Josephian messiah.[67]

---

64 Isaiah 53:4.

65 This idea is based in the Zohar. See there for example, III, 246b.

66 *Megaleh Amukot Al Hatorah*, Leviticus, 29.

67 An interesting description of the infant-messiah is found in the writings of R. Chaim Luzzato's followers. R. David Vali, one of the group's leaders, explained why it was that 'infants and children' were chosen to hasten the redemption instead of older sages. Tishbi argued that Vali's claims were actually apologetica for the fact that Luzzato's group, who saw themselves as a messianic vanguard, was composed of the young. Even though they do not relate directly to R. Nachman, Vali's claims constitute another layer in our understanding of the messianic-infant phenomenon in general.

' This great repair God desires to effect through infants and children, who are the righteous menders even though they are young in years. For even so, they suckle the milk of higher wisdom, the hidden wisdom. This is the secret of the verse, 'from the mouth of children and infants You established power' (Psalms 8:3) and not through the old sages as would have been appropriate. The reason is to destroy the enemy and the revenger... for if they were old sages who dealt with this wisdom, the repair would not suffice to shut the mouth of the enemy prosecuter and to arouse compassion to bring redemption. For the way of these [older sages] in arousing the lower spheres does not force the power of the upper spheres as the way of the children and infants does whose way is not like theirs. Even so, they choose hidden wisdom and holy ways against nature and the evil urge which is strongest in the flower of youth .... It is a wonder that these children and infants should arise to effect the repair of the world and so from them are chosen the messiahs and prophets and those who fight against the shallow outer world... About this great thing spoke Isaiah [based on 29:23, with a few changes] Not now will Jacob be ashamed, not now will his face burn, but upon seeing his children, his actual children, the work of his hands, those closest will he sanctify My name. They sanctify His name in their proper

The second is the numerological connection between the year 5566 (1806) and the Josephian messiah. It is difficult to exaggerate the import that this equation held, as we see that R. Nachman neither needed to make this connection on his own nor account for its meaning. Rather he found it ready-made in a kabalistic work of a respected mystic, R. Natan Nettah Shapiro of Krakow.[68] All that was left for him was to link the number with the year.

Third, and of equal importance, we find here the possibility of the pairing of the two messiahs – the Josephian and the Davidian. Only their union reaches the perfect number 1000 – '1000 to Solomon'. This idea became an integral part of R. Nachman's understanding of the Moses-like tzadik's incorporation of both of the messiahs.

The fact that R. Natan Shapiro's influence on R. Nachman is apparent in other places strengthens our supposition that R. Nachman made use of this work. We find, for example, that R. Nachman adopted other numerological equivalences and acronyms brought by R. Natan.[69] Additionally, because we are dealing here with an unusual thematic package found first in *Megaleh Amukot* and afterwards in R. Nachman's own work it seems even more likely that R. Nachman was directly influenced by R. Shapiro.

---

choice and give themselves over to God. This is how they strengthen the holy enabling it to grow and spread throughout the world....' (Isaiah Tishbi, *Studies in Kabbalah and its Branches* (Jerusalem: 1993), vol. 3, 850-51).

68 It seems that R. Nachman's grandfather, the Baal Shem Tov himself, also used *Megaleh Amukot*. R. Gedaliah Melintz testifies on a particular sermon of the Besht, 'and afterwards his words were found in the work *Megaleh Amukot*' (Rav Gedaliah of Lintz, *Teshuot Chen* (Brooklyn: 1982), 91.

69 Here are a number of examples of numerological equivalences found both in *Likutei Moharan* and *Megaleh Amukot* from parshat Ve'etchanan: Moses (Moshe) is equivalent to anger (charon-af) [Nemirov, *Sefer Likutei Moharan Hamenukad*, 18:1; Rav Natan Netah Shapiro, *Megaleh Amukot Al Parshat Ve'etchanan* (Bnai Brak: 1992), 111a]. Moses is an acronym for argument between Hillel and Shamai (Nemirov, *Sefer Likutei Moharan Hamenukad*, 59:8; Shapiro, *Megaleh Amukot*, 53a. The letters of Iyar stand for My enemies will back-down, embarassed in a moment (Nemirov, *Sefer Likutei Moharan Hamenukad*, 277; Shapiro, *Megaleh Amukot*, 98b).

Taken together, these three ingredients: 5566, the messiah as infant, and the union of the two messiahs, add up to make the year 5566 into the annus mirabilis of unsurpassed import for the Breslav Chasidim who saw in R. Nachman's child (born one year earlier) the long-awaited savior - the combination of the two messiahs.

> As is accepted practice, in the naming of his child, Shlomo Efraim, our Master hinted at the souls of the two messiahs – the Josephian messiah in Efraim (the son of Joseph) and the Davidian messiah in Shlomo (the son of David).[70]

There is no doubt that despite 'his containing part of the soul of the son of David, he is mainly comprised of the son of Joseph.'[71] In the year of the Josephian messiah, 5566, he was certainly 'an infant who suckles from his mother's breast.'

There are other discourses found in *Megaleh Amukot* in which similar themes appear.

> Ishmael was the reincarnation of Joseph the righteous. He was that child spoken of by R. Yehoshuah (TB Gittin 58a) – 'Who plundered Jacob and spoiled Israel? He answered – Is it not God against whom we have sinned?'[72] [It is] because of the sin of Joseph which resides in each generation. He was the very likeness of the youth Chanoch, like Joseph and a child of his old age, 'I was a youth and have grown old'[73] (TB Yevamot 16) this verse was spoken by the heavenly minister of the world [Metatron]….[74]

---

70 Kramer, *Toldot Moharnat: Be'aish Uvmayim*, 582, fn. 6. See also *Siach Sorfei Kodesh*, vol. 4, 48.

71 See R. Avraham Chazan, *Sichot Vesipurim (Printed with Kochvei Or)* (Jerusalem: 1983), 123 and Rav Avraham Chazan, *Chochmah Utvunah (Printed Together with Sipurei Maasiot)* (Hanekudot Hatovot, 2004), 496. This is R. Nachman's own explanation.

72 Isaiah 42:24. The Talmud tells us that this infant was R. Ishmael son of Elisha (TB Gitten 58a).

73 Psalms 37:25.

74 *Megaleh Amukot Al Hatorah*, Parshat Shmot, 6c.

From the context of this sermon it seems that here too we are dealing with the Josephian messiah, the reincarnation of Joseph the righteous, who appears as both child and youth. At the conclusion of this discourse the numerological equation of the Josephian messiah with 'an infant who suckles from his mother's breast' appears again.[75]

The most surprising connection between R. Nachman and the Josephian messiah, though, is found in one of R. Shapiro's sermons on the weekly Torah reading *Chukat*.

> 'The flowing river-beds' is numerically equivalent to 'messiah king'[76] and 'the flowing river-beds which go to the place of Ar'[77] is an acronym [standing] numerologically for Joseph,[78] for he is the flowing fount the source of wisdom[79] and from this river-bed he will drink – from the river-bed 'on this path he will drink'[80] is an acronym for messiah son of Joseph.[81]

In the next sermon the connection is made between 'from the river-bed "on this path he will drink" as an acronym for messiah son of Joseph' who will become 'the flowing fount the source of wisdom.'[82]

The verse, 'the flowing fount the source of wisdom' whose first letters of each word in Hebrew are the same as the letters of the name Nachman, is used as a sobriquet by Breslav Chasidim for the Rebbe. R. Natan addresses his letters – 'Our holy, awesome master, of blessed and righteous memory, the flowing fount the source of wisdom'[83] and we find this phrase in untold

---

75 Ibid.

76 River-bed=messiah king=448.

77 Numbers 21:16.

78 Both equal 156.

79 Parables 18:4.

80 Psalms 110:7.

81 *Megaleh Amukot Al Hatorah*, parshat chukat, 31b.

82 Ibid.

83 Rav Natan of Nemirov, *Alim Letrufah* (Jerusalem: 1981), 18, 31 and other places.

other Breslav works throughout the generations.[84] However, it is important to recall that R. Nachman himself made the connection between this verse and his own name. This is found in the work known as the 'Secret of R. Shimon bar Yochai'.[85]

This work was discovered by R. Nachman during his journey to Uman in 1810 and a censored version is found in the second edition of *Likutei Moharan* as an introduction.

> Go and see the works of God, a wondrous revelation of the secret[s] of the divine sage R. Shimon bar Yochai.
> R. Shimon bar Yochai promised that he would keep Israel from forgetting the Torah, as is found in the words of our Sages of blessed memory: When our rabbis gathered in Kerem Beyavneh they said, 'In the future the Torah will be forgotten in Israel'[86]. Rabbi Shimon bar Yochai said, 'It will not be forgotten, as it says, "It will not be forgotten from the mouths of his seed"' [87] and as it is explained in the *Zohar* (Naso 124b): With this work, the *Book of Splendor*, the diaspora can be left.[88] Now come, see and understand the hidden wonders of our holy Torah, for R. Shimon bar Yochai referred to himself with this verse, 'it will not be forgotten from the mouths of his seed.' Truthfully this verse itself holds and hints at this very same thing. For thanks to the seed of Yochai, R. Shimon bar Yochai, the Torah will not be forgotten. The last letter of each word of this verse spell out Yochai – that is, the verse itself informs us on account of whose seed the Torah will not be forgotten, from his seed specifically, that is from the seed of he who is

84 See Piekarz, *Studies in Bratslav Hasidism*, 14 R. Avraham Chazan opens a number of sermons with this same phrase playing on R. Nachman's name: 'Now we have understood only a drop from the sea of the one called the flowing fount the source of wisdom…' (R. Avraham Chazan, *Chochma Vebina (Bound with Kochvei Or)* (Jerusalem: 1983), 102). Another example is found in in the introduction written by R. Alter Tepliker to the *Scroll.*

85 On the secret of R. Shimon bar Yochai, see Piekarz, *Studies in Bratslav Hasidism*, 13-15.

86 TB Shabbat 138b.

87 *Sefer Hazohar, Margolit*, 138b. The verse quoted is Deuteronomy 38:28.

88 Ibid., III, 124b.

The tombstone at R. Nachman's grave before the site was enclosed in a second structure of stone. On the tombstone appears not the name Nachman, but only the acronym taken from the first letters of each word in the verse, 'the flowing fount, the source of wisdom.' In Hebrew they the same as the letters of the name Nachman and were used as a sobriquet by Breslav Chasidim for the Rebbe. Today, the fabric covering the tomb also uses the same appellation. It reads: "The grave of the flowing fount, the source of wisdom: our Holy Rebbe, R. Nachman of Breslav - may the memory of the holy, righteous one be blessed." (ft 85)

himself mentioned and hidden in this verse – the Sage Yochai. On account of his seed, mentioned in this verse in the last letters of each word, R. Shimon bar Yochai - on account of him the Torah will not be forgotten. For 'with this work, the *Book of Splendor*, the diaspora can be left.' Know that the secret of R. Shimon himself is contained in another verse. For know that the holy Sage R. Shimon is akin to 'a holy watchman descended from heaven'[89] – the first letter of each word spells Shimon.

89 Daniel 4:1.

The connection between R. Nachman and R. Shimon bar Yochai is not made at all clear in this introduction. It is also not clear why this text was chosen as the opening to R. Nachman's book. The mystery, though, can be solved by tracing other mentions of R. Shimon bar Yochai in the Breslav oeuvre. In *Chayei Moharan* where R. Natan describes the discovery of the *Secret of R. Shimon bar Yochai* he details a piece of the conversation between him and R. Nachman which forms the basis of the above introduction.

> During our journey to Uman, he said, 'Despite everything God always aids Israel - no generation is ever orphaned. Like R. Shimon answered when one of the Sages said that in the future the Torah would be forgotten from Israel, "No, because with this work, the *Zohar*, the diaspora can be left. For it will not be forgotten from the mouth of his seed."' So he referred to himself with the verse and revealed then the secret printed in the beginning of my book – see there the greatness of R. Shimon bar Yochai. I then answered him, 'Certainly R. Shimon himself profits from this, that is from this wonderful novel interpretation. He answered, 'Yes' and afterwards said that R. Shimon himself is another matter, for R. Shimon is the holy watchman who descended from heaven as printed there. Now there is a flowing fount the source of wisdom, etc. It was also heard that he referred to himself as the river which purifies all stains.[90]

From the elliptic 'etc.' we can surmise that this version was also censored and did not report on all that the discussion contained. An addendum to this text was published in *Hashmatot Mechayei Moharan* by R. Shmuel Horowitz in 1933: 'Even the holy watchman needs to receive from there. Understand this.'[91]

R. Nachman wants to create a parallel between himself and R. Shimon bar Yochai: just as R. Shimon's masterwork, the *Zohar* would take Israel out of the

90 *Chayei Moharan Im Hashmatot*, 214-15.

91 *Hashmatot Mechayei Moharan*, (Jerusalem: 1893), 195.

diaspora,[92] so too would R. Nachman's *Likutei Moharan*. We are well aware that R. Nachman claimed that, 'when my book is accepted by the world it will be time to prepare for the messiah'[93] and that the appearance of his 'holy book *Likutei Moharan* in the world was the beginning of redemption.'[94] In light of this it is clear why the choice for the introduction to his book would be praise of the one other work which played a similar role in the hastening of Israel's redemption.[95] We should recall that *Likutei Moharan* ranked above even the *Zohar*, however, as R. Shimon bar Yochai himself needed to 'receive from there' – the flowing fount, the source of wisdom.[96]

It is important for us to note that R. Nachman himself helped foster his identification with the messianic. He adopts the verse 'flowing fount, the source of wisdom' as his own, reordering its letters such that it spells out his name. This is a continuation of the numerology with which he connected various verses to the names Shimon and Yochai. It was not his followers who saw him as the 'flowing fount,' but he himself – just as he himself drew the parallel to the earlier messianic figure, R. Shimon bar Yochai.

We may conclude that when R. Nachman found the numerological and acronymonic connections between the Josephian messiah and this very

---

92 On R. Shimon bar Yochai as the messiah, see Yehudah Liebes, "*Hamashiach Shel Hazohar: Ledemuto Shel R. Shimon Bar Yochai*," in *The Messianic Idea in Jewish Thought* (Jerusalem: 1990). On the role of the Zohar in messianism in general, see pp. 104-5.

93 *Siach Sorfei Kodesh*, vol. 3, 83.

94 *Chayei Moharan Im Hashmatot*, 314-19, 44-5. R. Natan also supports this in his letters: Sell his books there, this is the beginning of redemption (Nemirov, *Yemei Moharnat*, II,211).

95 Libes shows that the Besht and others saw in R. Shimon bar Yochai a messianic archetype. See Liebes, Hamashiach, 102.

96 The claim that R. Nachman is greater than R. Shimon bar Yochai is found in other deleted texts, as well. 'Once he spoke to me and said with longing: How does one lead a group like those who followed R. Shimon bar Yochai? I would stick my head among them and, I think, become their Rebbe' (*Chayei Moharan Im Hashmatot*, 223 together with Rav Alter Tepliker, "*Hashmatot Mechayei Moharan*," (1898), 195). Derivative of this claim is that R. Nachman is himself greater than Moses, as R. Shimon bar Yochai saw himself as greater than Moses. For sources on this, see Zvi Mark, "*Ma'aseh Mehashiryon (The Tale of the Armor) – from the Hidden Chambers of Breslav Censorship*," *Zion* 70, no. 2 (2005): 209 fn. 87. Chasidei Breslav were aware of this. See, for example, Chazan, *Sichot Vesipurim*, 124.

same verse, drawn by a noted mystic, R. Shapiro,[97] he surely took notice. This strengthened his own self-focused messianic conceptualization. R. Nachman, it is worth noting, believed in such numerological equivalences quite strongly, even mentioning that of all his discourses, those built around such calculations were the most important that he had written.[98]

However, it is difficult to be sure whether R. Shapiro's words were the catalyst which changed R. Nachman's self-perception or whether they merely served as an affirmation of that which he already was certain – his identity as the Josephian messiah. Likewise, we cannot be certain whether the naming of his child, Shlomo Efraim, was the result of a conscious identification of the boy with those numerological calculations found in *Megaleh Amukot* and the messianic importance of the year 1806. In any case, the combination of those instances where R. Nachman and the 'flowing fount' were identified as one together with the numerology which pointed to the year 1806 as the year of the Josephian messiah (also known as the 'infant who suckles from his mother's breast' and the 'child'), do provide us with more background against which to measure the messianic tension which was part and parcel of the Breslav community at the time that R. Nachman's son was born. Additionally, it serves to help us better understand the portrayal of the messiah as child found in the *Scroll.*

4. THE DEATH OF THE INFANT, SHLOMO EFRAIM, AND THE CALMING OF THE MESSIANIC FERVOR

We might speculate that after the death of R. Nachman's son, the entire messianic sequence outlined in the *Scroll* needed to be understood very differently. No longer was the *Scroll* to be read as a description of the sure-to-

---

97 *Megaleh Amukot Al Hatorah,* Chukat 31b.

98 *Sichot Haran,* (Jerusalem: 1995), 53, 248. The weight given to numerology provided the impetus to R. Natan son of Yehuda, a student of R. Natan, to write his book *Kuntras Hatzirufim.* This is a list of all the instances of numerology and acrynoms in R. Nachman's works. See Rav Natan Zvi Koenig, *Neveh Tzadikim* (Bnei Brak: 1969), 158; David Asaf, *Breslav: an Annotated Bibliography* (Jerusalem: 2000), 51.

arrive messianic future, but rather as a depiction of what might have been if Shlomo Efraim had lived. The coming of the messiah may be certain, but it may unfold very differently. However, according to the conversation held between R. Nachman and R. Natan after he first related the *Scroll*'s contents, it seems clear that R. Nachman's messianic expectations as therein outlined were not dashed.

> After the first telling of this matter, a great joy descended upon us. He had already left. Afterwards, when he returned to his house we spoke with him about this and he said that he too had become extremely happy after telling us this story. I asked him, 'This is a truly wonderful thing, but when, when will it come to pass?' He answered that the telling of the tale itself is a great thing. When that which is hidden away comes to be discussed in this world – that itself is something great. Thank goodness that we merited to hear such secrets which have never before been heard. (Until here I copied from the manuscript.)[99]

R. Natan's question as to when the events in the Scroll will take place show us clearly that he understood them not as a description of what could have been, but rather as an account of the actual future. R. Nachman's answer does nothing to dissuade him of this, but concentrates on the very revelation of the tale as important in itself – even if it depicted events which would only take place far in the future. The happiness which enveloped R. Nachman and his followers felt after his recitation of the Scroll also indicates that it did not detail a paradise lost (which would only arouse feelings of disappointment), but rather one waiting to materialize sometime in the future - with the coming of the righteous redeemer.

However, the 'great joy' which the telling of this tale occasioned presents us with a few questions. As we saw above, the death of R. Nachman's son ended the aspirations for a soon-to-arrive messianic age and brought with it a painful realization that more than 100 years may have to pass before its

---

99 Nemirov, *Yemei Moharnat*, I, 11.

advent.[100] Why then, after this tragedy did R. Nachman continue to occupy himself with the messianic themes found in the *Scroll*? And why did this lead him to the aforementioned 'great joy'?

Even though the immediate messianic hopes died along with Shlomo Efraim in 1806, R. Nachman did not come to see them as false. How is it though, that, after the events of 1806 R. Nachman not only did not lose his own self-confidence, and continued to teach discourse after discourse but also, without letting up, began to tell the incredible series of tales which would come to be collected in his other major work, *Sippurei Maasiot*? In light of all that we have seen, we can suggest a possible answer.[101] All of the messianic tensions surrounding the arrival of the messiah, as well as the infant's connection to the year 1806, were based on the conception of the Josephian messiah – a messiah whose death, in addition to his arrival, was something to be expected.

R. Chaim Vital's description of his teacher, R. Yitzchak Luriah as the Josephian messiah demonstrates this nicely.

> One day when we set out to pray at the tomb of [the Sages] Shemiah and Avtalion, my teacher, may he be remembered in the world to come, admonished us twice that we must remember in each and every prayer, to intend [upon reaching the blessing of the *Amidah* prayer] 'your servant David' that the Josephian messiah live, and not die by the hand of Armilus the evil one, called the 'throne of David'. This is the secret 'he requested life from you' - as it is written in the *Riayah Mehemana*[102] that in the future the Josephian messiah will die. We did not understand his words - God knows the hidden. But as the end explains the beginning, my teacher, the tzadik (may he be remembered in the world to come), died due to our many sins …[103]

100 Ibid.

101 See Piekarz, *Studies in Bratslav Hasidism*, 80-2.

102 Seemingly referring to *Sefer Hazohar, Margolit*, 448.

103 Rav Chaim Vital, *Sefer Pri Etz Chaim* (New York: 1995), 245-6. On R. Luria as the messiah, see Tamar, "*Luria and Vital as Messiah Ben Jose*ph".

In a gloss on this text we find the following explanation.

> As it written in the *Tikkunim*,[104] in every generation the incarnation of the Josephian messiah arrives. If there are righteous men in that generation who protect him, he does not die. If no one is found to protect him, he himself must die.[105]

In every generation there is an individual who is the incarnation of the Josephian messiah upon whom death is decreed. Only exceptional actions, such as the mobilization of the righteous, can save him from his fate. Because of this, R. Luriah as well as R. Nachman knew of the dangers that awaited them. R. Nachman, like R. Luriah, asked that his disciples pray in order to forestall the end.

> He warned me often to pray for his infant, the holy child Shlomo Efraim. He also exhorted and warned the one to whom he gave the book mentioned above that he should pray for the child for he knew that they [others] would work evil against the child. But, due to our many sins, our prayers did not help and the child died after Shavuot of that same summer… May God console him, us and all of Israel, over this tragedy and great crisis which has struck the world as he said explicitly and repeatedly, 'May we be consoled,' and bring us the righteous messiah speedily in our day, amen.[106]

It may have been that this request for prayer came before the infant's sickness, as R. Nachman well understood both his son's constitution and the dangers which awaited him.

R. Chaim Vital provides us with another example of the danger of death which awaits the Josephian messiah of each generation. A Rabbi Masoud

---

104 Perhaps he is referring to *Tikunei Zohar*, trans. Rav Yehudah Edrei (Jerusalem: 1998), 728, 69.

105 Vital, *Sefer Hachizionot*, 246.

106 Nemirov, *Yemei Moharnat*, I, 19.

Cohen told him in the name of a 'great sage who can see into the future, that he [R. Vital] is the Josephian messiah…and that the Sages have said that the fate of this messiah is to die. I will try with all my strength to save him from this decree, for of him it is said, "He asked of You life and You have given it to him.'[107]

The death of Shlomo Efraim, like that of R. Yitzchak Luriah, did nothing to diminish their stature as Josephian messiahs. On the contrary, it served as firm proof that they were in fact messiahs as this provided an explanation for their untimely death. Shlomo Efraim was not the first messianic child to perish. He joined a long line of different Josephian personalities who died before their time, whether as infants, youths or still young adults with much left to accomplish.

The hopes that R. Nachman and his followers held out for 1806 were ultimately undone, but this did not affect their basic messianic orientation. The death of the potential Josephian messiah was an already understood part of messianic theology. As such, the fact that at a particular time the messianic ideal was not actualized did not mean that all was lost nor that R. Nachman's own view of himself and his mission needed to be drastically altered. That he or his offspring could still play an essential role in bringing the Josephian messiah was still a given. He therefore continued on his original path, sure that even if success was still far off, in the end he would surely succeed.

We may also speculate that if the child had lived, he may have come to actualize the Davidian messianic aspect of his personality – the Shlomo (son of David) side. In his death, however, the Efraim (son of Joseph) aspect of his messianism was actualized, while the other side remained as mere potential.[108]

---

107 Vital, *Sefer Hechizionot*, 5. On the possibility of seeing R. Mazalotshov as a deceased messiah, see Mor Altschuler, *The Messianic Secret of Chasidism* (Haifa: 2002), 124-8.

108 This explanation leaves some hope for Chasidei Breslav that even the potentiality of the Davidian messiah can still be fufilled in the future. Perhaps this is the intent of R. Nachman's claim that he influenced God to allow for the messiah to be one of his descendants. As far as I know, some Chasidim today hold this belief.

Both the *Scroll*, first revealed in Av of 1806 a mere two months after his child's death, and the *Secret of R. Shimon bar Yochai* first spoken of a few years later in 1810, deal with the messianic ideals of R. Nachman, despite the fact that the great expectations for soon-to-come redemption had passed. R. Nachman did not give up his messianic mission, even though he knew that the messiah himself may tarry. R. Shimon bar Yochai's secret was also R. Nachman's. Both of them held a messianic self-consciousness which did not require that it be realized in any immediate fashion. Rather their hopes were long term. Their messianic missions were meant to be multi-generational, spanning the years from Yochai to Shimon and from Nachman to Shlomo Efraim, and to succeed through their written works, the *Zohar* and *Likutei Moharan* respectively. The world-wide dispersion of both of these books was meant to be instrumental in redeeming Israel from her own long sojourn in the diaspora. Their aim was to usher in the messianic age.

5. THE SECRET SCROLL OF R. YITZCHAK YEHUDA YECHIEL SAPARIN OF KUMARNA

In the year 1806 a child with messianic potential was born who did live to a ripe old age - R. Yitzchak Yehuda Yechiel Saparin of Kumarna. In a mystical diary that he kept, known also as *The Scroll of Secrets* and first published in 1944, he reveals his own messianic self-conception. The year of his birth (which numerically corresponds to 'Josephian messiah') held great import for him and he saw himself as a Josephian messiah. He often mentions R. Chaim Vital's *Book of Visions* and identifies with the latter's messianic world-view and visions. One of the more interesting pieces of his diary details the time when he first began to have visions and to answer public queries.

> From the time that I was two years old until the age of five, I saw wondrous visions and was blessed with the holy spirit. I spoke prophecies when asked for the word of God and I saw from one end of the world to the other. My teacher, my uncle, the holy man, R. Zvi of Zeditshav

would give me two coins a week so that I would tell him and answer any question which he would ask me. I spoke clearly in answering all of his questions and I distributed the money to charity.[109]

Here we have another example of a messianic child, like the son of R. Chaim Vital[110] and the child messiah of R. Nachman's *Scroll.* R. Yitzchak gained prophetic abilities at the age of two and like Adam and Moses could see from one end of the world to the other.[111] His uncle, R. Zvi of Zeditshav, a mystic and an important Chasidic rebbe in his own right, could ask him anything, and he knew what to answer.

This messianic child could not have served as a template for R. Nachman's depiction in the *Scroll*, for R. Nachman had died before he had reached the age of six and two-hundred years before his diary was published. On the other hand, it was not possible that R. Nachman's *Scroll* inspired the rabbi from Kumarna as it was kept well hidden by Breslav Chasidim until recently. The fact, then, that we see another example of a connection between a child, the Josephian messiah and the year 1806, is all the more interesting. It may very well be that the common inspiration for both of these works is the *Megaleh Amukot* by R. Shapiro which first drew together all of these themes.

6. GIFTED CHILDREN IN SIPUREI MAASIOT

R. Nachman's creation of the child messiah in the *Scroll* has certain parallels to the gifted children who appear in his *Sipurei Maasiot*. In the 'Tale of the Master of Prayer' one of the characters is a child who already at the age of three is a serious scholar able to decide halachic issues for all of Israel. This, of course, is reminiscent of the *Scroll*'s depiction of the messiah.

---

109 Rav Yitzchak Yehuda Yechiel Saparin, *Megilat Setarim (First Published in Manuscript by Naftali Ben-Menachem)* (Jerusalem: 1944), 9.

110 See note 50 above.

111 On Adam, see TB 12b; *Yalkut Shimoni*, (Jerusalem: 2000), 823.

> The king's daughter bore a child and this child was very beautiful – beyond the likes of human loveliness. His hair was blond with varied highlights; his face was like the sun, his eyes luminescent. He was born already fully intelligent. This was observed even at the moment of his birth. When people spoke around him, when it was appropriate to laugh he laughed, etc. Thus they understood that he was a genius – lacking only in adult physical abilities such as speech and the like.[112]

This beautiful golden-haired child is suggestive of the Davidian messiah as David is quite similarly described in the *Tikunei Hazohar*.

> David had seven shades of gold in his hair. Greenish gold, golden gold, grayish gold, Parveyian gold, closed gold, gold of Tarshish, pure gold – all the shades including Shebian gold.[113]

R. Adin Steinsaltz has commented on R. Nachman's description.

> The child born to the hero and the king's daughter is the highest actualization of the redeemer. This is the Davidian messiah who from birth realizes both human and divine perfections. His description of the infant here and in other places in the story is related to that described in the Book of Isaiah,[114] 'a child has been born to us....'[115]

Later on in the story, this perfect child is stolen. This in itself brings this character closer to some of the other infant messiahs who we have already met.

> On that day, there was a huge storm throughout the world ... The wind burst into the king's castle, but did no damage – it just swept up

---

112 *Sefer Sipurei Ma'asiot Hamenukad*, (Jerusalem: 1985), 193-4.

113 *Tikunei Zohar*, 690.

114 Isaiah 9:5.

115 Rabbi Adin Steinsaltz, *Six Stories of Rabbi Nachman of Bratzlav* (Jerusalem: 1995), 140.

> the infant and bore him away. In a clap of thunder just as the precious infant was swept away, the king's daughter chased after him, as did the queen and king each [running] in a different direction, and they all went lost.[116]

This storm wind is reminiscent of the wind that snatched the infant Menachem son of Hezekia, the messiah king, in the Talmudic story. R. Avraham Chazan, in his book *Chochma Vetvunah* (Wisdom and Understanding), a commentary on R. Nachman's *Tales*, quotes R. Natan's comments on this story.

> The matter related in the tale 'The Master of Prayer', where the master of prayer told about the great storm-wind which entered the king's castle, harming nothing but snatching the king's daughter away, etc. [This relates] to the summer of 1806, the middle of the conflict with the well-known elder. There was false witness brought against our Rebbe. This strengthened the Accuser such that the holy infant, may his merit protect us, passed away.[117]

According to R. Natan's interpretation,[118] Shlomo Efraim is the perfect messianic infant: born with complete intelligence, but snatched away by the winds of conflict against R. Nachman. The movement from this character to the child messiah of the *Scroll* seems natural and easy. The *Scroll*'s messiah is a prodigy who becomes a halachic authority, the king of Israel and world emperor all while still a child. This was to be R. Nachman's son's own destiny –but he was stolen by the evil winds whipped up by his accuser, the 'Saba of Shpola,' here merely called the well-known elder.

---

116 *Sefer Sipurei Ma'asiot*, 196-7.

117 Chazan, *Chochmah Utvunah (Printed Together with Sipurei Maasiot)*, 539. See Piekarz, *Studies in Bratslav Hasidism*, 79.

118 R. Natan offered an in depth interpretation of this tale, yet did not make this identification. See Rav Natan of Nemirov, *Likutei Halachot* (Jerusalem: 1984), vol. 1, 172-80.

Another infant, important and wondrous, appears in the 'Tale of the Seven Beggars'. The first beggar, ostensibly blind, describes himself thus:

> You think I am blind? I am not blind at all. Rather all time for me is but an instant (therefore he seems to be blind, for he doesn't look at the world at all, for all the world's time is like the blink of an eye so it makes no sense that he view or look at this world at all). I am very old, but I am still very young. I have not yet begun to live, yet despite that I am very old. This is not just my own claim; I have proof of this from the great eagle. I will tell you a story.[119]

The blind beggar is an eternal youth who has not even begun to live, for all time is but an instant for him. In the dimension in which he lives, his biological clock has not yet started running.[120]

The story which he proceeds to tell describes how as a 'mere infant' he was on a ship at sea when a fierce storm came and destroyed the vessel. He and some others survived and reached a tower. At the end of his story, the great eagle does in fact testify that, 'You are like me, you are very old, but still very young; you have not yet begun to live at all.'[121]

These descriptions of the blind beggar match that given by R. Nachman of the messiah in his discourse, 'Blessed God is Above Time.' In this discourse he argues that time and space are both relative, and as an example of this he offers his description of the messiah.

> Therefore the messiah, who has undergone all that he has experienced, suffered all that he has suffered since the very creation of the world, is still

---

119 *Sefer Sipurei Ma'asiot*, 243.

120 His 'blindness' is the result of his not being to 'see' beyond the immediate instant of his own existence.

121 The eagle represents eternal youth and rejuvenation, as in the verse: 'your youth will be renewed like an eagle' (Psalms 103:5). R. Nachman also uses the eagle in this way in one of his discourses: 'The eagle is akin to the soul – this is the rejunivation that the soul undergoes as it rises from infancy, eagle-like – "your youth will be renewed like an eagle". The eagle in the Torah, this is akin to Torah novela, 'renewed like an eagle' (Nemirov, *Sefer Likutei Moharan Hamenukad*, 13:5.

> told by God: 'You are my son, today I have fathered you.'[122] This seems incredible – but due to his great genius, in accord with his stature and great intelligence, he has become so great that all the time that has passed since the creation of the world until then is like nothing. It is as if he was born on that day, for all time collapses in his mind, as he is so great. Therefore God tells him, 'today I have fathered you' – today, for all the time that has passed is as nothing at all. This is my understanding.[123]

Here is a direct discussion of the messiah as child, in fact as a newborn. It seems that the 'today' under discussion is the day of the messiah's coming or coronation. On this day the messiah arrives at an incredible intellectual grasp of things, such that it is as if he has just been born. In the messianic consciousness, all of time is 'like nothing' and so he remains an eternal newborn. He is also, though, as old as creation itself. This follows the Talmudic aphorism that the name of the messiah was one of the seven things created before the world itself.[124]

In *Chayei Moharan* R. Nachman is quoted as identifying with the blind beggar.

> Once he uttered a word ... about himself and he said, 'I am the *saba desabin* (grandfather of grandfathers).'[125] If you look and understand the awesome tale of the seven beggars, in the first beggar's tale, the first beggar who was blind was told by the great eagle that he was very old, but still very young and had not yet begun to live at all, etc. He was the oldest of all the elderly mentioned there. Think on this matter a bit.[126]

---

122 Psalms 2:7.

123 *Sefer Likutei Moharan Hamenukad.* R. Natan explains the connection between the character of the blind beggar and the Torah. See *Likutei Halachot*, YD, 73-8.

124 TB Pesachim 54a.

125 R. Natan often refers to R. Nachman like this. See *Alim Letrufah*, 9, 18, 94, 162, 353, 421, 24 and others. This expression is from the Zohar.

126 *Chayei Moharan Im Hashmatot*, 275-6.

So not only is the child messiah of the *Scroll* a depiction of R. Nachman's lost son, but also of R. Nachman himself.[127] R. Nachman constructs a parallel between himself and the blind beggar who is akin to the messiah – the grandfather of grandfathers, as old as the world, yet an eternal newborn at one and the same time.

7. THE SCROLL OF SECRETS AS ONE OF R. NACHMAN'S TALES[128]

The thematic unity found in the variety of R. Nachman's oeuvre regarding gifted children raises the question whether the description of the child messiah in the *Scroll* should be read as another literary depiction of this motif. The answer to this question impinges directly upon whether the *Scroll* is to be read as a chronicle of the messianic future or as yet another of R. Nachman's tales, which like the majority of these stories, is concerned with the coming of the righteous redeemer.[129] We get a hint at the answer in a conversation which took place between R. Nachman, R. Natan and R. Naftali a few weeks after the revelation of the *Scroll*. The three discussed their excitement at hearing secrets of the messiah's arrival revealed.

> After the first telling of this matter, there descended upon us a great joy. He had already left. Afterwards, when he returned to his house we spoke with him about this and he said that he too had become extremely happy after telling us this story. I asked him, 'This is a truly wonderful thing, but when, when will it come to pass?'[130]

---

127 Weiss comments on R. Nachman's self-conception as a old-youth: 'I cannot fully explicate all the psychological and messianic intricacies of one whose own self-image combines that of an elder with eternal youth as found in R. Nachman's writings and other Breslav works' (Weiss, *Studies in Bratslav Hasidism*, 49 fn. 15.

128 Weiss correctly hypothesised that the Scroll would have the 'form of a story' (ibid., 213).

129 See ibid., 152; Piekarz, *Studies in Bratslav Hasidism*, 136-50.

130 *Yemei Moharnat*, I, 20-1.

We need to remember that the excitement and joy here was not due to any soon expected arrival of the messiah. The *Scroll* had been revealed after the death of Shlomo Efraim and after R. Nachman's resignation that the messianic age would only arrive in the far future. The almost paradoxical tension between the feelings of joy on the one hand, coupled with knowledge that the time of redemption was still far off may have been what led R. Natan to ask his question.[131] R. Nachman's answer, however, does not relate at all to chronology.

> He answered that the telling of the tale itself is a great thing. When that which is hidden away comes to be discussed in this world – that itself is something great.[132]

His answer focuses on the literary aspect of the *Scroll* – its weight lies in the telling, not in its power of prediction. His answer may, in fact, have contained a measure of criticism at even being asked R. Natan's prosaic question, for it misses the very point of revealing the *Scroll*'s secrets – the uncovering of what had until then been hidden. For R. Nachman the importance of the *Scroll* is that it is part of the messianic discourse itself. The telling of the *Scroll* is the addition of one more tale concerning the righteous redeemer – 'that itself is something great'. Another part of the messianic tale has been brought to light. As R. Nachman concludes, 'Thank goodness that we merited to hear such secrets which have never before been heard.'[133]

The connection between the *Scroll* and the *Tales* is also reflected in the decision made by R. Nachman of Tscherin regarding the placement of his discussion of the *Scroll* in *Yemei Moharan*. At the end of the section in which the *Scroll* is discussed, he adds:

---

131 ibid.

132 Ibid.

133 Ibid., 21.

> In the year 1806, after the death of the infant, he traveled to Medvedevka and its environs. There he began to tell the first tale of his tales. When he returned from his journey, I visited him and he retold us this same tale, telling us that on his journey he had told the story, etc. as it is printed in his book *Sipurei Maasiot.*[134]

Now, as we already know that the first rendition of the *Scroll* occurred in the wagon while setting out from Breslav during R. Nachman's second journey throughout the Ukraine, we see that this same journey was the occasion for the telling of the first of his fabled tales, 'The Tale of the Lost Princess.'[135] This being the case, we see how the same journey yielded both one of his tales which deals with a number of aspects of the redemptionary process,[136] as well as the *Scroll*'s unique depiction of messianic times. It appears that the *Scroll* contains but one of the variegated pieces of messianic lore on which R. Nachman held forth in his many sermons, stories and discourses. In light of this, the *Scroll* may need to be read less as prophecy and more as another literary statement by R. Nachman concerning the coming of the redeemer. However, the *Scroll* remains unique in that it has neither the form nor the literary content of one of R. Nachman's marvelous tales. Perhaps its simplest of readings, taking this into account, is as a future description of the messianic age and not as symbolic literature.

---

134 Ibid., 20-1.

135 According to R. Schick's chronology, the Scroll was related on Sunday, the 5th of Menachem-Av and on the following Saturday, in Tscherin, he told the first of his Tales. See Rav Eliezer Schick, *Pe'ulat Hatzadik* (Jerusalem: 1944), 346-7.

136 See Piekarz, *Studies in Bratslav Hasidism*, 132-50; David G. Roskies, "The Master of Prayer: Nachman of Breslav," in *A Bridge of Longing: The Lost Art of Yiddish Storytelling* (Cambridge, MA: 1995).

CHAPTER THREE
The Nature of the World in Messianic Times

It is not as some claim that when the messiah comes the world will change[1]

One of the basic questions concerning the messianic era concerns the nature of the world: will it change or stay the same? Is the prophecy 'the lamb will lie down with the wolf' meant literally as a fundamental change in the natural order? Or will the world continue to function as it always has? These questions relate both to the natural physical world as well as to the social and psychological nature of men. The attitude evinced in the *Scroll* leans towards continued stability and not radical difference. Both physical and human nature are depicted as essentially unchanged in the days of the messiah.

1. THE PHYSICAL WORLD

> He will make an orchard and growing in it and he will make new compounds. The daily schedule will be an hour in which he will eat and will drink and he will practice contemplative religious introspection. He will walk amongst all the sick that come and quickly command each what he should take – each effective things from the same orchard, from the new compounds.[2]

---

1 *Chayei Moharan Im Hashmatot*, (Jerusalem: 2000), 461.

2 Section I, line 25.

> And he will announce what he will do each day – at this hour such an activity, etc. For three hours he will treat the sick that will come, as even then there will be illness. The sick will come to him and he will instruct them to take from the orchard which he will make containing the new compounds the likes of which
> have never been before. He will go among the sick and instruct each of them to take that which he knows according to the powers of the appointed angels which daily visit each blade of grass.[3]

The practice of medicine occupies a permanent place in the messiah's daily schedule. He is, in fact, depicted as both a master healer as well as an innovative pharmacologist to whose door the sick beat a path. The need for medicine continues for 'even then there will be illness.' Medical cures will not rest on the supernatural – on mystical amulets and the like – rather the messiah's new medicinal 'compounds', the product of his own agricultural ingenuity, will offer the key to health. The efficacy of messianic medicine, however, does depend upon the messiah's special spiritual knowledge – he knows the divine source of each and every herb – but their actual function is quite natural. It seems, then, that the physical world is not subject to change in the messianic age. The regularities of nature, as well as their disturbances (such as sickness), will be constants. However, new drugs will be available to fight them.

The human condition, circumscribed by birth and death, will remain the same as well. Even the 'messiah himself will die, but he will have many children. Ten generations will he see…'[4] It may be that behind this unusual longevity lies the classic Maimonidean depiction of the messianic era.

> The messiah will die and his son will reign in his stead and his son after him. The prophet has already described how despite his death, 'he will neither fail nor stumble until he has brought law to all the land'. His

3 Section II, line 59.

4 Section II, line 49.

kingdom will last for many days. Men will live long lives, for when the worries and troubles of men are removed this aids longevity.[5]

Maimonides understands that 'there is no difference between the messianic era and this world except for the nations' subjugation alone'.[6] While the messiah's years will stretch well beyond today's average, this can easily be attributed to the salubrious effect of that peaceful time's tranquility.

The claim that the messiah is mortal also appears in *Chayei Moharan*: 'Most people believe that when the messiah comes he will not die. This is not so, even the messiah himself will die. He said this in public'.[7] R. Natan's emphasis on the fact that this was stated in public may indicate that if not for R. Nachman's willingness to divulge this opinion he himself might have kept it a secret. Perhaps the inclusion of the messiah's mortality in the *Scroll*'s depiction led him to believe that this too was to be kept hidden. It was only R. Nachman's making this claim in public which allowed him to do the same. Might R. Natan have felt that this view would somehow tarnish the expectations that the multitudes held for the messiah and his kingdom – despite the fact that this was the opinion of Maimonides himself? The reasons that R. Natan had for keeping the *Scroll* secret may have included not only a desire to keep the identity of the messiah (suspiciously close to R. Nachman and Shlomo Efraim) hidden from the masses, but also respect for the difference regarding their supernatural expectations of the messianic age and its depiction in the *Scroll*.[8]

---

5 Rav Moshe ben Maimonides, *Shelosh Hakadmot* (Jerusalem: 1940), 118.

6 Maimonides, MT Hichot Melachim 12:1; 11:12.

7 *Chayei Moharan Im Hashmatot*, 277.

8 A fuller discussion on the question of the Scroll's concealment is found below. Regarding this comment by R. Natan, see Joseph Weiss, *Studies in Bratslav Hasidism* (Jerusalem: 1995), 197-8 fn. 17. On the tradition of a 'golden tree' which was once part of the Scroll found in *Avneiha Barzel*, see below appendix six.

2. THE NATURE OF MAN AND SOCIETY

> The evil inclination and the Sanhedrin and all those things that [once] were will be [again] but each thing will be much more pleasant than before. Each and every one according to his station will have his eyes opened in wisdom and will gain great new understanding, better than before – each in accord with his station.[9]

In opposition to the reading of the prophetic verses 'I will give you a new heart and a new spirit within you'[10] as promising a change in the nature of humankind, the *Scroll* offers a perhaps less sanguine depiction of the messianic era. Man's evil inclination will not disappear[11] – guaranteeing that neither sin nor crime will either. The need for an extant judicial system, headed by the Sanhedrin, is then a given. Even as these things remain the same, however, they will be 'more pleasant than before.'

The societal evolution of the messianic era will not lead to the complete breakdown of intellectual differences between people. The promise that 'the earth will be filled with the knowledge of God as the seas with water are filled,'[12] was understood by some as suggesting that the messianic age would be uniquely egalitarian, wherein all people's knowledge of God would be complete. The *Scroll*, however, describes a hierarchy: the knowledge of God depends upon the 'station' or level of each individual. R. Nachman emphasizes this – 'each according to his station'. This position is detailed earlier quite clearly in the discourse, 'Atika Tamir'(The Hidden Ancient One) which offers an interpretation of Isaiah's promise that the world will be filled with knowledge of God.

---

9 Section II, line 81.

10 Ezekiel 36:26.

11 R. Nachman follows the Zohar in accepting that 'the evil inclination will never be exterminated,' despite that in the world to come it will be 'lightened' some. See *Sefer Hazohar*, Reuven Margolit ed. (Jerusalem: 1984), 273-5. More sources are brought ad loc.

12 Isaiah 11:9.

In the future all will know God, even the gentiles as mentioned above, 'the earth will be filled with knowledge.' However, the knowledge that they will posses is comprehensible and can be discussed, but that which we will have then, it is beyond words...

Know – that also in the future when the earth is filled with knowledge, and that known through the 'superficial' intellect will become known with the 'in-depth' intellect, there will still be other superficialities. For of course, they will not know the essence of God. Rather, each person will understand according to his station and in accord with his effort, exertion and trouble in this world for the sake of God...

Also among the Jews themselves there will certainly be a large difference between *tzadikim*, and all the more so between the righteous and the wicked, for what will be superficial for one will be in-depth for the other. This is the meaning of the verse, 'the earth will be filled with the knowledge of God as the seas with water are filled.' As far as the 'common' intellect, all will be equal: everybody will know God, even the gentiles. However, regarding deeper wisdom, all will be hierarchical, 'as the seas with water are filled.' On the surface, the level is equal in every place. However, it is in the depths that there are differences. In one place the water is shallow and close to the earth, in another it is even deeper – and in another it reaches the bottomless deep. So will be the understanding of God in the future.[13]

Despite the great advances in theological knowledge throughout the world, the differences inherent in stratified human nature remain the same. The future still finds differences between Jew and gentile, as well as between the righteous and wicked who naturally do not inhabit the same spiritual plane. Some will expend a great deal of energy in their theological search, others little. Human nature and society, even in the messianic era of wonders, stays the same.[14]

---

13 Rav Natan of Nemirov, *Sefer Likutei Moharan Hamenukad* (Jerusalem: 1994), 21:11.

14 This understanding is reflected elsewhere, as well. Regarding the questions of free will and human hierarchies in the world-to-come R. Nachman wrote: 'The reward of the world-

3. THE CHILD MESSIAH AND THE NATURE OF THE WORLD

The *Scroll* depicts the messiah both as a uniquely gifted child and as an elder who lives to see the tenth generation of his offspring. These descriptions seem to conflict with the general picture of the unadulterated course of nature found in the messianic world which is not, in R. Nachman's words, 'a world different than ours now.'[15] We can explain this seeming contradiction by proposing that the unique qualities of the messiah are not exceptions to the laws of nature,[16] but rather examples of unusual maximalization of the human potentials which already exist therein. This approach is close to that suggested by Maimonides' explanation for the attainment of advanced age in the messianic era.[17]

We should remember that the Chasidic hagiographies contain many stories of the *tzadikim* who even in their infancy were revealed as extremely gifted – able to make blessings before nursing, and who exhibited ethical behavior well beyond their years.[18] R. Nachman was purported to have desired a life of asceticism from the age of six.[19] Already at this age, he attempted

---

to-come, "no eye has seen" (Isaiah 64:3), as all will be one, there will be no eye to see – only God alone ('save for You God'). Then he said: Also regarding this there is extreme difficulty which cannot be understood. How can reward be meted out according to each individual's standing and good works in this world? It must be that also in the end not all will be equal. As all will be one, how is it possible to differentiate between one and his fellow according to standing? This is an unfathomable ancient mystery' (Ibid., 51).

15 See the text adjacent to note 36.

16 This is similar to Maimonides' description of the material plentitude and prosperity which will characterize the messianic age (MT Hilchot Melachim 12:5). This does not imply any reversal of nature, however, only its successful cultivation.

17 See above the text adjacent to note 5.

18 See, for example, the stories concerning R. Yitzchak Meir of Gur and R. Avraham Borenstein of Sukatchav in Rav Avraham Issakar Meir Eleyahu Alter, *Me'ir Eynei Hagolah* (Pietrakov: 1925), 6 and R. Zvi Yehudah Halevi Momlok of Kolish, *Abir Haro'im* (Pietrakov: 1935), 9-10 respectively.

19 For example his efforts at swallowing his food without tasting it so as to not get any pleasure from eating. See *Shibchei Haran*, (Jerusalem: 1995), 5.

to attain mystical visions and may have even succeeded.[20] We know that he married shortly after reaching the age of bar-mitzvah,[21] and then began his career of 'outreach' – drawing people close to the worship of God in such an authoritative fashion that many felt 'he was sure to become a famous *tzadik*.'[22] Of course, there is quite a gap between these details and the depiction of the messiah as a three-year-old halachic authority. However, they help to place messianic wonders in a context where wondrous deeds by children are well-known. These children's abilities may be exceptional, but they need not be considered as any miraculous alteration of the fundamental laws of nature.

However, even if we do understand the wondrous capabilities of the child messiah as supernatural, this will also be true in the messianic context as well. Even in the messianic age it will not be usual for infants to speak and teach or for youths to become world rulers. The messiah is exceptional even in the messianic era. The world continues to behave as it always has. While the messiah qua child prodigy may be unique, in other ways he is quite normal.

4. 'POLITICAL ZIONISM'

The *Scroll* details a unique and novel way by which the messiah obtains possession of the Land of Israel, gathers the exiles and consolidates his rule. To the best of my knowledge, no similar depiction can be found in the entirety of Jewish literature before R. Nachman.

> .... And he will send epistles to all of the wise-men and they will send him the sons of the kings and each one will write to his father until each

20 *Chayei Moharan Im Hashmatot*, 252. On this see Zvi Mark, *Mysticism and Madness In the Work of R. Nachman of Breslav* (Jerusalem: 2003), 246-7.

21 On this see Arthur Green, *Tormented Master* (New York: Schocken, 1987), 34; Rav Eliezer Schick, *Pe'ulat Hatzadik* (Jerusalem: 1944), 59-60. On the childhood matrimony among Jews in Europe in this period, see David Biale, *Eros and the Jews* (Berkeley, CA: University of California Press, 1997), 167-70. For a different description see Gershon David Hundert, *Jews in Poland-Lithuania in the Eighteenth Century: A Geneology of Modernity* (Berkeley: 2004), 131-7

22 See *Chayei Moharan Im Hashmatot*, 139.

one will give. Afterwards he will exchange with the Sultan and if it is too far then he will exchange it with another and another with another. And he will go there with all Israel and then he will be the king of Israel....[23]

The second section of the Scroll is more explicit.

Each of the kings will give him a present – or a country or a people
And some will give him a stipend and he will exchange with each of them until
he receives through barter the Land of Israel. That is, he will give to each the country near his border and receive for this a country closer to the Land of Israel until he receives through barter the Land of Israel. He will travel to the Land of Israel and in that year in which he travels to the Land of Israel then the ingathering of the exiles will occur and then all will travel to the Land of Israel and the Land of Israel will have room for all. Afterwards the Land of Israel will expand.[24]

Neither through might nor war will the messiah return the land to its people, but rather through what would one day be called 'political Zionism.' By way of a chain of agreements for territorial transfers based on economic-political considerations, the messiah is able to establish his kingdom in Israel legally in accord with the nations. Only then does the ingathering of the exiles begin as the Jewish nation streams to the Holy Land to become part of his kingdom.

The redemption of the land is carried out with neither miracles nor supernatural means. The acceptance of the messiah as king of Israel and ruler of the world is a gradual process, which requires no exceptions to any natural law. This path of action allows for Israel to return to their land with no worry that they have overstepped the famous 'oaths' holding them to the diaspora and prohibiting any revolt against the gentiles.[25] All of the mes-

23 Section I, line 13.

24 Section II, line 25.

25 For sources on this subject, see Aviezer Ravitsky, *Messianism, Zionism and Jewish Religious Radicalism* (Tel Aviv: 1993), 277-305.

siah's actions are taken with the full political and economic cooperation of the rest of the world's nations.

5. THE APOCALYPSE IS NOT MENTIONED IN THE SCROLL

The political leadership that the messiah displays in bringing the people of Israel back to its land reveals another interesting aspect of the *Scroll*, which we mentioned above – the lack of any apocalyptic struggle in the end of days. No wars, acts of violence or natural disasters are needed to change the face of humanity.

In *Avneiha Barzel* R. Natan is quoted as describing the peaceful nature of the messianic revolution. 'Our master, R. Natan, would say that the war of Gog and Magog is not mentioned in the *Scroll of Secrets*. This means that heresy will be commonplace. This will be our test and that of the messiah.'[26] It seems that R. Natan could not completely dismiss the notion of struggle as part of the messianic process, for it is mentioned by the Prophets. The war, however, will entail a spiritual and not a physical struggle.

Interestingly, however, no mention of even a spiritual war can be found in the *Scroll*; not one mention of heresy meant to test R. Nachman's followers and the messiah himself. We do find, though, a call to the faithful to stand strong in the face of difficult times to come. Near the end of the Scroll the following is written: 'Happy will be the strong of faith in those days';[27] 'Happy is he who merits this – may he strengthen his faith [until] then.'[28]

Aside from these somewhat abstruse declarations, it may be that the messiah's mission can be read as essentially one of a spiritual struggle

26 R. Avraham Chazan, *Avneiha Barzel* (Jerusalem: 1983), 72. On the apocalyptic war of Gog and Magog as a spiritual struggle, see Rav Chaim Menachem Kramer, *Toldot Moharnat: Be'aish Uvmayim* (Jerusalem: 1996), 584 fn 8.

27 Section II, line 76.

28 Ibid., line 95. It can be inferred here that the belief that needs strengthening is that regarding the messiah and not God. See Section II, lines *.

against those who have abandoned a life of faith. The messiah's high station in Israel and throughout the world is the result of his spiritual charisma and not physical power. His great wisdom, his powerful sermons to Israel and the nations, his horticultural skill and medical prowess – these are his divisions with which he conquers the world, drawing close to him those who thirst to hear his songs of faith. This tradition is also found in *Sod Sorfei Kodesh* where a Breslav adage is quoted: 'The messiah will take the world with nary a shot fired.'[29] Other Breslav works repeat the notion of the bloodless revolution as well.[30]

As opposed to the Maimonidean conception that outlines messianic times as beginning with an individual 'who fights the wars of God,' and who only then is considered a 'presumptive messiah,'[31] the Scroll describes the messianic age in terms which are the very antithesis of war. The messiah awakens in his followers feelings of love and the longing to be close to him.[32] His greatness is not measured in military might, but in his success as healer, poet and musician. The Scroll contains no mention of battle or violence: the messianic age is ushered in 'with neither war nor struggle.'[33] His minions obey him not out of fear, but out of love.[34]

While war is not a supernatural event, the destruction of the old usually signals the shaking up of the established order so that the new can be built upon its ruins – all the more so the apocalyptic battle of Gog and Magog. The fact that the Scroll carries no mention of such well known prophecies of violent struggle would seem to indicate that the messianic era will be less a revolution and more an evolutionary process. Rather than tearing down the old, the messiah improves upon it – making everything 'much more pleasant than before.'

---

29 *Siach Sorfei Kodesh*, vol. 1-5 (Jerusalem: 1994), vol. 2, 17.

30 Kramer, *Toldot Moharnat: Be'aish Uvmayim*, 116, 584 fn 8.

31 MT Hilchot Melachim 11:4. However, regarding the nature of the natural world, the *Scroll* follows Maimonides. See MT Hilchot Melachim 11:3.

32 See Section II lines 40 and 68.

33 Ibid., line 67.

34 Ibid., line 68. This opposes the Maimonidian coercion mentioned above.

Other statements by R. Nachman support the conception of the messianic era as a continuation of our own familiar world.

> I once heard in his name that the messiah will arrive suddenly. Word will go out that he has come and every one will put aside whatever business dealings he is involved with. The money changer will put aside his table, the candle-maker his wax. As it is written in Isaiah – 'he will put aside his gods of silver and gods of gold.'[35] It is not as some think – that the world will be different than ours once the messiah arrives, as mentioned above. Rather, everyone will be embarrassed by the frivolity of his daily life – each according to his own actions. (More research must be done to find who actually heard this from his holy mouth.)[36]

The suddenness of the messiah's appearance might indicate that something of a revolution occurs upon his arrival. However, R. Nachman explains that this is not the case. The changes that his presence effect are not in the nature of the world, but rather those that result from deep embarrassment – the suddenly unbearable lightness of being reflected by his presence.[37] The messiah need not harangue; there is something about his very being there which engenders in those that experience his closeness a desire to drop what they are doing to draw close to him. The world stays the same, but what changes is how people see themselves in it; how they value their own lives.

The picture which the *Scroll* paints (which I have expanded on here), of a messianic world which retains all the characteristics of our current familiar home, is not the only description offered by R. Nachman. Some of his discourses describe the messianic age as a

> ...renewal of the world in the future. Then the world will follow a supernatural course. That is, only through divine providence – wonders and

---

35 Following Isaiah 2:20.

36 *Chayei Moharan Im Hashmatot*, 461.

37 This is equivalent to the ending of the 'Tale of the Master of Prayer'.

> not the way of nature. In the future, the entire world will be renewed like the Land of Israel, as mentioned above, and then the entire world will function according to divine providence alone, like the Land of Israel. Then the natural will vanish, replaced by the divine alone – a world of wonders and not nature.'[38]

It may be that for R. Nachman the future is large enough to contain two separate eras. In the first, the world still runs according to the laws of nature; in the second it changes and God rules the world directly, essentially eliminating the natural order. This second wonder-full era, while not detailed in the *Scroll*, may, nonetheless, be hinted at. The second section of the Scroll mentions how the land of Israel will 'expand' after its exiles return to it in the days of the messiah. The meaning of this expansion is left curiously enigmatic. However, in the discourse, 'Teku Tochacha' (Blow a Reproach) we find help in understanding this short statement. There R. Nachman discusses the stage of expansion as being a part of redemption when the whole world becomes 'akin to the Land of Israel' and the natural order is overturned. This is the change from natural law to direct divine providence.

What is not clear from the *Scroll*, however, is when this stage will occur. According to the *Scroll*, it occurs 'after' the ingathering of Israel – but we are not informed if this means that it occurs immediately afterwards or in the far away future. If the former, the miraculous expansion of the Land of Israel seems to be part of the same sequence of redemption outlined in the *Scroll*. If, however, it will take place at some unspecified time in the far future, it may be that it constitutes a different stage in the redemption which is not included in the messianic world depicted in the *Scroll*'s time-frame. I will return to this question below.

---

38 *Sefer Likutei Moharan Hamenukad*. This discourse was related on Rosh Hashanah of 1810. On the meaning of the Land of Israel, see Mark, *Mysticism and Madness In the Work of R. Nachman of Breslav*, 281-93.

CHAPTER FOUR
The Temple

> In the end of days the mount of the House of God will stand above the mountains and tower over the hills. To it, all the nations will stream. Many peoples will say, 'Let us go up to the mount of God, to the house of the God of Jacob. He will teach us his ways and we will follow him.' For from Zion will the Torah go forth, the word of God from Jerusalem.[1]

> I will bring them to my holy mountain, gladden them in my house of prayer. Their sacrifices and offerings will be accepted on my altar - for my house will be called the house of prayer for all peoples.[2]

One of the central symbols connected to the end of days and the coming of the messiah in Jewish consciousness is the establishment of the Temple. It is depicted as the holy center of worship for both Israel and the nations.[3] The words of the prophets describe the Temple as the place where God will make the nations rejoice as He accepts their sacrifices. There they will all come to pray.

The Temple, its destruction and anticipated rebuilding, has held a prominent place in Jewish thought, custom and liturgy for thousands of years. The request, 'return the sacrifices to the inner court of your house,'[4] is mentioned

---

1 Isaiah 2:2-3.

2 Ibid., 56:7.

3 Ithamar Gruenwald, "*Mezricha Leshkiah: Ledmutan Shel He'escatelogia Vehameshichiut Beyahadut*," in *The Messianic Idea in Jewish Thought* (Jerusalem: 1982), 26-7.

4 The Amidah prayer.

in every prayer. On the Sabbath and holidays, a complete additional prayer service devoted to recalling the Temple worship and asking for its reinstatement is inserted into the liturgy. The connection between the messianic age and the reestablishment of the Temple has been codified into law by Maimonides. For him, one of the essential tasks of the messiah is the rebuilding of the Temple. Without it, the messiah cannot be acknowledged as Israel's true redeemer.[5] In light of all this, the complete absence of any mention of the Temple in the *Scroll* is quite unusual.

The *Scroll* describes the entire career of the messiah from the time that he begins to teach Torah until he becomes the king of Israel and finally emperor of the world. We learn how the messiah succeeds in acquiring the Land of Israel, gathers the exiles and builds a series of palaces in his capital. Artisans from the across the globe arrive to create the complex of palaces meant to house the messiah and the princes of the nations. Despite all this construction, not a word is mentioned concerning the building of the Temple. Not in the first or in the second recitation do we find any mention of what has been traditionally considered to be the crowning achievement of the entire messianic age: the rebuilding of the Temple – the universal house of God.

The lack of the Temple in the *Scroll* highlights what *is* found therein – a well developed depiction of the messiah with many details of his personality and daily life. This stands in stark contrast to the Lurianic tradition which, despite its attention to messianism, gives little notice to the actual messiah. The messiah plays no role in the process of spiritual repair which occurs in the end of days. Rather he is more a symbol of the change which has taken place as the world has moved into its messianic state.[6] The *Scroll*, however, is focused first and foremost on the messiah as the instigator and catalyst who brings these long-awaited changes to the entire world.

---

5 See Maimonides MT *Hilchot Melachim* 11:4.

6 The exception to this is the description of the messianic soul's various incarnations in the works of R. Yitzchak Luriah. See Gershom Scholem, *Explications and Implications* (Tel Aviv: 1975), 213; Isaiah Tishby, *The Doctrine of Evil and the 'Kelippah' in Lurianic Kabbalism* (Jerusalem: 1992), 142-3.

More than this, the *Scroll*'s messiah is not just an agent who serves as the catalyst for the messianic era, fighting Israel's enemies and building its spiritual center as Maimonides suggests. Rather he himself remains at the very center of the redeemed world.[7] We may even sharpen this and say that the role which the Temple plays in other messianic visions of the end of days is replaced by the person of the messiah in R. Nachman's. The messiah, who is drawn along the lines of the Breslavian *tzadik*, is the center of the entire world's attention and longing. It is not the Temple of God around which the world's princes come to build their palaces, but around the messiah's abode. Not to the mountain of the Almighty does the world beat a path, but rather, '… everyone will live nearby him due to their great yearning for him such that they cannot be without him.'[8]

Here we are witness to the exchange of the holy place with the holy personage. This is not a mere temporary measure, meant as a substitute until that time when the Temple can be built, as other strands of Chasidic thought have held;[9] rather this is a permanent transfer which lasts throughout the messianic era. The complete realization of human perfection is found in the very person of the messiah, the ultimate *tzadik*. According to the *Scroll*, the messianic age, whose very essence is the gathering of humanity around the messiah, is forever centered on this *tzadik*.

---

7 Although we are informed that the Sanhedrin will be re-established in the days of the messiah, it will be the messiah-king, and not the Sanhedrin who will enact the socio-religious changes of the period. The Sanhedrin will function only as a non-activist judiciary.

8 Section II, line 40.

9 The idea that the individual – the holy person – can replace the holy place as the nexus of God's presence can already be found in some of the early works of Chasidic thought. For example, R. Yaakov Yosef of Polnoy wrote, 'the tzadik is called the Hall of God and the Temple of God as He dwells within him as is well-known from the words of the elders. When one cleaves to the sage in whom the Divine Presence dwells, he cleaves to the [Divine] itself' and 'the sage is called the Temple of God… (Rav Yaakov Yosef of Polnoy, *Tzafnat Panei'ach*, Gedeliah Nagal ed. (Jerusalem: 1989), 223, 329). R. Nachman also quotes the well-known midrash on the verse, 'I will dwell among you,' (Exodus 25:8): 'Within it [the Tabernacle] is not mentioned, but among/within you. This teaches us that God causes his presence to dwell in each individual….' [Rav Natan of Nemirov, *Sefer Likutei Moharan Hamenukad* (Jerusalem: 1994), 141:94].

Theoretically, we could explain the lack of the Temple's appearance in the *Scroll* by reasoning that the *Scroll* is devoted to detailing the '*coming* of the messiah' – an early stage of the messianic era. Perhaps the building of the Temple is merely beyond the scope of the *Scroll*'s chronology. However, we know that the *Scroll* contains not merely a depiction of the messiah's arrival, but also the early stages of Israel's redemption. Israel has returned to her land, the messiah is crowned king and appointed world emperor. Even the tenth generation of the messiah's offspring warrants mention, along with his death after a long and fruitful reign. The nations of the world assemble around him, not the Temple. In light of this, just as R. Natan noted that the 'war of Gog and Magog is not mentioned in the *Scroll*,'[10] and so concluded that this apocalyptic battle will not occur, being replaced by a spiritual struggle instead – so too we may surmise that the lack of the Temple points to its lack of importance in the messianic scheme.

However, the sanctification of place is not wholly missing from the *Scroll*. The Land of Israel is the focal point for messianic times. Jerusalem

---

10 This subject has received much attention in the literature. See Arthur Green, "The Zaddiq as Axis Mundi," *Journal of American Religion* 45 (1977). He stresses that in Chasidic thought the *tzadik* was not viewed as a replacement for the holy place, but rather as an additional site of the holy. The hope to return to Israel and the Temple remain a part of the Chasidic world-view. Rivkah Shatz-Oppenheimer stressed that there was no abandonment of the traditional hope for the arrival of the messiah who would rebuild the Temple as evidenced by the prayers and texts found throughout the Chasidic genre. However, she felt that these texts were representative of the movement's formal connection to the tradition and were not an expression of the actual spiritual vibrancy of Chasidic thought [Rivka Shatz Oppenheimer, *Chasidism as Mysticism* (Jerusalem: 1988), 168-77, esp. 175]. Margolin, however, understands that the centrality of the *tzadik* represents a more actual transformation of the concept of the holy from place to person. This is in line with the general internalization characteristic of the movement. He does not feel, however, that this entails the abandonment of actual commandments or hope for the eventual building of the physical Temple [Ron Margolin, *The Human Temple: Religious Interiorization and the Structuring of Inner Life in Early Chasidism* (Jerusalem: 1995), 127-38, 390-8]. See also Samuel H. Dresner, *The Tzadik: The Doctrine of the Tzadik According to the Writing of Yaakov Yosef of Polnoy* (New York: 1974), 122-3, 276-7; Moshe Idel, *Chasidism Between Ecstasy and Magic* (Tel Aviv: 2001), 356 fn. 37. For a different understanding of the relationship of the Baal Shem Tov to messianism, see Haviva Pedayah, " *The Baal Shem Tov's Iggeret Hakodesh*," *Zion* 70, no. 3 (2005), esp. 350-4.

itself becomes the messianic capital city – a model of an ultimate Chasidic court - built up with the palaces of the world's leaders who flock to be near the messiah king. Even if we assume that the messiah builds his estate on the Temple Mount, next to the Temple, it is to him that the world's minions flow and not to the Temple itself. So overshadowed is the Temple that it does not even warrant being mentioned by name.

In light of all this, the focus of the *Scroll* on the person of the messiah as a Breslavian *tzadik* receives yet another layer of meaning. It is not the return of the Jewish people to their land, or the rebuilding of the Temple, or the establishment of sovereignty which are the most important aspects of the messianic era. Rather, it is simply the central presence of the messiah, the holy *tzadik* upon which all rests. All of the good which comes to the entire world in the end of days rests squarely upon his shoulders alone.

The *Scroll*'s messiah, despite his reign as emperor of the world, spends his days in ways more befitting a holy man than a world leader. He arouses not fear and respect in his followers, but love. He is not enclosed in his palace, but acts as a compassionate *tzadik* - walking about among his people, healing the sick, preaching to the masses. He offers new prayers and customs to his followers; he innovates in the arts and sciences, all the while reserving time for daily *hitbodedut* and prayer. As a charismatic leader, he sweeps an entire generation off their feet. He is the world's foundation stone, its axis mundi – replacing the Temple itself in the time of redemption.[11]

---

11 It is worth noting that over the years Breslav Chasidim have continued to mourn the destruction of the Temple and to pray for its rebuilding. This reflects the wishes of R. Nachman himself, expressed in several of his works. 'Now, when God is expecting to return to us and rebuild our Temple, it is suitable to not encumber, heaven forbid, its construction. We must work for its rebuilding by being careful to arise at midnight and to mourn its destruction' (*Sefer Likutei Moharan Hamenukad*, II 67). Before the establishment of the State of Israel, the Jerusalem Breslav community was known for its devotion to mourning the Temple's destruction at the Western Wall. (Agnon describes the meeting between one of his characters with a group of Breslav Chasidim in *T'mol Shilshom* (Tel Aviv: 1945), 376). The importance of the Temple and the dreams of its rebuilding are clearly seen in R. Natan's works as well. 'The fundamental completion of the redemption entails the completion of the rebuilding of the Temple. Therefore, each time that we request redemption, we request that the Temple be rebuilt speedily in our day … for it is akin to an awakening from slumber as

We find no complete parallel to the idea that the *tzadik* will replace the Temple in *Likutei Moharan*. However, there are a number of discourses which contain the foundational notion that the holy person of *tzadik* can fulfill the role of the holy place. For example, we find in 'Chadi R. Shimon' (R. Shimon Rejoiced) that R. Nachman compares the *tzadik* to the foundation stone of the Temple and its Holy of Holies which are the true objectives of those who make pilgrimages to the Holy Land.

> This is akin to traveling to the *tzadik* on Rosh Hashanah. Rosh Hashanah is the day of judgment for the rest of the coming year and each individual approaches the generation's *tzadik* (who is akin to the Holy of Holies, to the foundation stone) with his own holiness and 'contractions.' Everyone comes to be included in this *tzadik* who is akin to the foundation stone.[12]

In his discourse 'Breishit,' we discover that for R. Nachman the true *tzadik* is what illuminates the Temple and that its very existence depends upon him.

> The *tzadik* is akin to Shabbat.... Therefore in every place that the construction of the Sanctuary is mentioned so too Shabbat. As in: 'Keep my Sabbaths and honor my Temple.'[13] And also in each warning regarding

---

in "I will not let my eyes sleep, my eyelids rest – until I find a place for God" (Psalms 132:4) – that is the building of the Temple.... [Rav Natan of Nemirov, *Likutei Halachot* (Jerusalem: 1984)]. R. Natan also wrote prayers which expressed the hope for the rebuilding of the Temple and the restoration of the Service therein. See Rav Natan of Nemirov, *Likutei Tefilot Hamenukad* (Jerusalem: 1989), 241.

12 *Sefer Likutei Moharan Hamenukad*, 61:7. The description of the *tzadik's* functioning as a substitute for the Temple is found in many Chasidic sources. For example, R. Avraham Yehoshuah Heschel of Apta writes: 'My uncle... was sick ... and recovered. After this, he saw R. David Halevi Segal in a dream and he asked him why he had not brought a thanksgiving offering. He replied that the Temple was destroyed. R. Segal replied, "In Lublin there is a small-scale Temple ... and he went to Lublin"' (Menachem Mendel Walden, ed., *Niflaot Harebi* (Bnei Brak: 1944), 83.). For other sources, see note 9 above.

13 Leviticus 26:2.

> the construction of the Sanctuary, [we find] a previous warning concerning the Sabbath. For the Sabbath illuminates the Temple....
> The true *tzadik*, who is the beauty and nonpareil of the world ... it is through him that the Temple and the homes and dwellings of Israel are sustained....[14]

In the first section of the *Scroll*, we learn that at some stage the messiah will sanctify the Holy Land. The need for this sanctification relates back to a Talmudic discussion concerning the question of whether the sanctity of Israel has remained extant despite the dispersion of the Jews. All agree that the sanctity of the land which devolved upon its conquest by Joshua dissipated with the first diaspora. The second conquest in the time of Ezra re-sanctified the land. The question is whether or not this sanctification remained after the second diaspora. This point is debated in the Talmud.[15] By claiming that the messiah will re-sanctify the Land of Israel, R. Nachman apparently sides with the opinion that the sanctity of the land was not extant, but needed to be renewed.

The fact that the messiah sanctifies the land also teaches us that the return of the Jewish people to Israel is not in itself enough to re-establish its holiness. Rather, a specific initiative on the part of the messiah would be needed as well.[16] On the other hand, the fact that the messiah does so, shows us that the place of Israel as the center of holiness is indeed fortified.

The second section of the *Scroll* carries more information about the Land of Israel. After the messiah arrives there and gathers all the exiles we find that 'the Land of Israel will have room for all. After this the Land of Israel will expand.'[17] At first, the land seems to be a small vessel holding much

---

14 Nemirov, *Sefer Likutei Moharan Hamenukad*, 67.

15 This is a legal point which is still debated among scholars today. See in *Haencyclopediah HaTalmudit* (Jerusalem: 1987), 213-18.

16 For a discussion of whether the Land of Israel need be specifically resanctified or whether its physical conquest serves this purpose, see ibid. 217.

17 Section II, line 30.

– the entire Jewish people are able to settle there. Afterwards, the land itself expands beyond its original borders.

The expansion of Israel may, in accord with traditional sources, be understood in two different ways. The first relates to geo-political territorial expansion resultant of the military conquest of surrounding territories. This is the midrashic interpretation of the Biblical promise 'every place upon which you step, I will give to you.'[18] According to the Sages, this means that Jewish settlement in surrounding lands lends them the same holy status enjoyed by Israel itself.[19] Understanding the expansion of the Land in this way limits it to those places where there will be actual settlement. It does not seem to correspond to the depiction of the messiah's activities in the *Scroll* which do not include any military conquests, however.

The second possibility is to understand that the Land's expansion is meant as R. Levi, the Talmudic Sage stated: 'In the future Jerusalem will be like the Land of Israel and the Land of Israel like the entire world.'[20] He refers not to any geo-political consequences of conquest, but rather to a spiritual process of expanding sanctity which encompasses, in the end, the entire world. This option seems closer to the ambiance of the *Scroll*'s non-violent, spiritual concerns. R. Nachman's teachings in *Likutei Moharan* also point in a similar direction. He notes that 'in the future, the entire world will be renewed [and become] like the Land of Israel.'[21] We see that his meaning, which also includes the entire world, is spiritual and not political. No conquest is needed. Rather here is a promise for the future – a promise that God will turn the entire world into the Promised Land.

Unlike the absence of the Temple proper from the *Scroll*, the Land of Israel does feature prominently in the messianic future. Its role and status

---

18 Joshuah 1:3.

19 See "Otzar Eretz Yisrael," 212-3.

20 *Pisikta Rabati*, Meir Ish Shalom ed. (Tel Aviv: 1963), Parsha 1; *Yalkut Shimoni*, (Jerusalem: 2000), 809. See also, *Sifrei Al Sefer Devarim*, Finkelstein ed. (New York: 1993), 1.

21 Nemirov, *Sefer Likutei Moharan Hamenukad*, II 8:10. For more on this promise, see Zvi Mark, *Mysticism and Madness In the Work of R. Nachman of Breslav* (Jerusalem: 2003), 281-93.

seem to grow. However, paradoxically, this growth works in the opposite direction - marginalizing its importance as it expands. As the entire world attains the sanctity of Israel, the Land of Israel proper looses its unique standing as a holy place defined in space. The *Land of Israel* is no longer the name for a particular local, but rather signifies a qualitative status of sanctity which embraces the world at large.

This de-placement of the centrality of the Land of Israel also reinforces the different nature of messianic times: The center to which all turn will not be a place, but a person – the messiah himself. Paradoxically, then, the climax of the process through which the importance of the Land of Israel is raised is in actuality its replacement by the person of the messiah.

CHAPTER FIVE
King Solomon and the Scroll's Messiah

When read against the background of King Solomon's reign, the messianic vision found in the *Scroll* takes on another layer of significance. Both in the broad focus of the Scroll, as well as on the more particular level, we find that the biblical-midrashic depiction of King Solomon and the *Scroll*'s own messiah-king share much in common.

The second section of the *Scroll* opens with the pronouncement that the twelve-year-old messiah 'will become emperor over the entire world.'[1] According to the midrash this is the same age at which Solomon began his reign: 'At the age of twelve Solomon began his rule.'[2] The depiction of the child messiah is similar to that of the child king who is blessed with outstanding wisdom which brings him fame throughout the world. Solomon, the 'wisest of men,'[3] received his gift of wisdom at the start of his reign, perhaps to compensate for his youth. While praying for help he mentioned that 'I am but a small youth,'[4] and was answered by God with the gift of knowledge. He becomes known as, 'a wise man – intelligent and intuitive.'[5]

---

1 Section II, line 3.

2 *Seder Olam Raba Hashalem Latana Rabi Yosi Ben Chalafta* (Bnei Brak: 1990), 237; *Yalkut Shimoni* (Jerusalem: 2000), Samuel II 149:15.

3 Kings I 5:11.

4 Ibid., 3:7.

5 Chronicles II 2:11. The basis for this comparison is found in the midrash which describes how, when Solomon's wisdom was known, 'they asked whether he was the messiah

Just as the kings of the world will eventually send their children to learn at the side of the messiah, so too do we find that Solomon's court became the address for those wanting to gain wisdom. 'From all the nations they came to hear the wisdom of Solomon, from all the lands' kings who had heard his wisdom.'[6] And just as the messiah was the recipient of many gifts, so too did those who arrived at Solomon's court come bearing gifts. Aside from the exotic collection of presents brought by the Queen of Sheba, 'All of the lands' kings approached Solomon to hear his wisdom which God had placed in his heart. Each brought his gift – gold and silver vessels, clothing, weapons, spices, horses and donkeys – year by year.'[7]

The *Scroll* describes the important geopolitical results which the world's fascination with the messiah and it leaders' respect for his wisdom bring. He receives gifts (including lands) and through careful barter he is able eventually to gain control of the Land of Israel and bring its scattered people home. King Solomon, esteemed for his wisdom, likewise made mercantile connections with the surrounding nations which included territorial exchanges. He gave to Hiram, the king of Tzur, 'twenty cities in the Galil' in payment for the supply of lumber used in building the Temple.[8] The king of Egypt granted Solomon the city of Gezer.[9]

The horticultural expertise evinced by the messiah also echoes the work of Solomon in planting 'gardens and orchards' in which he cultivated 'trees bearing all manner of fruit (Ecclesiastes 2:5).' R. Nachman mentions the midrash which describes the extensive horticultural knowledge of Solomon in one of his discourses. '... the foundation stone upon which the very world

---

and began to stream to him' ("*Midrash Breishit Rabati Nosad Al Sifro Shel R. Moshe Hadarshan*," ed. Chanoch Albeck (Jerusalem: 1967), 103.

6 Kings I 5:14.

7 Chronicles II 9:23-4. Gifts of gold and silver are mentioned in the *Scroll*, I line 46. A midrash describes the gifts brought to Solomon, 'The nations brought offerings and in the future they will bring to the messiah-king' ("*Midrash Rabbah*," ed. M. A. Merkin (Tel Aviv: 1987), 66.

8 Kings I 9:10-13.

9 Ibid., 9:16.

rests, from which all the arteries of the world extend to all the lands. King Solomon, exceedingly wise, knew all the particulars of all these arteries, and would plant trees bearing all manner of fruit.'[10]

One of the more distinctive features of the messiah detailed in the *Scroll* is his functioning exclusively through peaceful means. His revolution occurs with nary one bullet being spent. Likewise, Solomon, whose name in Hebrew is from the same root as peace – Shalom/ Shlomo[11] – is noted for leading his kingdom to greatness with no need for war. As opposed to his father, David – a warrior who established his reign with much bloodshed – Solomon's reign is completely peaceful. It was this very lack of bloodshed which made him suitable in the eyes of God to build the Temple.[12]

King Solomon, despite commanding a large kingdom, found the time to compose the verses of 'five and one-thousand' poems.[13] Like the *Scroll*'s messiah, his devotion to the arts and wisdom were exceptional. He authored Proverbs, Ecclesiastes and the renowned Song of Songs[14] regarding which R. Akivah claimed that the day of its creation was on par with the very creation of the world. R. Akivah taught that if the rest of the Scriptures were holy, the Song of Songs was the holy of holies.[15]

We should also remember that R. Nachman gave his son the name Shlomo – Solomon. If only he had lived, the *Scroll* would have described his own life.

Despite all the similarities, however, Solomon and the *Scroll*'s messiah differ in important ways as well. King Solomon, desirous to strengthen his court's strategic alliances with other kings, married many foreign

---

10 *Sichot Haran* (Jerusalem: 1995), 75. See also, *Midrash Tanchuma Hashalem*, 2 vols. (Jerusalem: 1988), vol. 2, 99.

11 The Hebrew can be read as 'peace is his'. See *Yalkut Shimoni*, 1072.

12 See Chronicles I 22:7-10.

13 Kings I 5:12.

14 Song of Songs 1:1. See *Yalkut Shimoni*, 1064 for an explanation of its name.

15 *Shir Hashirim Rabba* (Jerusalem: 1994), 40-41.

wives – the daughters of kings and ministers.[16] These he brought to his palace where he even built a separate home for the Pharaoh's daughter.[17] Even if his intentions were to 'house the words of Torah and bring them under the wings of the Divine spirit'[18] in the end his wives swayed his heart to worship foreign gods.[19] Solomon was punished and his house split in two, leaving his once mighty kingdom a torn shadow of its former glory.[20]

The messiah found in the *Scroll*, despite his strict monogamy, does bring the children of the world's leaders to live in his midst. They come to study at his side and he orders them to build their palaces in proximity to his own. Even before his arrival in Jerusalem, his capital, this building commences as the world's kings chose to make it their home, 'Because everyone will live nearby him due to their great yearning for him such that they cannot be without him.'[21]

We can see the stark contrast between the connection that Solomon had with the world's princes and that endorsed by R. Nachman's messiah. While Solomon brought foreign women to his court as wives and concubines, this erotic connection is completely different from the way that the messiah relates to the nations' sons. He is their teacher – they his students; he their rebbe – they his followers. It may very well be that R. Nachman consciously set out to correct the sins of Solomon in this regard by offering a picture of the proper connection between the king of Israel and his foreign subjects. This connection is established through wisdom, religion, liturgy, poetry and song – not through conjugal relations. Thus the messiah rebuilds the former glory of the Solomonic empire including its global ties with the nations in the proper fashion.

---

16 Kings I 3:1; 11:1.

17 Ibid., 7:8.

18 TY Sanhedrin 13b.

19 Kings I from 11:4.

20 Ibid., from verse 11.

21 Section II, line 40.

This platonic relationship, based on friendship and not eros, is part of the Breslav ethos which sees the reigning in of the erotic as an essential part of the true religious experience in general and of the messianic process in particular.[22] R. Nachman deals with this issue in a wide variety of discourses – the discussion of which would unfortunately take us far afield from the *Scroll*. It will suffice to say that the fall of the Solomonic empire could have been prevented if his erotic attachment to foreign women had been properly controlled. It is for this reason that the children of kings are under the care of R. Nachman's messiah – as a preventative measure taken against the excesses that brought down Solomon.

Our comparison of the *Scroll*'s messianic vision to King Solomon's world again shows up the striking lack of attention that the *Scroll* gives to Solomon's crowning achievement – the building of the Temple, the House of God. Solomon invested the resources of his own country and others in building the Temple, even completing it before his own palace.[23] However, as mentioned above, the Temple is absent from the *Scroll*, even though the building of the palaces of the messiah and his royal neighbors are clearly described.

In spite of the important differences between the two, it does seem that many aspects of the Solomonic empire did serve as a model for R. Nachman's messianic kingdom. His vision recalls for us Solomon's days of glory when his kingdom and influence stretched far and wide beyond the narrow confines of the Holy Land. For R. Nachman, though, the messiah's purpose is to build both a more spiritual and more universal

---

22 R. Nachman discusses the importance of sexual propriety and its connection to the messiah in several places and composed his *Tikkunim* around this topic. See Yehuda Liebes, "*Hatikun Haclali Shel R. Nachman Mebreslav Veyachaso Leshabta'ut*," in *On Sabbateanism and its Kabbalah* (Jerusalem: 1995), esp. 246-8, 54-9. For more information, see Appendix 4 below; Zvi Mark, "*Ma'aseh Mehashiryon (The Tale of the Armor) – from the Hidden Chambers of Breslav Censorship*," *Zion* 70, no. 2 (2005); Zvi Mark, "*The Formulation of R. Nachman of Breslav's 'Tikkun ha-kelali,' the 'Tikkun for Nocturnal Pollution,' and Pilgrimage to the tomb of R. Nachman, and Their Relationship to Messianism*," *Da'at* 56 (2005).

23 Kings I 6:38-7:1.

empire than Solomon had done. The messiah-king who stands at its head possesses the wisdom of Solomon as well as his love of the arts and architecture. He builds a kingdom which encompasses the entire world and exceeds that of Solomon in its stability and endurance. The messiah himself will live to see ten generations of his offspring rule the empire which he established.

CHAPTER SIX
Is There a Secret Belief that R. Nachman Never Died or Will Return from the Dead?

> Before the messiah will arrive, the grandchild/ren of the Baal Shem Tov will come before all the kings and master their written and spoken languages.[1]

While no exact description of the grandchildren's activities with the kings are recorded, it may very well be that as their stay with them precedes the messiah's arrival, their actions constitute some type of preparation for that day. The importance of linguistic competence as a method of establishing rapport with the world's leaders is one of the central themes found in R. Nachman's 'Tale of the Wise-Man and the Simple-Man.' The simple-man of this story, who eventually ascends to great heights, took upon himself the task of learning 'wisdom and languages' because 'the way of the king's speech is to tilt in a certain direction, to speak wisdom and other languages. Therefore, it is good (and good-manners) that you should be able to answer him.' The simple-man learned different languages and when he conversed with the king, the king was suitably impressed with him. So much, in fact, that he made him his chief-minister.[2]

---

1 Section II, line 89.

2 *Sefer Sipurei Ma'asiot Hamenukad*, (Jerusalem: 1985), 94-5.

According to this tale, linguistic skill is one of the keys in establishing a real relationship with those in power – one that moves beyond formalities. This opens the way for positive developments of the kind found in this tale wherein the simple-man becomes a powerful minister of the king.

The original text found in the copy of the *Scroll* – *nech' habesh'* seems to indicate the words – *nechdei habesht*, the grandchildren of the Baal Shem [Tov]. The plural here fits with the continuation of the sentence '[they] master their written and spoken language.'[3] The plural refers to the offspring of the Baal Shem Tov, which may in fact also mean those of R. Nachman as well; he himself was a great-grandchild of the Baal Shem Tov. Another less likely possibility is that the first word is the singular, grandchild. If this is the case, we might ask if a specific grandchild is meant – perhaps R. Nachman himself? If this is the case, perhaps this is a hint that R. Nachman himself will return from the dead. Not as part of the general messianic revival of the dead, but rather before the arrival of the messiah. He will have some type of task vis-à-vis the world's leadership at that time.

Now, if we follow this string of assumptions we come to separate the person of R. Nachman from that of the messiah. The Baal Shem Tov's grandson (or –sons) arrives before the messiah, and from the lack of information concerning his actual activities in the *Scroll*, seems to be destined to play a relatively minor role by comparison. All we are told is that he will master the languages of the kings.

Both the actual textual evidence and the fact that the *Scroll* offers no other description of the 'revival of the dead' as part of the messianic experience point to the plural 'grandchildren' as the better reading here. This way, there is no confusion that R. Nachman himself is meant to be the harbinger of the messiah mentioned.

Some of the scholarly research, though, has claimed that there remains a secret belief that the Rebbe never really died, or alternatively, will come back to life and play a major role in the coming of the messiah among Breslav

3 This is the version found in the Sichot Me'anash manuscript as well.

Chasidim.[4] In light of these claims, it is reasonable to question whether we can in fact find support for them amongst the Breslav community and whether the *Scroll* itself is the source for this secret belief. (If we do find that this is the case, we may decide that the singular 'grandchild' that is R. Nachman reading,seems to gain more credence.)

Joseph Weiss hypothesized that there is an 'esoteric belief that R. Nachman, in fact, did not die.'[5] The evidence that he finds for this theory is in R. Natan's description of his Rebbe's death as something nearly incomprehensible: 'But his actual passing is something which cannot be spoken of, it is completely incomprehensible.'[6] However, it is difficult to understand such utterances as actual evidence of any secret belief. This sentence and others like it are familiar expressions of grief and disbelief upon the death of a loved one. The suspension of belief may be all the more understandable regarding one so admired and esteemed by his followers. Asserting that this is proof for a belief that R. Nachman did not actually die seems to be off the mark.

Weiss also finds other quotes by R. Natan which indicate his continued connection and communication with R. Nachman after his Rebbe's

---

4 Joseph Weiss, *Studies in Bratslav Hasidi*sm (Jerusalem: 1995), 231-3 fn. 42; Mendel Piekarz, *Studies in Bratslav Hasidism*, expanded ed. (Jerusalem: 1995), 139 and fn. 19a, 32-50, 209-16; Arthur Green, *Tormented Master* (New York: Schocken, 1987), 197, 217 fn. 32; Jonathan Garb, *The Chosen Will Become Herds: Studies in Twentieth Century Kabbalah* (Jerusalem: 1995), 130-1. On the tradition of the Baal Shem Tov's resurrection and becoming the messiah, see below Appendix Five.

5 Weiss, *Studies in Bratslav Hasidi*sm, 232.

6 'All those who witnessed [his death], the majority of the holy fellowship and all of those great rabbinic assistants who deal with such things, all said that they have seen those who died pure deaths, but a death like this they had never witnessed. This is only in accord with our understanding, but essentially we can not describe his passing at all, for it is inscrutable. Anyone who understands even a bit of his greatness through his holy books, discourses and the stories we heard from him ... will understand that it is impossible to discuss his death for it was a wonderously new and unique event, the likes of which had never been seen before and never will be again. This is mentioned elsewhere – "What can we say, how can we thank God for meriting to be present at the moment of his holy soul's departure"' [Rav Natan of Nemirov, *Yemei Moharnat* (Jerusalem: 1982), I 76].

death.[7] However, even these statements are not really exceptions to usual expressions of the continued influence and attachment felt towards the departed by those who were close to them. This is all the more so true regarding a religious milieu wherein actual death is considered to be the mere destruction of the body alone. There are many descriptions of visitation by the dead's spirit in dreams and visions, yet none of these are meant as indications that physical death had not actually occurred. In such a culture, it is only natural to turn to the departed after death. We find reference to such communication in R. Nachman's world in the following text.

> Once [we] heard a woman crying at her father's grave, 'Father! Father!' in a bitter voice. R. Nachman's own daughter was with him at the time and he turned to her and said: 'This woman is crying with great intent, 'Father, Father,' but actually her father is not here.' He then said that when coming to the graves of one's forefathers it is best to address those dead who lie in the surrounding graves and to request that they announce that [living] relatives have arrived. Certainly not all of the dead leave their place of burial ... many are still near their graves. Therefore it is proper to ask them to call one's departed family members. He then said, 'But regarding the *tzadik* there is no need to worry about this – whether he is not there. For the death of the *tzadik* is like moving from one room to another.' He made a parable for his daughter about himself, 'It is as if I am now in one room and afterwards I leave it for another room and close the door behind me. If you come to the door and yell, "Father, father," won't I hear you?!' Similar things were heard from his holy mouth several times. He hinted

7 Regarding the death of R. Nachman's son, R. Natan wrote, 'May God comfort you' (Ibid., I 19). It seems that this was written after the death of R. Nachman. Weiss brings further evidence: 'The goodness and mercy of our Rebbe was beyond measure. His left hand would push away a bit, but his right would strongly draw near. This duality was in itself a great drawing near for anyone who truly wanted and desired it. He still acts like this" (*Yemei Moharnat*, I 14-5). According to Weiss, the line 'He still acts like this' represents some denial of R. Nachman's death. However, R. Natan's words are not a denial of the fact that his Rebbe is dead and buried, but rather a description of his own feelings that at times R. Nachman draws him near and at times pushes him away.

to all about the great level of anybody who would be privileged to come to his terribly holy grave for he would surely hear his words and do all he could to aid him.[8]

The dividing line between the living and the dead is not one which divides existence from non-existence, but rather separates different types of existence. From this follows the possibility of conversing with the dead.[9] It would be a mistake to assume from statements describing such communication that it is indicative that a certain individual has been somehow buried alive.

Weiss points to the language used by R. Nachman in his sermons regarding the death of the *tzadik* – referring to himself – 'the departure of the *tzadik*' or 'disappearance and departure' as further proof for his theory. For instance, in the discourse 'Bereishit' (Likutei Moharan II 67), which R. Natan interprets as relating both to the death of R. Levi Yitzchak of Berditchev which occurred in that year and to the Rebbe's own death one year hence,[10] R. Nachman uses the phrase 'disappearance, the *tzadik* vanishes.'[11] However, such language is in fact quite common and has no bearing on the factual state of R. Nachman's own death. Actually, this discourse may serve to counter Weiss' claims. If the use of 'disappearance' refers both to R. Levi Yitzchak of Berditchev and to R. Nachman, and means something other than physical death, then we should assume that R. Nachman understood

8 *Sichot Haran*, (Jerusalem: 1995), 204-5.

9 In this context the following should be read: 'Before leaving Breslav for Uman to die there, as he left the house to alight upon the wagon he placed his hand on the mezuzzah and said: "Make sure to gather together and pray together. If you pray with the proper intention you may just be able to draw me back here again"' [*Chayei Moharan Im Hashmatot*, (Jerusalem: 2000), 214]. The claim that R. Nachman may return can be understood as meaning his return to Breslav, but it may also be understood as referring to his return from the dead.

10 Weiss, *Studies in Bratslav Hasid*ism, 232-3.

11 Weiss also claimed that 'it is not impossible that this discourse about the disappearance of the *tzadik* contains traces of Sabbatean theology regarding the messiah's disappearance' (ibid., 233).

that R. Levi Yitzchak of Berditchev was still alive. There is no doubt that such language expresses the understanding that the actual death of an individual is something other than non-existence. This is all the more so the case regarding *tzadikim* (who in death are called living[12]) and even more so regarding R. Nachman, the ultimate *tzadik* who promised to hear and to come to the aid of any who visited his grave.[13]

Piekarz also addresses this subject and attempts to find support for the claims of Weiss in latter Breslav texts which mention the 'departure and disappearance of the *tzadik* from our midst.'[14] In my opinion, there is no real connection between these expressions and the belief that R. Nachman will return from the dead as the harbinger of messianic times. However, Piekarz ties this theory to the understanding that R. Nachman is the messiah and as such is destined to return and redeem us. He believes that this idea can already be found in the writings of R. Natan.

> Little by little, R. Natan's faith reaches the boiling point, bubbling over, as his language becomes more revealing. No more talk of the plural 'greatest of the *tzadikim*' or '*true tzadikim*'; no understatements such as 'Moses-like.' Rather, 'the true *tzadik* who is the Moses-messiah, the first redeemer who will be the last redeemer.'[15] The concrete meaning of this 'true *tzadik*' needs no explanation. We may – we must – add those two words to the sentence – 'Rabbi Nachman'![16]

---

12 *Yalkut Shimoni*, (Jerusalem: 2000), 989. In this context R. Natan wrote: 'As is known, this is the essence of praying at the graves of *tzadikim*. For *tzadikim* are greater in death than in life; *tzadikim* in death are called living' [Rav Natan of Nemirov, *Likutei Halachot* (Jerusalem: 1984), YD 221].

13 *Sichot Haran*, 204-5. It is clear that in the discourse, 'Breishit,' R. Nachman stresses the continued spiritual existence of the *tzadik* in heaven after his death, while his offspring and students represent his legacy on earth.

14 Rav Avraham Kochav-Lev, *Tovot Zichronot (Bound with Yerach Eitanim)* (Bnei Brak: 1978), 135.

15 *Likutei Halachot*, OH 221.

16 Piekarz, *Studies in Bratslav Hasidism*, 144.

However, here too, reading these statements in their proper cultural and literary context gives us a better indication of their true weight in R. Natan's own messianic scheme of things. In his own words:

> Afterwards [in the blessings between the *Shemah* and the *Amidah*] we say 'true and stable, etc.' in order to link redemption to prayer. This is, to receive the strength of the true *tzadik*, that is the Moses-messiah who is the first and final redeemer. For only through his power are we able to continue until we can reveal his full majesty before the entire world.[17]

From the context here it does not appear that R. Nachman is destined to be reborn, but rather that as the true tzadik, the 'Moses-messiah', is already active in helping his people survive until that time when the final redemption arrives.[18] This is true irregardless of whether or not he will return in the flesh. His fire will burn in the hearts of his followers and students until the messiah comes, and only through it will the kingdom of God be revealed. Piekarz reads too much into the fact that R. Natan makes a more direct identification asserting that R. Nachman *is* the Moses-messiah and not *akin* to the Moses-messiah. Using the same logic, we might assume that there is a secret Breslav belief that Moses himself never died – just disappeared and will return for the final redemption.

Piekarz even claims that 'the hidden Breslav belief, that the death of R. Nachman was but his hiding and disappearance, and in the future he will return once again to enact the final redemption, found explicit expression in the aforementioned booklet [of R. Avraham Chazan].'[19] Beyond this, according to Piekarz, R. Avraham Chazan reveals an accepted Breslavian prophecy which details the exact date upon which the Rebbe was due to return. He claims that R. Avraham reports that the 'Breslav "watchmen" predicted that this appearance would take place forty-five years after his

17 *Likutei Halachot*, 221.

18 Ibid.

19 Piekarz, *Studies in Bratslav Hasidism*, 139.

death.'[20] Despite the fact that R. Avraham Chazan wrote many years after this date had passed, this still did not disturb the faith of those who believed that eventually the Rebbe would return from the dead.

> Even though the prophecy was disproved, as he [R. Avraham Chazan] wrote, 'nearly twice the forty-five years ... which the watchmen said regarding this hiding' having already passed, he did not give up his faith that R. Nachman, the redeeming messiah, who had not completed his mission and had brought about redemption in his first coming, due to the 'haughtiness[21] of the foolish old king' – a clear reference to the 'Saba' of Shpola – would in the end, gather strength [to succeed] ... 'For the man will not be silent until he completes that which he said,[22] 'to redeem us and to heal us from our terrible ills.'[23]

On the surface, we have here the fascinating testimony of Breslav prophets who not only predicted that R. Nachman would return to life as the redeeming messiah, but even knew the exact time that this would occur. However, the details of who exactly these people were and how they expressed their prophecy are not dealt with by Piekarz. The description of Breslav 'watchmen' sounds odd to anyone who is familiar with the court and its important personalities. It is difficult to fathom a guess who these might have been. However, even if there was some prophecy which was passed on in the Breslav tradition, we need ask why its actual failure to be fulfilled did not incur a crisis of faith in the community.

---

20 Ibid. See also note 19a there. Piekarz also noted in his editor's comments on Weiss that, 'According to Breslav tradition, the death of R. Nachman was only a matter of concealment. In the future he is destined to return for a second and final time for the final redemption forty-five years after his departure' (Weiss, *Studies in Bratslav Hasidi*sm, 233 fn. 42).

21 The Hebrew contains a mistaken correction here.

22 Following the Book of Ruth 3:18. This is also in context of redemption.

23 Piekarz, *Studies in Bratslav Hasidism*, 139 fn. 19a.

If we examine the fuller context of R. Avraham Chazan's remarks we find that these difficulties are avoided.

> In any case, there is much blessing, for he will always have the upper hand. This despite the weight of the war. (note 44: If one checks TB Sanhedrin 111 regarding the Sages' commentary on the verse 'I will take one from the city' …, and on the verse 'she will answer there'[24] – one should not be surprised or afraid[25] that one sees that even today the entire community wants to stone the two out of 60,000 who believe in the greatness of [R. Nachman] and cling to his wondrous words…. Recall the days of yore, the generations past, look at the tribes of God in whose merit we live – they too hated their brother Joseph, who was exalted above them all…. Let us look at the generation of Moses' himself, of whom we speak, it is clear in the written and oral Torah that the 250 heads of the Sanhedrin – the chiefs of their tribes, men of God – together with the entire community … they all fought and complained against Moses, the head of all prophets, who spoke directly with God and saw His visage. Even after all the signs and wonders, the strong hand and awesome things that he did in the eyes of all of Israel, [which they saw] with both their spiritual and physical eyes, how – how did slander and ignorance gain the upper hand so that they could actually suspect him of adultery, as our Sages tell us?) It forced him to hide and take his departure from us – and even led to lengthening the days of his leaving to nearly double the 45 which the watchmen referred to regarding this departure. (note 45: See the poem of R. Eleazar Kalir in the reading of 'This month' and Rashi in the Book of Daniel on the verse 'Happy is he who waits.') But, God will not ignore us forever, nor forever be angry even if there is

24 'R. Simay says: It says, "I will take you to me for a people" and it says, "I will bring you". The exodus from Egypt is likened to the coming to Israel. Just like only 200 out the 600 thousand arrived in Israel, so to did only 200 out of 600 thousand leave Egypt. Raba said: So too in the days of the messiah, as it says, (Hoseah 2:17) "[Israel] will answer there like in the days of her youth and like on the day that she went up from the land of Egypt"' (TB Sanhedrin 111a)

25 Following Judges 13:5.

much fury and might...even if difficult, he [R. Nachman] has not left us completely. [While] from long ago, no man has known the site of his [Moses] grave, who upon him our redemption depends.... Therefore, even if the haughtiness of the foolish old king reaches the heavens, from there they will pull him down. For the man will not be silent until he completes that which he said, to redeem us and to heal us from our terrible ills. (This entire section I took from the words of R. Natan which I heard from my father ..., now let us return to our previous discussion for God will have the last word).[26]

When we read the passage quoted by Piekarz in its entirety, we see that there is no discussion of Breslav 'watchmen' at all. Rather this is one of the Talmudic expressions used for the Biblical prophets[27] from whom the Sages learned of the departure of the messiah.[28] In Midrash Ruth we find a midrash transmitted by R. Brachiah in the name of R. Levi: 'As the first redeemer, so shall be the final redeemer. The first redeemer, this is Moses who was revealed to them and hidden from them. So the final redeemer, [will be] revealed to them and hidden from them. How long will he be hidden from them? R. Tanchuma in the name of R. Chama the son of R. Hoshiah said, "forty-five days."'[29] Similarly (although he exchanges days for years) we find in Rashi's commentary on the Book of Daniel on the verse, 'Happy is he who waits': 'Forty-five additional years were added to the above calculation that in the future our messiah will remain hidden, after first being revealed, until he will be revealed again. So we found in Midrash Ruth and also R. Eleazar Kalir

---

26 R. Avraham Chazan, *Chochma Vebina (Bound with Kochvei or)* (Jerusalem: 1983), 119-20. The comments are R. Chazan's as we can see from his comment 34 and 38 on pp. 116-7.

27 See TB Megilah 2b and the Tosphot ad loc, 'od'.

28 Piekarz suggested that the number forty-five quoted by these 'watchmen' stemmed from Daniel 12:11-12 (Piekarz, *Studies in Bratslav Hasidism*, 139 fn. 19a). However, R. Chazan himself noted these same sources in the very edition and page number mentioned by Piekarz. Piekarz could have himself inferred from this that there are no 'watchmen' to speak of.

29 Rut Rabbah 5:14 and in other midrashim.

established this....'[30] The watchmen discussed by R. Avraham Chazan who spoke of forty-five days or years were not Breslav watchmen at all.[31]

It seems, then, that no concrete prophecy concerning the return of R. Nachman exists. It may be that the connection made between the midrashim regarding the return of the messiah and R. Nachman was in fact first made by R. Avraham Chazan himself, even if he based his claim on the messianic theories which he heard from his father in the name of R. Natan. Additionally, we not only have no evidence of a crisis over the non-appearance of the messiah (be he who he may) forty-five years after R. Nachman's death, but this number contradicts a statement made by the Rebbe himself. After the death of his son, Shlomo Efraim, he said, 'The messiah will definitely not come for another 100 years.'[32] In his book *Yemei Hatlaot* (Days of Hardship), R. Avraham Chazan quotes R. Natan regarding a disagreement with R. Moshe Tzi of Sovron: 'The redemption must be 100 years later than it was supposed to have been.'[33]

R. Avraham Chazan's words, then, must be understood not as pointing to a secret Breslav belief passed down by 'Breslav watchmen' concerning the return of R. Nachman in forty-five years, but rather as a literary device used to tie the conflicts faced by the Rebbe with the midrashim which discuss the disappearance and reappearance of the actual messiah. He realized that this forty-five-year time-frame did not actually apply to R. Nachman. It had long since passed at the time of his own writing and conflicted with other statements by R. Natan.

---

30 Daniel 12:12. See Ephraim E. Urbach, *The Sages: Their Concepts and Beliefs* (Jerusalem: 1998), 617-8.

31 The motif of the disappearance and return of the messiah is also found in later sources. R. Chaim Vital discusses the disappearance of the messiah, how he will rise up to heaven and later return. He ties this to the Zohar's paralleling the messiah's disappearance with that of Moses' disappearance in the clouds of Mt. Sinai [Rav Chaim Vital, "*Arba'ah Meot Shekel Kesef*," (New York: 1995)].

32 *Siach Sorfei Kodesh*, vol. 1-5 (Jerusalem: 1994), vol. 2 36; Rav Chaim Menachem Kramer, *Toldot Moharnat: Be'aish Uvmayim* (Jerusalem: 1996), 112.

33 Rav Avraham Chazan, *Yemei Hatlaot* (Jerusalem: 1933), 150.

We still need to clarify, however, what exactly R. Avraham meant when he discussed the disappearance and return of the messiah. Actual death is but one of the manifestations of this disappearance. The major part is what he described as the 'slander and ignorance', that is the persecutions, troubles and belittlement that was the lot of R. Nachman and his followers. These are what prevented the general public from drawing close to him and finding true redemption in his words. This is part of the paradoxical situation in which Breslav Chasidim have found themselves from the time of their Rebbe's death until some thirty odd years ago. While they have always fervently believed that their Rebbe was the one true *tzadik* of the ages who would muster all of Israel to his side for the final redemption, in actuality, their court was but a tiny remnant – 'one from the city', 'two out of 600,000' which was often hounded by others and whose Rebbe's works were often ignored. This stark difference between their faith and their reality was what prompted R. Avraham to look for other examples from the tradition where despite public condemnation, the messianic hero returns to save his people. Even Moses suffered this very same treatment. Despite his own true unique personal status, his own people treated him with lack of faith and much suspicion. This was also the case with Joseph who was abused by his brothers, thrown into a pit and sold into slavery. However, the messianic figure is vindicated in the end: just as with Joseph and Moses, so too would R. Nachman eventually come to be recognized as the great character that he was. More than this, while the burial place of Moses remains a secret, that of R. Nachman's is at least known.

This last point is especially important if we take into account a midrash which explains the reason behind the hiding of Moses' burial site.

> And R. Chama bar Chanina said: Why was the burial site of Moses hidden from the eyes of flesh and blood? It was known by the Holy One that in the future the Temple will be destroyed and the Jewish people dispersed from their land. Lest they come to his grave at that time in

> tears and beg Moses to pray for them saying, 'Moses our teacher, stand and pray for us,' and Moses will stand and cancel the decree.[34]

The well-known grave-site of R. Nachman is the opening to redemption. That which could not be done at the burial site of the first redeemer may be accomplished at that of the final one.

Additional aspects regarding the knowledge of R. Nachman's grave site are mentioned in the introduction that R. Tepliker added to his manuscript of *Chayei Moharan*.

> The copyist says: Regarding the matter of the hiding of the great and wondrous light of our Master, the likes of whom never existed even in the earlier generations (this we heard directly from his holy mouth), yet who was lost and hidden in the most dire way so that most of the world does not even merit to come to his grave upon which they can be utterly healed. We find a hint of this in his holy words. He said that all that he did was concerned with Rosh Hashanah. About Rosh Hashanah it is written, 'on the concealed holiday' (as our Sages said).[35] Therefore the great and wondrous light is concealed and covered so much that all of the world cannot merit coming to his grave to pray. This is like that which is written regarding the hiding of Moses' grave (in Tractate Sotah). We learn that no one knew of his burial site so that they would not be able to pray there. This is the same reason that the grave of our Master has vanished as well (even though its location is known) due to the great conflicts. This is so it is impossible to come and pray there. May it be His will that his truth be revealed to the

34 TB Sota 14a following the *Hagaot Habach*.

35 R. Abahu said: What is the verse, 'Blow the shofar on the [new] month, on the covered day of our holiday'? Which holiday is that in which the month is covered? This is Rosh Hashana (TB 16a).

world and his holiness made known throughout the world. Then the redemption will quickly come in our day.[36]

The end of the era of concealment for R. Nachman is not his return to life, but rather the revelation of his great holiness which can heal those who are willing to follow his path. When this revelation occurs, 'then the redemption' can quickly follow. R. Nachman was, and remains, the final redeemer, yet the redemption must wait for the revelation of his greatness. The messiah is a manifestation and actualization of this itself. This we saw in our reading of the *Scroll.*[37]

It is in this same spirit which other statements of R. Nachman about his 'return' in messianic times need be understood. When he claimed that 'In the future, I will sing a song which will be the World-to-Come for all the *tzadikim* and Chasidim,'[38] he did not mean that he would actually arise from the dead

---

36 Rav Alter Tepliker, "*Hashmatot Mechayei Moharan,*" (1898), 2; *Chayei Moharan (Hashmatot Chadashot),* (Beit Shemesh: Hanekudot Hatovot, 2005), 4; *Chayei Moharan Im Hashmatot,* 344-5. R. Alter here expanded upon the words of his brother-in-law, R. Avraham Chazan, brought in the opening of Rav Avraham Chazan, *Chochmah Utvunah (Printed Together with Sipurei Maasiot)* (Hanekudot Hatovot, 2004), 491.

37 Another example quoted by Piekarz as proof for the secret belief in R. Nachman's resurrection can also easily be read quite differently once we check the actual sources. He quotes from *Biur Halikutim*: 'Also our Rebbe, after all of his comprehension, after his taking leave ... until he returns and appears as the redeemer for whom we wait to reveal the faith....' (Piekarz, *Studies in Bratslav Hasidism*, 139 fn. 20). However, when we place the quote in its fuller context we find that it does not serve as ready proof for Piekarz's thesis. 'According to this it is possible to explicate more *...but in truth it appears from his holy words that this was due to the reasons that it was decreed upon Moses to expire, and also upon other exceptional individuals of their generations like R. Shimon bar Yochai, etc. Also, our Rebbe after attaining all of his understanding, the battles against the general populace – in their wars and impurities (as mentioned above) – took their toll until he left completely in order to attain even higher understanding afterwards (*tzadikim* are greater in death than in life) until he returns and appears in the redeemer for whom we wait to reveal faith before the eyes of all' [Rav Avraham Chazan, *Biur Halikutim* (Jerusalem: 1993), 5:8]. That is, the greatness of R. Nachman will be revealed in the redeemer who will rule the world in accord with R. Nachman's wisdom, so justifying before all belief in the *tzadik.*

38 This is brought in *Chayei Moharan Im Hashmatot,* 272 and also in similar language on p. 312 and in other manuscripts.

with musical accompaniment. Rather, the spiritual values expressed through his words and songs represent those which will make up the spiritual good for these *tzadikim* in the future.[39] Similarly, his statement that the conclusion of the 'Tale of the Seven Beggars' will only be heard when the messiah comes,[40] should be understood as suggesting that the messianic age itself comprises the end of this story; not that he will return to finish its telling.[41]

Green accepted the claims of Weiss and Piekarz regarding the Breslavian faith that R. Nachman would one day return, but tempered it by adding that 'such an expectation in itself is not at all odd in a world where people believe in reincarnation.'[42] This suggestion fits well with the statement by R. Avraham Chazan, 'While no prophet like Moses has ever arisen among Israel, he himself will again arise to redeem us from this diaspora as well, for the messiah is Moses'. He continues to explain that R. Nachman was a *tzadik* 'who contained the messianic threads' of both the Josephian and Davidian messiahs. However, 'even though he contained something of the soul of the Davidian [messiah], he was mainly from the side of the Josephian messiah.'[43] It is clear that this description is connected to the notion of reincarnation. This notion, alongside of its complement – the 'combining' of souls – allows for a situation wherein a given *tzadik* may be comprised of the soul-matter of both of the messiahs. R. Chazan added that 'R. Yitzchak Luriah, as well as other exceptional luminaries were from the Josephian side.'[44] Additionally, he describes other cases where the souls of Jacob, R.

39 It is also possible to understand that R. Nachman meant that his return would be part of the general raising of the dead.

40 'The end of the tale, that which took place on the seventh day – the matter of the legless beggar … we did not merit to hear. He said that he would not tell us any more – a great loss, for now we will not hear the ending until the coming of the messiah, speedily in our day, amen' *Sefer Sipurei Ma'asiot*, 281-2. See also Green, *Master*, 198.

41 I heard in the name of R. Levi Yitzchak Brand that the intention of R. Nachman was that the messiah himself would conclude the telling of the story.

42 Green, *Master*, 197-8 and 217 fn. 32.

43 R. Avraham Chazan, *Sichot Vesipurim (Printed with Kochvei or)* (Jerusalem: 1983), 122-3.

44 Ibid., 127.

Shimon bar Yochai and the Baal Shem Tov were found in other individuals. However, he adds that R. Nachman was exceptional even among this company for 'he epitomized the verse,[45] "many daughters have done well, but you are above them all."'[46]

It is clear that the complex intermingling of the souls of Jacob, Joseph, Moses, David, R. Shimon bar Yochai, R. Yitzchak Luriah, the Baal Shem Tov and R. Nachman described here has really nothing to do with the actual return of the latter from the dead. In fact, R. Chazan himself warned against understanding the entire notion of reincarnation literally. In answer to a question concerning a seeming contradiction between his discussion of Moses as the final messiah with a tradition that he would not return to redeem Israel,[47] he referred his readers to one of R. Nachman's sermons which deals with the subject of reincarnation. 'God does not do the same thing twice. Even with reincarnation, this is not an instance of the [same] soul returning a second time. Rather, this is a case of this soul with this spirit and the like as is known. Now when this soul combines with another spirit and the like, this is not what once was – for God does not do the same thing twice.'[48] R. Natan added a note here – 'This is something else; a completely new thing.'[49]

It is clear, then, when one speaks of the soul of the tzadik as the soul of the 'Moses-messiah,' one is not referring to the actual return of a soul to a body that it once inhabited, nor to the return of the same spiritual object to a different body at a different time, but rather to the complicated co-mixture of spiritual entities which creates a 'completely new thing.' It is this new creation – which shares in something of Moses' soul – that will eventually come to enact the final redemption. Given all this, there is no reason at all to confuse the understanding that R. Nachman's soul contains parts of the spirit of the first and last redeemer with any secret belief that he will eventually return from the dead.

---

45 Parables 31:29.

46 Chazan, *Sichot Vesipurim*, 123.

47 See the commentary of Rashi on Exodus 4:13.

48 *Sichot Haran*, 70-1.

49 *Likutei Halachot*, OH 74.

For now, I would like to conclude this discussion with reference to another text written by R. Chazan which is found in a censored version in Koenig's *Neveh Tzadikim*.[50] (Appendix 3 contains an expanded discussion of the manuscript.)

> I heard from R. Avraham the son of Nachman of Tulchin who said in the name of his father who said in the name of R. Natan... who said that the need for the Josephian messiah is [because] of that which will happen to the Davidian messiah. He will need the merit of those *tzadikim* who have died. The Josephian messiah will die before him. Our Rebbe said, 'I have prepared a nice place for him' for our Rebbe was the Josephian messiah as he was completely pure regarding sexual matters.... Therefore he was akin to Joseph in terms of sexual purity and the Davidian messiah will need to use his merit. May the truth be relieved in the world, quickly in our day, amen.

Here is a clear statement: R. Nachman is the Josephian messiah and this messiah is destined to die before the Davidian messiah arrives. R. Nachman helped to prepare a 'nice place' for the Davidian messiah, who must rely upon the merit of the Josephian messiah and other dead *tzadikim*, suggesting that they too were akin to the Josephian messiah. Through this merit, the messiah will be able to reveal the truth to the world.

This description differentiates between the two different messiahs, identifying R. Nachman with the Josephian messiah alone. So while R. Nachman is not the Davidian messiah who brings the final redemption, he does take part in the final redemption by preparing its way. His merit is the tool that the final messiah uses in order to complete the redemption and reveal the truth to the world. In this sense, it is possible to see him as the final messiah.

We must mention, though, that this last text by R. Chazan does not completely eliminate the possibility of the actual resurrection of R. Nachman. If he is seen as the Josephian messiah who died in battle, perhaps it is still possible

50 Rav Natan Zvi Koenig, *Neveh Tzadikim* (Bnei Brak: 1969), 79.

to hope that he will be brought back to life by the Davidian messiah, as we find discussed in a number of sources which deal with the Josephian messiah.[51]

In conclusion, we can see that none of the sources external to the *Scroll* itself can really counter the explicit non-inclusion of R. Nachman in its depiction of messianic times. However, these sources do provide us with a better general picture of the role that R. Nachman himself will play during this era. Until the death of the holy infant Shlomo Efraim in 1806, R. Nachman and his Chasidim all believed that if only the world would follow the Master, then R. Nachman, or his son, would become the messiah. However, after the infant's death, R. Nachman concluded that this messianic potential would not be fulfilled in his own lifetime. Nonetheless, he believed that he would be the one who would prepare the way for the coming of the messiah in the future. Through his writings and other works, the actual messiah would be able to complete his mission which R. Nachman had begun. In this sense, R. Nachman is indeed the final redeemer – he is the path breaker who enables the messiah to reveal the kingdom of God on earth.[52]

Additionally we find that the belief among the Breslav community concerning the messiah's arrival is intimately connected to the spread of R. Nachman's philosophy and ideas. As depicted in the *Scroll*, it is clear that through them the messiah redeems the world. The actions of the messiah are, in essence, the return and resurrection of R. Nachman – the revelation of what had long been lost and discarded due to the conflicts which hounded R. Nachman during his lifetime. The messiah uncovers the smoldering embers that R. Nachman had lit, fans them into flames and lets their light again, more fully this time, illuminate the world. More than this, the very source of the messianic soul is R. Nachman. The persona of the messiah as outlined in the Scroll is that of R. Nachman – whether one considers his life, his works or the actions which he took to save the world.

---

51 The Book of Zerubavel tells of the return of the Davidian messiah together with Elijah alongside the Josephian messiah (83).

52 See above chapter * in the text adjacent to note 193.

CHAPTER SEVEN

The Scroll in Light of the Other Secret Writings of R. Nachman

After the publication of the censored sections from *Chayei Moharan*,[1] 'The Tale of the Armor'[2] and 'The Tale of the Bread,'[3] the *Scroll* remained the last secret work by R. Nachman hidden among his followers. With the publication of the *Scroll*, the last puzzle piece of the Breslav esoterica has been laid down, opening up more wholly the complexities of R. Nachman's thought.[4] I would like to briefly discuss this broader picture and the place of the *Scroll* in relation to the other esoteric works. This will be the first time that such a discussion can be

---

1 The large majority of the deleted sections from R. Nachman's works (with the exception of the 'Tale of the Bread') have been published in two different editions of *Chayei Moharan*, *Yemei Moharnat* and *Yemei Hatlaot*. Their publishers attempted to insert these sections into their proper places in the original texts. Both of these editions were published by the branch of the Breslav court associated with R. Yisrael Odesser. (For reasons which are beyond the purview of the present discussion, this group believes that the time for hiding these texts has past.) The first edition was published by Netzach Yisrael in Jerusalem followed by an expanded edition published by Nekudot Tovot in Beit Shemesh. Regarding the nature of the materials deleted from Chayei Moharan, see Zvi Mark, "*Ma'aseh Mehashiryon (The Tale of the Armor) – from the Hidden Chambers of Breslav Censorship*," : 211-12 and in the sources cited therein and in Zvi Mark "*The Tale of the Bread – a Hidden Story of R. Nachman of Braslav*,". For another example of the purposeful deletion of text, see Zvi Mark, "*Why Did R. Moses Zvi of Savran Persecute R. Nathan of Nemirov and Breslav Chasidim?*," *Zion* 69, no. 4 (2004): 487-500.

2 See Zvi Mark, "*Ma'aseh Mehashiryon (The Tale of the Armor) – from the Hidden Chambers of Breslav Censorship*," *Zion* 70, no. 2 (1995).

3 See Mark, "*The Tale of the Bread – a Hidden Story of R. Nachman of Braslav*."

4 See above in the Introduction.

held with actual knowledge of the esoteric corpus instead of relying on guess work regarding the contents of the *Scroll*. What follows, however, is a brief sketch and is not intended to be a comprehensive treatment of this material.

The majority of the excised portions of material from *Chayei Moharan* consists of quotes from R. Nachman concerning his status as well as the status of other *tzadikim* from times past such as the Baal Shem Tov, R. Shimon bar Yochai, Moses and Adam. From the general tenor of these comments, it seems that R. Nachman felt that he was not just on a par with these other *tzadikim*, as the *tzadik* of his generation, but in fact considered himself to be *the tzadik* of all time. We also find a good deal of sharp criticism directed to those with whom R. Nachman was in conflict. This includes not only those with whom he had direct confrontations, but even those with whom he had indirect disagreements, such as R. Shneur Zalman of Ladi the founder of Chabad. His major opponent, however, to whom he directed his deepest criticism was R. Arieh Leib of Shpola.

R. Nachman's high self-appraisal as the *tzadik* of all time is connected of course to his self-understanding as an equal to the Moses-messiah. It is only natural, then, that throughout such self-appraisals a number of subjects related to varied aspects of messianism bubble up even when not being directly addressed. The secret tales – the 'Tale of the Bread' (also known as 'The Tale of Receiving the Torah'), the 'Tale of the Armor,' and of course the *Scroll* – all reveal different aspects of R. Nachman's self-conscious world-view. In the 'Tale of the Bread', he presents himself as a Moses-like messianic figure who experiences a new Sinaitic revelation, eats manna again and relates the Ten Commandments, as well as the rest of the Torah, once more.[5]

In the 'Tale of the Armor' R. Nachman is portrayed as the fixer of the broken, who through his works is able to redeem the sinful individual from his sin, rescuing him from the personal hell in which he has found himself in this world and into which he may be cast into in the next. R. Nachman paves new paths to repentance, the likes of which have never been known

5 See Mark, "*The Tale of the Bread – a Hidden Story of R. Nachman of Braslav.*"

before. His abilities to effect repairs have definite implications for the cumulative healing of the world which ushers in the messianic age.[6]

The *Scroll* does not present a picture of R. Nachman, per se, but it is clear that his personality, history and philosophy are what stand behind the image of the messiah offered therein as the *tzadik*-messiah to whom the entire world flocks to be saved. Here we see that R. Nachman is part of the messianic history; he has prepared the path upon which the final messiah will arrive. We also know that the description of the messiah in the *Scroll* fits well with that which might have been of R. Nachman or his son, if not for the conflicts and struggles which in the end prevented the actualization of their messianic potential. This lost chance, though, does not diminish the hope that one day the messiah will in fact arrive: the messiah who is of Breslav lineage coming to complete that which R. Nachman began.

Taking into account the powerful mystical experiences that made up the life of R. Nachman from a young age and which placed him on a par with Moses himself, as detailed in the 'Tale of the Bread,' there is no need to search for the reasons behind his messianic ambitions in the winds of historical changes that blew throughout his lifetime. More than the seeming messianic underpinnings of Europe's tremulous convulsions at the end of the 18th century, the key to understanding R. Nachman's messianic psyche lies within these internal experiences themselves. His messianism sprung forth from within, as a natural expression of the mystical elements and nature of his personality. Historical circumstances played at best a supporting role in its development.[7]

These formative mystical experiences led to the development of a self-conscious portrait of R. Nachman as a *tzadik* able to redeem and repair the very souls of his Chasidim and followers in ways which had never before been possible. This mystical basis was the foundation for the development

---

6 Zvi Mark, "*Ma'aseh Mehashiryon (The Tale of the Armor) – from the Hidden Chambers of Breslav Censorship*".

7 On the typology of the messianic personality, see Moshe Idel, *Messianic Mystics* (New Haven: 1998), 245-7.

of his self-image as the Moses-messiah – combining both Moses' traits as the recipient of divine law and the redeemer of his people from Egypt.[8] As part of the Mosaic mission the second receiving of the law had already been fulfilled according to the 'Tale of the Bread' by R. Nachman. It was to the second part of this mission that he set his sights: the redemption of Israel by the righteous redeemer who would come to raise up the Jewish people along with the rest of the world.

From the esoterica of R. Nachman we can construct a picture of his own self-image as the *tzadik* of all time. This image is informed by the constitutive mystical experiences detailed in the 'Tale of the Bread'; his view of himself as capable of effecting repair and redemption in the world as described in the 'Tale of the Armor'; and his self-understanding as the messianic figure ready to redeem his nation and lead them to the messiah's long-awaited arrival as detailed in the *Scroll* itself.

---

8 On Moses as the original and final redeemer in *Tikunei Hazohar*, see Amos Goldreich, "*Birurim Beriato He'atzmit Shel Ba'al Tikunei Hazohar*," in *Massu'ot: Studies in Kabbalistic Literature and Jewish Philosophy in memory of Prof. Ephraim Gottlieb*, edited by Michal Oron and Amos Goldreich (Jerusalem: 1994).

CHAPTER EIGHT
THE SCROLL AS ESOTERICA: SOCIAL AND SPIRITUAL ASPECTS OF THE SANCTIFIED SECRET[1]

1. REVELATION, INNOVATION AND SECRET

In *Chayei Moharan*, we find the following discussion in which R. Nachman places himself in the chain of the ages' *tzadikim*.

> I heard in his name that he said: 'From [the time of] R. Shimon bar Yochai who himself represented a great innovation (as is known), the world lay quiet until [the time of] R. Yitzchak Luria. That is, from R. Shimon bar Yochai until R. Yitzchak Luria nothing truly new was revealed like those things which were uncovered by R. Shimon bar Yochai until the arrival of R. Yitzchak Luria who himself represented a great innovation (as is known). He [then] revealed completely new ideas which no one until R. Yitzchak Luria had done. And from [the time of] R. Yitzchak Luria until the Baal Shem Tov, the world was again quiet with no innovation, until the Baal Shem Tov who represented a great innovation and revealed great new things. And from [the time of the Baal Shem Tov] until now, the world was again quiet with no innovation at all functioning in accord with that which the Baal Shem

---

1 This chapter is based upon several of the ideas found in *Concealment and Revelation: The Secret and its Boundaries in Medieval Jewish Tradition* (Jerusalem: 2001).

Tov had revealed – until I arrived. And now I have begun to reveal great new things.'[2]

The chain of tzadikim which R. Nachman chose to present here includes neither halachic masters nor any learned Talmudists. Those mentioned are part of the chain of the esoteric kabbalistic tradition whose innovative works became the backbone of that genre. The end of the longer text from which the above quote is taken ends with an elliptical 'etc.' However, it appears that its conclusion is found in the book *Siach Sorfei Kodesh* which quotes, in the name of R. Avraham Chazan, a fuller description of the chain of tzadikim found above.

> He [God] sent our holy Rebbe who said that he had already prepared the instruments for the righteous messiah. He [R. Nachman] said that after him there will be no more innovation until the arrival of the messiah himself (may he come speedily in our day) bringing full redemption, amen.[3]

In light of the total picture which emerges from the esoteric Breslav literature we can better make sense of R. Nachman's inclusion of himself in this list. It will help us to concentrate on three central foci: revelation, innovation and messianic mission.

R. Nachman viewed himself as ranking among these three – R. Shimon bar Yochai, R. Yitzchak Luriah and the Baal Shem Tov – all of whom

---

2 *Chayei Moharan Im Hashmatot*, (Jerusalem: 2000), 278-9.

3 *Siach Sorfei Kodesh*, vol. 1-5 (Jerusalem: 1994), vol. 3, 172. This is found elsewhere in a slightly different version: 'He sent our holy Rebbe, who has already prepared until the righteous messiah' [Rav Avraham Chazan, "*Ma'asiot Umeshalim*," in *Kochvei Or*, ed. Rav Avraham Chazan (Jerusalem: 1983), 39.]. A more moderate statement was made in the name of R. Pinchas of Korvitz: Those who ascended to the highest level were not found from R. Shimon bar Yochai until Nachmanides and from him until R. Yitzchak Luriah and from him until the Ba'al Shem Tov and from him until myself and from myself until the messiah' [*Imrei Pinchas Hashalem: Otzar Torat Pinchas Mekorvitz Vetalmidav*, (Bnei Brak: 2003), I 272].

underwent profound mystical-prophetic experiences. R. Nachman believed that these experiences provided him with the basis to create a reawakening and renewal whose effects would continue to be felt well beyond the confines of his own life and generation – that would, in fact, pave the way for the entire messianic process.[4]

From the excised conclusion above we see that not only did R. Nachman consider himself part of the chain of mystical revelation which stoked the flames of religious yearning for the messiah, but more than that, he placed himself as its very endpoint. He was the last link in this chain of the masters of esoteric knowledge. No other *tzadik* would come after R. Nachman to represent or reveal another stage of innovation until the coming of the messiah. The messiah himself would actualize, through his actions and life, the spiritual path which R. Nachman himself had laid out. He would do so with the help of the very instruments that R. Nachman had prepared for him.[5]

This conclusion also helps to explain another one of the unique characteristics of the Breslav court. They remained steadfastly committed to their original Rebbe, even after his death refusing to name a replacement. This led to their being known in the Chasidic world as the '*toyta Chasidim*,' Yiddish for the 'dead Chasidim.' However, it becomes clear that if no new spiritual innovations will be made after his demise until the coming of messiah,[6] and R. Nachman had already prepared the way for his arrival, there is no need to appoint a new Rebbe in his stead.

---

4 On the messianic mission of R. Shimon bar Yochai in the Zohar, see Yehuda Liebes, "*Hamashiach Shel Hazohar: Ledemuto Shel R. Shimon Bar Yochai*," in *The Messianic Idea in Jewish Thought* (Jerusalem: 1990). On messianic concepts in the works of R. Yitzchak Luriah, see David Tamar, "*Luria and Vital as Messiah Ben Jose*ph," *Sefunot* 7 (1963). On the messianic layer of thought in the works of the Ba'al Shem Tov, see the introduction, text adjacent to note 5; regarding R. Nachman see above chapter 3, the text adjacent to note 26.*

5 However, the students of R. Shimon bar Yochai in the Zohar already made a similar claim. They saw themselves as unique trail-blazers for the messianic age the likes of which would never be seen again. See Melila Hellner-Eshed, *A River Issues Forth from Eden: on the Language of Mystical Experience in the Zohar* (Tel Aviv: 2005), 105.

6 *Siach Sorfei Kodesh*, vol. 3, 172.

The connections between the links in the chain of mystical tradition can be understood through this interesting statement by R. Nachman:

> He used to speak to me [R. Natan] concerning the innovative thought of the Baal Shem Tov who revealed new things in the world. The story of the Baal Shem Tov is something new that had not been revealed beforehand. Only in the writings of R. Yitzchak Luria were similar things found in a few places.[7]

While the root of some of the Baal Shem Tov's innovative thought exists in the work of his predecessor, R. Luria, there it is just found in 'a few places'. What the Baal Shem Tov did was to develop these thoughts and move them into a central place in the totality of his own thought. This was then akin to the creation of something completely new which had not been known before.

R. Nachman's own innovative work, then, is also in some ways a continuation of those who came before him. However, he warned against misunderstanding his work as only a clarification of the tradition which preceeded him. His thought was unique – it reached heights never before attained.

> He said that those who studied his books, if they possessed [only] a modicum of sense, thought that the kabalistic ways of R. Yitzchak Luria were also hinted at in his works. They think that the most profound parts of his work reach even until there. But they do not realize that the opposite is true. The kabalistic ways of the predecessors are also included in his words. He did not explain further, but his intention was clear. That is, he meant that his thought was the highest – although their holy words were also included in his words of Torah.[8]

---

7 *Chayei Moharan Im Hashmatot*, 279.

8 Ibid., 324.

R. Nachman's work contains the thought of the earlier kabalists, but innovates and reaches completely new places.[9] He expressed this quite clearly: 'I walk a new path upon which no one has yet trod (and not even the Baal Shem Tov, not any creature...). Even though it is an ancient path it is completely new.'[10]

This is an important point which needs to be understood in order to fully comprehend R. Nachman's own theory of the esoteric. The secrets of the kabalistic masters and those who delved into the esoteric are not secrets which were passed on from generation to generation. They are, in fact, new revelations of what was previously unknown. The innovative mystic does not merely rely on that which he received from his teachers, but rather makes a spiritual breakthrough to reach completely new understandings of the Divine.[11]

R. Nachman's description of the chain of transmission of the esoteric part of the Torah is nearly the opposite of that usually claimed for the exoteric. Regarding the latter, it is understood that, 'Moses received the Torah from Sinai and passed it on to Joshua; Joshua to the Elders....'[12] Each generation draws from the one previous, all the way back to Moses. However, esoterica is revealed anew, not passed on. The defining ethos of the esoteric is not its fealty to tradition – faithfully preserving that which was received

---

9 On R. Nachman's innovation, see Zvi Mark, *Mysticism and Madness In the Work of R. Nachman of Bratslav* (Jerusalem: 2003), 294-99, 317-29; Yehuda Liebes, "*The Novelty of Rabbi Nachman of Bratslav*," *Da'at* 45 (Summer) (2000).

10 *Chayei Moharan Im Hashmatot*, 338 and 74. The symbol < > is part of the original and represents a deletion added to this edition.

11 It is worth noting in this context R. Nachman's own words regarding his innovative inclination. 'He said: "I know the place of all the tzadikim from Adam until today – from which place they taught Torah, and at which place they stayed once they died." He began to calculate: "The Ba'al Shem Tov was [at the level] of *bina*, the Magid from *chochma*. Even though bina is lower than chochma, he taught from the bina which is actually above chochma. R. Baruch – the lower level of bina, but I teach Torah from a place which is above them all. Even if a thought comes to me from these [lower] places, I reject it <for I only want innovative teachings." He said that he recieves teachings from a place that no man before has ever done before>' (Ibid., 317-8).

12 Mishna Avot 1:1.

before, from Mount Sinai onwards – but rather its innovative force. The great masters of the esoteric are those who brought a new story to the world, who paved new paths not yet trodden upon. The secrecy surrounding these thoughts comes to cover-up their innovative quality. The greatest of secrets are those which expressed the greatest innovation and for this very reason, because they represented a new path, were kept under cover.[13]

The close connection of the esoteric to innovation causes tension on both the theoretical and social plane. Socially, it leads to internal conflict. While this is true in general it is all the more so the case in a society where the very basis of authority rests in the past. It is quite natural that in such a traditionally oriented society expressions such as, 'Innovation is prohibited by the Torah,' are coined to give voice to the anti-innovative stance. New revelatory ideas can stand on their own with no need for the support of authoritative tradition and as such constitute a threat to the traditional society – its texts, institutions and leaders. R. Nachman himself pointed out that his innovation was in fact one of the causes for the strife that shadowed him throughout his career.

> He said, 'How is it possible that they won't disagree with me. For I am traveling a new road upon which no one has yet trod. (And even the Baal Shem Tov did not, no creature has....) Even though it is an ancient path it is completely new.'[14]

It is clear why R. Nachman felt that he needed to cover his new path in secrets. Innovation is controversial; the greater the former, the greater the latter.

---

13 On the ways in which the esoteric conceals the innovative and innovation through tradition, see Halbertal, *Concealment and Revelation: The Secret and its Boundaries in Medieval Jewish Tradition*, esp. 98. It is important to note that these innovations were in the realm of the theoretical and exoteric. They were not connected to the actual practice of halacha. Regarding the importance of this distinction, see Zvi Mark, " *The Tale of the Bread – a Hidden Story of R. Nachman of Braslav*," *Tarbiz* 72, no. 3 (2003): 447-50.

14 *Chayei Moharan Im Hashmatot*, 338 and 74.

The esoteric and innovation are connected in an essential way as well. Only that which was hidden can be discovered, only that which is discovered is new. The exoteric is already known and can offer no attraction of dynamic spiritual renewal. This can come only from the discovery of hidden layers of the world or the Torah, those things that were not known before. The act of discovery lends excitement to life itself and adds something that the experience of the exoteric lacks. R. Nachman gives expression to this in an extreme personal statement: 'If I knew that I would still be now what I was yesterday, I would not want such a life at all.'[15] Constant renewal is an essential condition for a valuable life. Without it, life is flavorless. Contact with that which was hidden is what makes life worthwhile.

2. THE REVELATION OF THE SECRET AND THE ESOTERIC IN THE EXOTERIC

A secret which is fully revealed to all loses its renewing potential. The renewing power of the esoteric is preserved only if even during the revelatory process the tension between the revealed and concealed is maintained. This means that some measure of secrecy must be kept. However, the very act of revelation brings with it the feeling of renewal and peaked interest for both the one to whom it is revealed as well as the one who is doing the revealing. This in turn means that there is a constant tension between the need to keep the esoteric secret and the desire to reveal it to others. This tension is difficult to maintain as the move from esoteric to exoteric creates an anti-climax where it is lost.

Even those masters of esoterica mentioned by R. Nachman eventually did publicize their works – making their once secret innovative thought available to all.

> He said to me: 'There are some things which were originally secret, but became known. For example, some of the kabalistic secrets that

15 Ibid., 343.

> preceded R. Shimon bar Yochai and R. Yitchak Luria were great secrets and were only discussed in the greatest of secrecy. Afterwards, in the days of R. Shimon bar Yochai and R. Yitchak Luria, they ceased to be so. They permitted their revelation to some degree. There are many things which are now secret, but in the future will no longer be so.[16]

The esoteric does not remain hidden for ever. The process of revelation continues throughout the generations. Even the secrets of R. Nachman, 'now secret,' are destined to be brought into the open. A puzzling text brought in the same context also points in this direction.

> He said to me: 'It may be, etc. just as etc. and in the fullness of time it will be forgotten.' He answered me: 'I know, etc. This too is now secret, but later will no longer be so.'[17]

The revelatory process of R. Nachman's own work began in his lifetime in accord with his own wishes. The best example of this is his *Likutei Moharan*. It is important to note that at the time that the contents of the *Scroll* were first revealed in 1806, all of the discourses included in *Likutei Mohoran* were treated as secrets which were not to be revealed to any outside of his innermost circle.[18] Thus R. Natan describes:

> On the day following the holiday [1807] .... He took from me the book mentioned above, that is the one containing his discourses which were written down now called *Likutei Mohoran*. I did not yet know what his intensions were regarding it, for he had not yet revealed to anybody his desire to publish any of his books. On the contrary, he would always

---

16 Ibid., 362-3.

17 Ibid. See also the version in Rav Alter Tepliker, "*Hashmatot Mechayei Moharan*," (1898), 19; Rav Natan of Nemirov, *Likutei Halachot* (Jerusalem: 1984), vol. 3, 234-5.

18 See Joseph Weiss, *Studies in Bratslav Hasidi*sm (Jerusalem: 1995), 216, 51-61.

> warn us not to reveal any of his works to others who were not part of our circle.[19]
>
> At that time he would constantly warn us against revealing his thought to strangers not of our circle. He told us a few reasons for doing so and we were extremely careful to hide the pamphlets which had been transcribed.[20]

Even the exoteric works of R. Nachman were first treated as secrets; he warned his followers against revealing them. Only two years preceding his death, after much deliberation, he decided to publish them.

> While he was in Lemberg he gave the book *Likutei Moharan* to a certain individual who had come from Medvedevka and told him to print it upon his return to our country. And so he did. At first he deliberated much concerning this matter for in previous years we were warned to hide any writings from the world.[21]

The definition of material as either esoteric or exoteric is not hard and fast, but flexible. This is the case with R. Nachman's work as well. He himself described once secret writings as having moved from one category to the other.[22]

Even after the revelation of once esoteric texts and their availability to all, there remains in them some element of the hidden. Just as the works of R. Shimon bar Yochai and R. Yitzchak Luria remain under the general rubric of 'esoterica' and their interpretations are categorized as '*sod*,' so too

---

19 Rav Natan of Nemirov, *Yemei Moharnat* (Jerusalem: 1982), I 43-4.

20 Ibid., 13.

21 *Chayei Moharan Im Hashmatot*, 209-10.

22 This seems to be the intention of R. Nachman's statement regarding his 'Tale of the Bread': 'This tale will be needed for those who are with us today, as well as those who are not with us today. See what will become in time of this tale. He warned not to tell it to strangers' (Mark, "*The Tale of the Bread – a Hidden Story of R. Nachman of Braslav*," 422).

are the teachings of R. Nachman. Even after their publication they retain an undisclosed element which requires decoding and interpretation.

> The teachings and the writings in his holy books… have very deep meaning, both on the level of *pshat* as well as *sod* and *nistar*. It is impossible to explain this.[23]

Libes has already commented that the great innovation of R. Nachman lie 'not in his teachings, but rather in himself': in his unique mystical personality.[24] R. Nachman himself contained the unique combination of secret and innovation. As he testified about himself: 'An innovation like myself has never before been.'[25] As part of the innovative force he stressed his own sense of self as a secret and a wonder: 'I am a man of wonder, possessed of a wondrous soul.'[26] In the same way he was described by his followers: 'He was something new and wondrous and awesome that no mouth could describe nor any heart discern.'[27]

The esoteric Breslav material, as well as the secrets interlaced in other discourses, teachings and stories, all confirm this. A large part of it is devoted to describing the unique greatness of R. Nachman himself as a wondrous secret. Even when facets of the man himself are revealed, there remains even more undercover. As R. Nachman described himself: 'I am an enigma, which even when uncovered remains secret.'[28]

The secret at the center of R. Nachman's personality and his teachings is not a secret in the conventional sense of esoterica or carefully guarded

---

23 *Chayei Moharan Im Hashmatot*, 323.

24 Libes, "*The Novelty of Rabbi Nachman of Bratslav*," 100.

25 *Chayei Moharan Im Hashmatot*, 263.

26 Ibid., 266.

27 Ibid., 262.

28 Following the version in "Pnu Lechem Tzefona," *Or Haorot* 14. See also Avraham Zogdon, *Eilu Yadativ Hiyativ* (Beitar Elite: 2002), II 420 and *Siach Sorfei Kodesh* vol. 2, 15; vol. 4, 114; vol. 6, 178.

knowledge. As described above in the Introduction, the Chasidic world treated the concept of 'the secrets of the Torah' and '*sod*' in distinctly new ways. In much Chasidic discourse these concepts no longer referred to kabalistic texts, esoterica, or personal paths for cleaving to the Divine, but rather to that which was inexpressible in words.

One of the primary aspects of the mystical outlook is the feeling that within the creation (and the Torah) there lies a more essential hidden level of meaning than that found on the surface. The mystic senses that that which meets the eye only represents some outer layer and not the essence of what is observed. The discovery of what lies beyond, of the more spiritual levels of existence, is the very mission of the mystical life. The basis of this outlook is the assumption that God is the 'hidden God'[29] whose presence in the world needs to be constantly sought out and uncovered. It is the belief that 'the world is filled with His Glory' that raises the question as to 'where is the place of His Glory.' It leads to the never ending search to uncover the holy and divine immanent in creation; it breeds the desire to make intimate contact with it.

R. Nachman was a part of the Chasidic trend which both broadened and changed the meaning of the secret. (I have dealt with this elsewhere.)[30] The focus of the discussion here, in regard to the *Scroll*, regards the more regular meaning of the secret: the *Scroll* as an esoteric work, guarded carefully by those privileged to know of it.

3. SOME COMMENTS ON THE SOCIOLOGY OF THE HOLY SECRET

The *Scroll* is perhaps one of the last secrets in the world of Jewish mysticism which actually functioned as such for a religious community. While there may be lost secret texts whose meanings will never be known, or even others of whose very existence we will never know, it seems that very few

29 Isaiah 45:15.

30 See Mark, *Mysticism and Madness In the Work of R. Nachman of Breslav*, 147-62.

esoteric texts, passed down through the generations and functioning as sacred secrets for those who knew of them, on a par with the *Scroll*, will ever be found. We live in a time when once carefully guarded esoteric mystic works are now published together with translations for any and all to peruse and purchase. In opposition to this state of affairs, the *Scroll*'s history as a text which was secretly preserved by a living religious community is even more unique. This community succeeded in keeping this text unpublished and closely guarded from outsiders for generations.

The study of the *Scroll* offers an opportunity not only to study it qua text, but also to investigate the social aspects of the phenomenon of the 'holy secret' of which it is a prime example. Not only is it representative of the 'hidden text,' but it has been uniquely situated in a vibrant Chasidic community which has over the past two decades experienced tremendous growth as its presence and influence have become known throughout a variety of cultural milieus both in Israel and elsewhere.

The hiding of the *Scroll*, detailing the coming of the messiah, needs to be understood not merely as a singular case of guarding a particular text, but rather as part of a general approach to the esoteric followed by R. Nachman.[31] As noted above, R. Nachman covered an entire corpus of his output with a cloak of mystery while at the same time discussing the theoretical implications of esoterica in other works. He was constantly concerned with the question of what to reveal and what to keep hidden.[32] He developed a many-leveled methodology aimed at secreting that which he desired remain unknown. One book was hidden away never having been read;[33] another

---

31 The subject of esoterica in the Breslav oeuvre has been given much attention in the literature. See Weiss, *Studies in Bratslav Hasid*ism, 181-258; Mendel Piekarz, *Studies in Bratslav Hasidism*, expanded ed. (Jerusalem: 1995), 10-7, 19, 51-3, 62, 111-17, 26, 27; Arthur Green, *Tormented Master* (New York: Schocken, 1987), 27, 187-228, Yehuda Liebes, "*Hatikun Haclali Shel R. Nachman Mebreslav Veyachaso Leshabta'ut*," in *On Sabbateanism and its Kabbalah* (Jerusalem: 1995), 238-61. On the 'Tale of the Bread' as an example of esoterica, see Weiss, *Studies in Bratslav Hasid*ism, 191-2; Mark, " *The Tale of the Bread – a Hidden Story of R. Nachman of Braslav*."

32 Weiss, *Studies in Bratslav Hasid*ism, 181-88.

33 Piekarz, *Studies in Bratslav Hasidism*, 63-4.

burnt;[34] teachings and tales were forbidden to relate to others;[35] and, of course, the *Scroll* was to be made known to only a single individual in each generation. The variety of his methods point to the importance that the secret played in the world of R. Nachman and to the importance that the meaning of the 'secret' played in his philosophy.[36] The Breslav court became known as one which enclosed itself in a veil of secrecy – always hinting at the existence of hidden works and hidden meanings in known teachings whose time to be revealed had not yet arrived.[37]

'So As Not To Increase Conflict In Israel'

One of the reasons for secreting texts has to do with the potential for adverse reactions on the part of those who are not part of the circle of believers devoted to their message. There is some worry that the revelation of certain texts will result in ridicule, anger or conflict which may fan the flames of already existing tensions or play into the hands of adversaries. Secrecy serves to protect a group or an idea from a potentially hostile environment. There is no doubt that such considerations played an important role in decisions made by R. Nachman and his followers regarding that which would remain hidden from others.

According to the sources in our possession, we know that when R. Nachman decided to secret a text he did not offer explanations for his decision. An exception to this rule is found regarding the conflict between him and the Saba of Shpola – a secret kept in the Teplicker manuscript of *Chayei Moharan* and only recently published in *Chayei Moharan Im Hashmatot*. This text is important not just owing to its actual content, but

---

34 Weiss, *Studies in Bratslav Hasidi*sm, 215-44, 45-8.

35 Mark, " *The Tale of the Bread – a Hidden Story of R. Nachman of Braslav*," and Zvi Mark, "*Ma'aseh Mehashiryon (The Tale of the Armor) – from the Hidden Chambers of Breslav Censorship*," *Zion* 70, no. 2 (2005).

36 Mark, *Mysticism and Madness In the Work of R. Nachman of Breslav*, 147-62.

37 Piekarz, *Studies in Bratslav Hasidism*, 10-16, 202.

because it preserved the directive for keeping texts secreted in R. Nachman's own words.

> Know that we have in our hands a manuscript of our Rebbe written by himself stating: 'Know my brothers and friends, I will reveal to you a secret, but keep it well hidden amongst you so as not to increase conflict in Israel. Know that the Zaide (grandfather) from the town of Shpola, the famous Yehuda Leib son of Baruch; know that I am holy and that he is my opposite in impurity. I am the true holy elder who has acquired wisdom of ancient things, but he is the impure elder. Therefore he is called Zaide – for he is the elder of the Other Side – the grandfather of all impurity. That is why he spent his entire life giving out charity – in order to negate the power of the Holy People Israel's charity which they give in order to neutralize the power of the impure, which stems from the impurity of the dead as in 'charity saves from death.' He through his charity attempted to conquer, heaven forbid, the power of the Holy People of Israel's charity.[38]

Here is a fine example of R. Nachman's insistence on secrecy due to the obvious inflammatory nature of that secret. This text describes the demonic essence of his primary rival, R. Arieh Leib of Shpola, who led the anti-Breslav attacks against him. Conversely, R. Nachman describes himself as the absolute pinnacle of holiness.[39]

This demonic description of the most elder of Chasidic masters in the Ukraine is not completely surprising given the less than subtle hints at the Saba's wickedness that R. Nachman mentioned in various other works. In *Likutei Moharan* he labeled the 'elders of the generation, those who have seen

---

38 Tepliker, "*Hashmatot Mechayei Moharan*," 9-10; *Chayei Moharan Im Hashmatot*, 161-2. On the nature of the conflict between R. Nachman and the Saba of Shpola, see Green, *Master*, 94-134.

39 On the development of this demonic motif in the works of R. Nachman, see Weiss, *Studies in Bratslav Hasidi*sm, 18-19.

many days' as nourishing the 'snake's brow' – which symbolizes dark knowledge and heresy.[40] In the continuation of the above text from *Chayei Moharan*, the writer lists a number of other teachings which contain hints of similar bitter criticism.[41] Despite the similarity between that found in the censored secret teaching and that published, the former is clearly much more strongly worded and lays out the accusation of working for the 'other side' in the most explicit of terms – even the seemingly charitable works of the Saba are, in fact, evil. We may assume that the readers of *Likutei Moharan* and other teachings knew to whom R. Nachman was referring when he spoke of the 'elder,'[42] but only in the censored text did he actually name his adversary.[43]

From this we learn something important. Part of the rationale behind the secreting of a given text may not be so much to keep its contents unknown, but to keep what is already known from being explicitly disseminated among the wider public. R. Nachman knew that his Chasidim, and even others who would read his teachings, could very well figure out for themselves who he was berating, yet he still wanted to keep some distance between his indirect argumentation and his much more explicit frontal attacks: between that which was whispered in the hallways and that shouted in the public square. It is also interesting to note that this harshest criticism of the Saba of Shpola was recorded not as a direct quotation, but was in fact written by R. Nachman himself with the intention that it never be published.

---

40 Rav Natan of Nemirov, *Sefer Likutei Moharan Hamenukad* (Jerusalem: 1994), II 4.

41 See ibid., I 242; II 4; I 22:4; II 67.

42 This is also the speculation of the scholarly literature. See the sources listed in note 39 above.

43 The harshness of tone in the esoteric literature is usually more muted in the exoteric. While R. Nachman accuses his adversaries of aiding and abetting evil through their deeds, he usually does not claim that they themselves are the embodiment of evil. They do 'hobble through their days and add no light of holiness or wisdom to them' (Nemirov, *Sefer Likutei Moharan Hamenukad* 4:8) thus feeding evil. However, in his esoteric writing, R. Nachman labels the Saba of Shpola as 'the elder of the Other Side – the grandfather of all impurity.' At times, though, even in exoteric works, R. Nachman does not pull his punches. He labels well-known tzadikim as 'famous liers ... akin to the chief of the Other Side' (Nemirov, *Sefer Likutei Moharan Hamenukad* II 67).

The fear of inflaming the passions of conflict not only kept this type of criticism from being published, but also served as a reason to keep other teachings, not even related to R. Nachman's foes, from seeing the light of day. As R. Natan wrote in *Likutei Halachot*:

> Every year, as the defect of faith in the Sages has not yet been repaired, we need to whisper, 'Blessed is the name of His royal presence forever,' in order, as our Sages said, not to antagonize the objectors.[44] For 'Blessed is the name of His royal presence forever' represents the Oral Torah which is, as we know, the novelae of the truly learned who compose many books, so we need to whisper this. For we need to cover and hide may of these novelae so as not to speak them out loud as it were, rather only whisper them. The Master said that there are many things which are now secret which will in another time not be so, etc. (as is written in *Chayei Moharan*). Therefore there were several holy books that were hidden away for many years, yet afterwards with the passage of time were revealed – like the Zohar and the writings of R. Yitzchak Luria. Also, there are still holy books hidden away and in the future they will be revealed. But even those works which are now being revealed need to be revealed slowly. And there are some things which need to be only hinted at. All this is because of the objectors and the scoffers, so that they will not be further antagonized. This is all connected to the secret of whispering 'Blessed is the name of His royal presence forever' throughout the entire year. But on Yom Kippur, when the High Priest enters into the innermost sanctuary etc., then the repair of the defect in faith in the Sages is repaired through the abundance of books, etc. as mentioned above. Therefore we say 'Blessed is the name of His royal presence forever' out loud. For when the truth is revealed and all know and believe in the holy wonder of the novelae of these holy books, then surely we will no longer need to hide them like a secret by whispering, for they will no longer be secret.[45]

---

44 TB Pesachim 56a.

45 Nemirov, *Likutei Halachot*, OH 234-5.

R. Natan describes the process of hiding and revealing which has taken place throughout the ages in terms of R. Nachman's claim that the reason behind it was to guard against unnecessary conflict with objectors and scoffers. Even though R. Natan relates to global historical processes exemplified in the treatment of the Zohar and the writings of R. Yitzchak Luriah, he concludes by returning to the more contemporary situation in which 'there are still holy books hidden away and in the future they will be revealed.' In this context he also mentions the need for patience in revealing them, as well as the necessity to, at times, only hint at them. It is more than reasonable to suggest that R. Natan is actually describing those writings of R. Nachman then in his possession and the proper way to publicize them. His last sentence, in fact, moves into the first person, 'For when the truth is revealed … then surely we will no longer need to hide them like a secret by whispering ….' This description of the proper treatment which the works of the 'truly learned' require corresponds to the way that R. Natan treated the secret texts of R. Nachman. Some of them he kept hidden, some were slowly revealed, while others were only written in ways that hinted at what they contained. 'All this is because of the objectors and the scoffers, so that they will not be further antagonized.'

It is worth noting that R. Natan differentiates between whispering secrets and declaring them out loud. Even when secrets are revealed, it may be that they will only be whispered; only hinted at. Then, only one who quietly and carefully listens will be able to discern them.

Another interesting point is found in the continuation of the above text.

> This is like what is written regarding 'in the eyes of all the nations.' That is, the secret stays [hidden] with us, and only enough is revealed so that others understand that the secret is still hidden with us. This is what is meant by whispering 'Blessed is the name of His royal presence forever' like a secret.[46]

46 Ibid.

Here is an interesting twist – suggestive revelation is used to let others know that secret writings do exist,[47] while not letting them have any access to the actual secrets themselves.

The Reasons For Hiding The Scroll

On the surface it appears that no special reason needs to be given for wanting to keep the *Scroll* secret. There is a longstanding Jewish tradition against calculating the end of days.[48] However, this tradition, as expressed in the Talmudic expression, 'May the spirit of those who calculate the end of days be destroyed' seems to be concerned mainly with attempts at determining when the messianic end of time will arrive and not with describing those days themselves.[49] Therefore, we still need to address the question of why R. Nachman insisted on guarding the *Scroll*'s secrecy.

Our previous description of how certain Breslav works were meant to be kept as a secret whispered among the inner circle, serves us well as an introduction to understanding the type of secrecy which surrounded the *Scroll*. It appears that the *Scroll* was destined to be closely guarded for fear

---

47 See also Piekarz, *Studies in Bratslav Hasidism*, 10-16, 202; Green, *Master*, 5

48 TB Sanhedrin 97b.

49 This Talmudic curse can be read as relating only to those who attempt to calculate when the messiah will arrive – thus sowing despondence if their timing proves false. For example, Maimonides describes some of the characteristics of messianic times while also mentioning the prohibition against calculating the time of its arrival (Maimonides MT Hilchot Melachim 12:2). This also seems to be the meaning of R. Natan's following statement on knowledge of the messiah's arrival: 'At first they asked me when the messiah would arrive. I answered that this is something hidden from the eyes of all the living for this is the wonder of the end. As Daniel said, "These things are hidden and sealed" (12:4). Even God Himself keeps it hidden in His heart – as it says, "I revealed it to my heart, but not to my limbs". They began to ask me about the meaning of this and I answered that there are those tzadikim who are akin to the heart and to them God revealed the wonders of the end of time, but there are those called limbs to whom he did not reveal it (Nemirov, *Yemei Moharnat*, II 210-11). His response was to the question regarding the time of messiah's arrival – this information was what was hidden even by God. However, R. Natan saw no problem with discussing other aspects of the messianic times.

of arousing conflict, while many parts of it were surreptitiously scattered throughout other exoteric works of R. Nachman.

We can list a number of the *Scroll*'s elements which seem to have been sufficient cause for R. Nachman's desire to keep the *Scroll* undercover so as not to inflame tensions. The publication of a work which purported to offer a complete description of the messianic age without anchoring each of its assertions firmly in authoritative Biblical or Talmudic texts, may have brought charges of unwarranted prophecy upon its author. R. Nachman's enemies may have been all too happy to label him as a false prophet. The depiction of the natural world as continuing to function as it always has, with sickness and death, not filled with daily miracles – despite continuing a strong line of traditional Jewish thought[50] – may have engendered further criticism. This view contradicted firmly held folk beliefs concerning the end of days held by the masses.[51]

However, it seems that the major worry behind the *Scroll*'s publication lie in other of its elements. The messiah, often thought of as 'above all men,'[52] is depicted in the *Scroll* as beginning his career as a mere child. Already at the age of three, people are corresponding with him concerning matters of halacha; before his bar-mitzvah, he is already crowned King of Israel. It is not difficult to imagine that this may have seemed absurd in the eyes of many. But further reservations could have sprung from the knowledge that this child-messiah was modeled after R. Nachman's own son, Shlomo Efraim. Despite his tragic death, it would have seemed odd that R. Nachman was still trying to crown him King of Israel.

This also presents a particular problem of seemingly Christian overtones to the entire messianic picture. The Christian infant-messiah motif was

---

50 For other views of messianic times, see Dov Schwartz, *Messianism in Medieval Jewish Thought* (Ramat Gan: 1997). For the understanding of this issue among *mitnagdim*, see Arie Morgenstern, *Redemption Through Return: Vilna Gaon's Disciples in Eretz Israel 1800-1840* (Jerusalem: 1997).

51 *Chayei Moharan Im Hashmatot*, 277.

52 Rav Yehudah Halevi, *Sefer Hakuzari*, trans. Yehudah Even Shmuel (Jerusalem: 1973), III 73.

well-known throughout the Ukraine even to the Jewish population as it featured prominently in public iconography (as it still does to this day). R. Nachman was correct in worrying that the *Scroll*'s depiction of the child messiah would leave him open to charges of christological influence. When this is combined with the fact that his own son had already died, this charge of influence is conflated with seeming support of a theology of resurrection, leaving him even more vulnerable to claims of false prophecy and Sabbatianism.[53]

The fact that the *Scroll*'s messiah closely resembles R. Nachman himself was another potential cause for discord and enmity. We now know that at the time R. Nachman transcribed the Scroll to his followers he had already resigned himself to the fact that he would not merit completing his messianic mission in his own lifetime. He drew a clear distinction between himself and the actual messiah. However, he still believed and expected that his teachings, his words and his followers would continue to keep his dream alive until the messiah would arrive.

Against this background, it seems that R. Nachman may have rightly suspected that the publication of the *Scroll* in his own lifetime could have been interpreted as his call for recognition of his unique status as the *tzadik* of his generation and for his crowning as the the potential Moses-messiah, King of Israel.[54] More than this, it may be that the *Scroll*'s depiction of the messiah as actually redeeming all of Israel from the diaspora and leading the world to recognition of the true God, would make it appear that R. Nachman was not just claiming the title of *tzadik* (helping individuals of his own court) and potential messiah – but that of the actual messiah king. This is the messiah who would function not just on the spiritual level, but on the

53 On the similarity between Christian and Sabbatean views on messianic resurrection versus those found in Breslav Chasidism, see Weiss, *Studies in Bratslav Hasidism*, 231-5 and fn. 42; Piekarz, *Studies in Bratslav Hasidism*, 215-16 fn. 46; Green, *Master*, 217 fn. 32. David Berger's anti-messianic polemic is devoted to the claim that it is just this belief in resurrection that differentiates Judaism from Christianity [David Berger, *The Rebbe, the Messiah and the Scandal of Orthodox Indifference* (New York: Littman Library of Jewish Civilization, 2001)].

54 On the tendency of the Breslav community to censor the belief in R. Nachman's own messianic status, see Green, *Master*, 197.

national stage of history for whom all of Israel had long awaited.[55] So while the publication of a detailed vision of messianic times may have exposed R. Nachman to charges of being a false prophet, the connection between the *Scroll*'s depiction of the messiah and his own biography could have led to charges of being a false messiah.

The lack of any mention of the Temple and the renewal of sacrifices in the Scroll would have also opened another path for criticism. R. Nachman's enemies may very well have seized upon this lacuna as evidence of heretical abandonment of the traditional picture of messianic times found in both the Bible and Talmudic literature. The liturgical longing that 'the Temple be rebuilt speedily in our day,' expressive of generations of prayerful hope, would not be so easily dismissed by his many detractors.

Other central motifs of R. Nachman's teachings – such as his claim that 'I have finished and will finish'[56] – together with the lack of the Temple in the Scroll may also have suggested overtly Christian concepts: A messiah arrives on earth, dies before completing his mission, yet still promises worldwide redemption. The messianic vision leaves no room for the Temple and the messiah himself seems to replace its centrality in daily life. R. Nachman, already having been embroiled in struggles with other influential Chasidic leaders of his day, such as R. Baruch of Mezibush and the Saba of Shpola, knew that his own legitimacy was not something to be taken for granted. Publicizing the *Scroll*, he knew, would offer ample opportunity for his detractors to renew their attacks against him and his followers. Even posthumous publication would not have stayed such attacks as the Christian-like motifs would not have been viewed with less suspicion. As long as Breslav Chasidim nurtured a hope that their Rebbe, even after death, would somehow have a role to play in the messianic process, it is understandable that these suspicions would have become even more acute, leaving his followers even more vulnerable.[57]

---

55 See Yosef Dan, *Apokolipsia Az Ve'achshav* (Israel: 2000), 310-12.

56 *Chayei Moharan Im Hashmatot*, 300.

57 See the sources in note 53 above.

R. Nachman may have suspected that the solid grounding in traditional Jewish sources upon which the *Scroll* is based (and which have been pointed out in this work[58]) would not have been enough to withstand the storm of accusations which his detractors would level against its author and his followers. Even though he knew that the basis of all of his claims could be found in traditionally authoritative sources – from the Bible through Lurianic kabalah and the teachings of the Baal Shem Tov – he also knew that in the hostile climate in which his own works were read, 'with a critical eye, searching for the every lack and defect,'[59] the *Scroll* could quickly be turned against him. It could be used to garner wide spread support for labeling his followers a messianic sect centered around their Master, himself. His awareness of the dangers that could result from the Scroll's publication – the bitter criticism and conflict that it would engender – seem to have been instrumental in his deciding that the *Scroll* should remain hidden, the most secret of the Breslav esoterica.

The Community of The Secret

> 'You, fellow man, my equal, my better, my friend – together we have sweetly shared a secret
> To the house of God, amongst the herdes, we have traveled together.'[60]

Even if the main purpose of the secrecy enforced by R. Nachman was to protect his followers from undesirable criticism, there were other rationale behind it and the shroud of mystery surrounding the *Scroll* fulfilled

58 We have discussed the sources relating to the motif of the messiah as infant, the replacement of the Temple with the person of the messiah and the return of the messiah in the previous chapters.

59 'The main problem caused by the leaders ... it is not enough for them that they do not know their place due to their thirst for position and honor, such that they grow jealous of proper men who will not surrender to them. So they undermine them and look at them with a critical eye, searching for the every lack and defect' (Nemirov, *Likutei Halachot*, YD 165).

60 Psalms 55:15.

other roles, as well. The very existence of esoteric literature in the Breslav ouvre helped to create an esprit de corps among those privy to it, while at the same time distancing those outside of this inner circle. I think that R. Nachman's language when discussing the secret of the Saba of Shpola serves as an indication of the former. 'Know my brothers and friends, I will reveal to you a secret, but keep it well hidden amongst you.'[61] R. Nachman emphasizes the fraternity of his audience. The secret that he reveals to them may be shared amongst them, but not to those outside of the group. A certain group modesty is required – in this case the modesty usual in expressions of intimacy: the sharing of something meant to be expressed only by those in most intimate contact.[62]

Other instructions regarding the keeping of secret texts also relate to this very point. After relating the 'Tale of the Bread,' R. Nachman added:[63]

> ...This tale will be needed for those who are with us today, as well as those who are not with us today[64] – see what will become of this tale in time.
>
> He warned not to tell it to strangers. 'If you tell it, even though I love you, this love will be empty.' He also added that all of the audience were responsible for each other so that no one would tell it to a stranger.

R. Nachman's words reflect the tension inherent in this communal secret. On the one hand, the tale needed to be recited so that it would remain

---

61 *Hashmatot Mechayei Moharan*, (Jerusalem: 1893), 9-10.

62 R. Nachman uses the Hebrew *lehatzniah* here for 'to keep hidden'. This Hebrew word is semantically connected to 'modesty' as well. The connection between hiding and modesty is also used by R. Nachman in describing other parts of the esoterica of the Torah as akin to the intimate relations between man and God. See Mark, *Mark, Mysticism and Madness In the Work of R. Nachman of Breslav*, 144-51.

63 I discuss this source at length in " *The Tale of the Bread – a Hidden Story of R. Nachman of Braslav*," 447-50.

64 Deuternonomy 29:14.

available for those who were not with the original group who heard it: its retelling was a necessity. On the other hand, it cannot be told to 'strangers.'[65]

The role that the communal secret plays can also be detected by observing the sanction with which R. Nachman threatens those who would reveal it. Keeping the secret is one of the conditions upon which his love of his followers is based. He does not threaten them with punishments or temper – not even with the loss of his love. Rather, those who break the code of secrecy will find only affection emptied of its true depth – an empty love. This is the loss of intimacy which the keeping of the secrecy expresses: the intimacy of those who share the secret amongst themselves. The communal secret serves to define who is part of the group and who stands outside of it. The group is defined by its mutual responsibility to keep the secret so. By retelling it only among their own, they reinforce their own group identity inwards, while strengthening the exclusion of those outside of their privileged group. R. Nachman treats his followers as a special community – emphasizing their group responsibility one for the other in guarding the secret. This too strengthens the communal bond amongst them.

The demand for secrecy, then, is not merely designed with the utilitarian goal of keeping a given text locked away, but has further reaching social consequences. It helps develop a group consciousness and reinforces the intimacy within that group and between it and R. Nachman.[66] A fascinating glimpse into this aspect of the communal code of silence is found in the personal introduction added to the 'Tale of the Bread' by R. Yitzchak Meir Korman[67] when he copied it from manuscript.

---

65 On the tension between the esoteric and exoteric as characteristic of Breslav Chasidism in general, see Piekarz, *Studies in Bratslav Hasidism*, 9-16. On this problem in general, see Halbertal, *Concealment and Revelation: The Secret and its Boundaries in Medieval Jewish Tradition*, 7-15, 96-100.

66 See *Chayei Moharan Hamenukad*, (Jerusalem: 1995), 225, 310-11; Rav Avraham Chazan, *Yemei Hatlaot* (Jerusalem: 2000), 174.

67 See Mark, "*Ma'aseh Mehashiryon (The Tale of the Armor) – from the Hidden Chambers of Breslav Censorship*," 212-15.

> Master of the World, You know that our holy Rebbe commanded us not to tell this tale to any strangers not belonging to the inner circle and his holy mouth even demanded that his audience take personal and communal responsibility for this. I know my trifling worth and my material [weaknesses], and You know them better than I. Great mercy you have shown in the face of my faults and failings and all the more so to the [physical] body known as man. To be more derided is that I, the unworthy, should be called one of the inner circle. Perhaps these worthy men were mistaken in entrusting this task to me. Therefore, I ask that you not blame them for this – for not out of opposition did they do so. This pig's leg I stretched out before them and so tricked them into thinking that I was fit. Woe is me – for those actions which are known to me and for those traits which are not. But I knew of the teaching of this *tzadik*, may his merit protect us, that there is no such thing as despair in the world at all – but one must pray and plead before You. Therefore, I ask of You – please God save me, your servant Yitzchak Meir son of Simah Mindel, that I will merit to improve my actions and thoughts in each and every way; that I will merit to walk in the ways of our holy Rebbe, the [author of] *Likutei Moharan*; that I may be truly called by his holy name: a Breslav Chasid.[68]

It is apparent that what is troubling the author is whether he is actually suitable to be a member of the exclusive inner circle of Breslav. Is he really worthy of the Breslav moniker, really worthy to be privy to their secrets? Or is he one of the 'strangers' – meaning that in revealing their secret to him, the members of the Breslav inner circle have broken their communal pledge? He longs to be called a true 'Breslav Chasid,' and becoming a part of the community of secrets serves as affirmation of this. However, he worries that his admittance was under false pretenses – he merely 'tricked them.'[69]

---

68 The copyist's introduction in Rav Yitzchak Meir Korman of Lublin, "*Ma'aseh Mehalechem* (Manuscript)," in *Machon Schocken* (Jerusalem).

69 R. Yitzchak Meir Korman wrote a similar introduction to another esoteric work as well. 'Master of the World: You know that at the time that the righteous rabbi from Tscherin,

The very existence of the hidden text and the desire to join the special fraternity privy to its secrets serves both as spiritual inducement and reward for those who become members.

From other testimony recorded by R. Korman, we see that those who revealed their secrets to him also had their doubts as to his suitability.

> The text of the teaching from Likutei Moharan chapter 267 which begins with the verse, 'If you enter the vineyard of your fellow... according to the tale ....' I asked several important members of the inner circle about this tale, but they knew nothing of it. However, when I was privileged to be in the city of Tscherin, where there resided a number of the inner circle, Chasidim, rich householders and a rabbi who was a scribe and a cantor, known by everyone as R. Avraham Sofer (the grandchild of our Master and of R. Nachman of Tscherin) – who was a Chasid and a wise scholar, I asked him about this tale and also for an interpretation of this entire discourse. At first, he did not want to tell me anything, but I pleaded with him, telling him I would not reveal any of this tale to a stranger.[70]

R. Yitzchak Meir did not grow-up in a Breslav family. He grew close to the Breslav world in Poland and joined a group of Breslav Chasidim in Lublin, who, like him, were for the most part other newcomers. This group naturally was most familiar with the well-known Breslav oeuvre and did not have access to esoteric materials. When he reached Tscherin, though, and came into contact with a much older and established Breslav community – some of whose members were actual descendants of the Rebbe – he was, for the first time, able to discuss Breslav texts with those who had direct

---

the author of the book *Parparaot Lechochma* and other works, gave me the book *Chayei Moharan* to publish, he did not give me the entire book because it is meant only for the inner circle of the tzadik.... I knew my lowly worth... can I be called one of the inner circle... ("Sefer Chayei Moharan (Manuscript)," in *Machon Schocken.*

70 Rav Natan Zvi Koenig, *Neveh Tzadikim* (Bnei Brak: 1969), 207-8.

access to the entire range of teachings, including the esoteric and oral traditions. His opportunity to find answers to questions which had troubled him in Lublin had arrived. He knew that the erasure of the tale alluded to in *Likutei Moharan* had been done purposefully; he assumed that it was one of R. Nachman's esoteric works which had been preserved only orally and only for those of the inner circle.[71] Therefore he concluded that in order to convince R. Avraham Sofer to reveal the actual tale to him, he would first need to convince him that he, a newcomer from the west, was worthy of being counted as one of the inner circle himself. By promising not to reveal the tale to any strangers, he is arguing, in effect, that he himself is no stranger – he can be trusted; can be considered one of the inner circle.

It may be that even after he heard the tale, or read it, the notion of actually writing or copying it raised doubts as to whether this was proper. For not everything that is said should be written and not everything written should be copied. It was told that once R. Avraham Sofer 'saw one of his students holding a booklet in which were copied a number of teachings which had been passed along orally among the inner circle. R. Avraham was cross with him that he was not afraid to copy those things for which silence was best. He said: "Should such things be written?!"'[72]

This type of atmosphere and the level of discourse concerning the esoteric texts and their transmission shows us how they were important social tools of communal solidarity. The right of access to them was an expression of admittance into the world of 'real' Breslavers; denial meant exclusion and 'stranger' status. Being in the know meant being responsible for the guarding of these secrets; being responsible for the solidarity of the inner circle. This was the dream of R. Yitzchak Meir – to improve his 'actions and thoughts in each and every way' so that he may be worthy of being 'called by his holy name: a Breslav Chasid.'[73]

---

71 I am presently working on a study of the relationship between R. Nachman's discourse and his mystic visions.

72 The introduction in Rav Avraham Chazan, *Biur Halikutim* (Jerusalem: 1993), 33-4.

73 The copyist's introduction in the Korman manuscript of the 'Tale of the Bread'.

Another interesting case sheds light upon the dynamics of the communal secret in the Breslav world. In a letter written in answer to a student, R. Eliezer Shlomo Schick[74] wrote regarding the rumor 'that you heard, that there exists a "Tale of Bread" and you are not familiar with it,'[75] R. Schick not only revealed the secret, but also proceeded to criticize the practice of keeping such things hidden amongst the inner circle.[76]

> Due to our great sins, the elders of the inner circle do not respect the wishes of our Rebbe who stated (*Sichot Haran* 209) that all of his teachings and discourses were not meant for us alone, but rather for those who are with us today, as well as those who are not.... Several times we discussed this with him and he hinted to us that we should make all the great works of God that He has done for us known to the coming generations. Once he said this explicitly – [that we should] make known to your children all the wondrous and awesome teachings and discourses and tales which he revealed to us. Then he quoted this verse with great excitement, burning like an ember, 'You shall make them known to your children and grandchildren....' Actually, this tale has made the rounds amongst the entire inner circle – immediately upon becoming privileged to know our Rebbe [each] should reveal it and publicize it to all of Israel. All the more so, the elders of the inner circle should take great pains to uphold [the verse] 'To every generation I will make known your faith orally (Psalms 79)' and 'father to son, I will make known your truth (Isaiah 38).' But more than this, they hide discourses and stories – each [thinking] that the more [secret] discourses he possesses, the greater his stature. However, thank God that now a new generation has arisen – thousands of youth who thirst after the stories and words of our Rebbe.

---

74 R. Schick is a leader of a large group of Breslav Chasidim – most of them newly religious. For more on him, see Piekarz, *Studies in Bratslav Hasidism*, 199-218.

75 Rav Eliezer Schick, *Asher Banachal*, vol. 14 (Jerusalem: 1984), 336. The thousands of letters contained in *Asher Banachal* are not given exact dates.

76 See Piekarz, *Studies in Bratslav Hasidism*, 202.

> We must make every effort to print everything so that we may be privileged to bring them life.[77]

It must be made clear that there was never any disagreement in the Breslav court that the publicizing of R. Nachman's exoteric works was of the utmost importance. However, R. Schick is here relating to those discourses and teachings which were hidden under instruction of R. Nachman himself, for example the 'Tale of the Bread,' which is the subject of his letter. He makes the radical claim that the inner circle, who felt that these texts were meant for their eyes only and were not to be exposed to those outside of this close-knit group, was actually transgressing the express wishes of R. Nachman himself. The Rebbe had dictated that his work was intended even for those absent at the time of their original recitation.

R. Schick's quotes regarding the access to R. Nachman's works were taken from his instructions regarding the very story that was the subject of his interlocutor's letter – the 'Tale of the Bread.'

> ...This tale will be needed for those who are with us today, as well as those who are not with us today[78] – see what will become in time of this tale. He warned not to tell it to strangers.[79]

As we noted above, the tension between the need to promote R. Nachman's unique teachings and to keep them hidden them due to potential problems is obvious.[80]

The latent claim in R. Schick's argument seems to be that the first part of R. Nachman's instructions is still valid, while the latter prohibition is not. This is due to the change in circumstances wherein 'thousands of youth' are

---

77 Rav Eliezer Schick, *Asher Banachal*, vol. 6 (New York 1978), 136.

78 Deuteronomy 26:14.

79 See Mark, "*The Tale of the Bread – a Hidden Story of R. Nachman of Braslav*," 422, 47-50.

80 We should note that the majority of the Breslav court does not agree with R. Schick's interpretation that the time for revealing what had been hidden has arrived.

waiting to hear the words of R. Nachman; it seems that there is no longer any fear of controversy. The status of R. Nachman and of Breslav Chasidism has vastly changed since he required the secreting of certain works. Therefore, it has become obligatory to publicize all of his works through printing them – thus making them available to all.

R. Schick also points to another aspect of the inner circle's jealous and zealous guarding of the esoteric texts: their very possession has become a status symbol. 'But more than this, they hide discourses and stories – each [thinking] that the more [secret] discourses he possesses, the greater his stature.'[81] Here another social function of the esoteric is uncovered. Among the inner circle hierarchies of status are determined through a sort of competition to see who has amassed the most esoterica. Through R. Schick's critique of this behaviour, the phenomenon is brought to our attention. Knowledge of the esoteric, then, functions to create a hierarchy among the inner circle – adding yet another reason to keep this material under wraps. It is clear, then, that R. Schick differentiates between the original intent – which aimed at hiding certain materials from outsiders in order to prevent dangerous confrontation – and what the secreting of Breslav texts had become: a matter of prestige. It was unconscionable, given the change in circumstances, that this continue.[82] As we will see, the secret that offered the most prestige to those who closely guarded it was, by far, the *Scroll* itself.

Secrets and Authority

The *Scroll* gained pride of place in relation to all of the other Breslav esoterica. Those who knew its contents were also considered to be special, even among the inner circle who knew of other secret works. We know that R. Nachman himself took care not to reveal it to all of those who were privy to other

81 Schick, *Asher Banachal* 6, 136.

82 Despite the impression that R. Schick revealed all the Breslav secrets that he knew, this was not actually the case. He possessed the Scroll, but never published it. See Mark, " *The Tale of the Bread – a Hidden Story of R. Nachman of Braslav*," the section on manuscript versions.

of his secrets. R. Aaron, the rabbi of Breslav, who himself was privy, along with R. Natan, to the secret 'Tale of the Armor', was purposefully excluded from the relating of the scroll. We recall how R. Nachman waited until he exited the study hall before reciting the *Scroll* to R. Natan and R. Naftali.[83]

Without a doubt, the *Scroll* was secreted even from some of the closest of R. Nachman's followers. They were certainly not 'strangers.' We can deduce that knowledge of the *Scroll* was not the regular ticket of admission to the inner circle, but something much rarer and therefore much more precious.

The fact that after R. Nachman's death the Breslav court functioned with no formal Rebbe or official institutions, created a situation in which whatever group hierarchy did exist was not formalized by office, but rather (amongst other things) by knowledge – including knowledge of the secrets left behind by R. Nachman. Despite the best efforts of any member of the court to master as much of the exoteric material as he could, without knowledge of the esoterica, including the many censored sections within the exoterica, success was sure to be limited. Only those who had in their possession the most complete collection of the varied 'missing' tales, teachings, discourses and the like could hope to arrive at the most complete picture of the Rebbe's message.

Against this background, it seems that whoever was entrusted with the *Scroll*, was considered to be the highest interpretive authority regarding the mysteries of the Breslav worldview and R. Nachman's teachings. The social repercussions of this stance are apparent if we consider how only the smallest group had access to most of these writings, but are even more so, when we recall that the *Scroll* itself was to be entrusted to only one individual in every generation. In this context it really does not matter whether this tradition was initiated by R. Nachman himself, or was the product of later generations. In either case the Breslav court believed that the *Scroll*'s secret had been entrusted to only one individual and this Chasid was destined to serve as the keeper of the Breslav 'crown-jewels' – the most precious of esoteric texts. It was only natural that the individual selected for this task would be the most

83 R. Avraham Chazan, *Avneiha Barzel* (Jerusalem: 1983), 29-30.

qualified in all ways, both regarding knowledge and personal traits. His selection would confer upon him top authorative status regarding the world of Breslav, and especially everything related to messianism.

An example of this status is found in the person of R. Avraham son of Nachman Chazan who was believed by his peers to be the select one in possession of the Scroll.[84] Anything that he said regarding the future redemption and the messianic age was understood as completely authoritative; it was assumed that he knew the secrets of the end of days that lay in the *Scroll*. There exists an entire series of his statements which were attributed to the *Scroll* despite never actually being connected to it by R. Avraham himself. It was related that he once visited the Chasidic master R. Gershon Chanoch of Radzin. After reading his work on the identification of azure dye used in *tzitzit* (ritual fringes) he told R. Gershon: 'We have better proofs than these.' The Breslav court understood that he was referring to the *Scroll* in his possession, meaning that even before the arrival of the messiah the matter of azure dye would become known. [85] It was related that 'not a few in Uman knew that R. Avraham knows many things regarding the end of days, but does not reveal them. There were those in Uman who claimed that even the exact hour at which the righteous redeemer would appear (speedily in our day) is known to him. This was no mere exaggeration; for he is great in knowledge … they allowed him to receive the traditions of our Rebbe in their entirety – including this important particular hinted at in the *Scroll*.'[86] 'It was known to the court that R. Avraham son of R. Nachman was familiar with the Scroll of our Rebbe. Once when they talked with him concerning

---

84 R. Avraham was the son of R. Nachman of Tulchin, the main student of R. Natan. He wrote many commentaries on the works of R. Nachman, as well as historical books on R. Natan and the Breslav court. See Chazan, *Biur Halikutim*, 3-45.

85 Ibid., 29. A different version reads: When the Rav from Radzin's book on azure dye was published, R. Avraham said that there was no need for proofs for he has an even stronger basis for proving that one needed to wear azure. It seemed from what he said that he knew this from our Rebbe's *Scroll of Secrets*. *Siach Sorfei Kodesh*, vol. 3, 201-2. On the connection between azure and messianism in Breslav thought, see S. Z. Sargai, *Pa'amei Geula* (Jerusalem: 1967), 115-6.

86 Ibid., 31.

the end of the diaspora and the coming of the messiah, he replied: "I have not yet seen the messiah's grandfather.'"[87]

Now that we know what the *Scroll* actually contains, it is clear that these statements really had nothing to do with it. The *Scroll* never mentions azure, nor does it discuss exact timetables. The secret *Scroll*, however, excited the imaginations of the court and became the imagined source of any of R. Avraham's statements about the messiah. This gave them an air of utter authority – even though it was based on false pretenses. It was to him that many seeking answers to questions concerning the end of days turned. Such questions predated R. Avraham as well. R. Aaron Lipovetzki asked R. Naftali, 'You have heard the Scroll from our Rebbe. Where does this matter stand?'[88] We also know that R. Avraham was under pressure to reveal the Scroll or at least parts of it.

R. Levi Yitzchak Bander testified that in conversation with 'several important members of the inner circle' R. Avraham was asked by R. Mordechai, who was the head of the rabbinic court in Sokolov, 'Please…but R. Avraham turned the discussion to other matters…. Afterwards, I heard that R. Avraham entered into a discussion about the messiah king. R. Mordechai asked to know any particulars about the end of days, but he was not answered.'[89] This situation in which 'several important members of the inner circle' look to R. Avraham for answers to their questions concerning the end of days, exemplifies the status that his possession of the *Scroll* granted him.

At times, the pressure put upon him was not completely proper. In one of his visits to Uman it is told that 'one of his fellows insisted that he tell him something of the end of days. When he pleaded with him, R. Avraham told him one particular. Afterwards, R. Avraham regretted what he had done, wondering why he had not remained silent concerning such sublime matters. He prayed greatly that this individual would forget that which he was

---

87 *Siach Sorfei Kodesh*, vol. 3, 172.

88 Ibid., 83.

89 Chazan, *Biur Halikutim*, 31-32.

told. The next year, when R. Avraham returned to Uman, he tried to determine what this person knew and realized that he, in fact, knew nothing of what he had told him the previous year.'[90]

This 'miracle' follows similar ones which R. Nachman caused to occur regarding other secrets which he revealed, including the *Scroll.*

> The copyist said: I heard that at the time he said you are guarantors one to another that nothing will be revealed, another was also present. They were worried lest he tell someone, for he was known to be a chatterer. Although they thought this, they said nothing out of respect for our Rebbe. Our Rebbe answered – I am his guarantor. Afterwards they began to question this individual concerning what he knew of the tale and he knew nothing. They understood that this is what our Rebbe had told them – I am his guarantor – he had caused him to know nothing of the entire story.[91]

We recall another miracle of this type when he revealed the contents of the *Scroll.* In *Avneiha Barzel* R. Avraham relates:

> Our Rebbe began to tell of us of Russia and what would transpire until the coming of our redeemer and from then until the resurrection of the dead. Seated by our Rebbe was Reb Yoske, his son-in-law, with R. Natan and R. Naftali. Also two men from Teplik sat on the wagon's step – one on either side. Afterwards, when R. Natan engaged R. Yoske in conversation, he saw that that he knew nothing of what had been told .... The two others had also heard nothing.[92]

---

90 Ibid., 31. See also Rav Eliezer Schick, *Pe'ulat Hatzadik* (Jerusalem: 1944), 344-5.

91 *Hashmatot Mechayei Moharan*, 195. In a homily, 'R. Shimon began,' which deals with his tales, R. Nachman asserts that if one tells a story with the proper intention, 'then God ensures that one's words will not be remembered by an unsuitable student, rather he will forget them' (*Sefer Likutei Moharan Hamenukad*, I 60:7.

92 Chazan, *Avneiha Barzel*, 29-30.

In *Siach Sorfei Kodesh* the story is brought in a slightly different version, perhaps moving what is told regarding the *Tale of the Bread* to the *Scroll.*

> He commanded R. Natan and R. Naftali not to reveal this to anybody. Concerning R. Yoske, he said: I am responsible and his guarantor.[93] And so it was. Afterwards, when R. Natan engaged the rabbi, R. Yoske, in conversation, he saw that he knew nothing.[94]

We see that the cloud of mystery which surrounded the *Scroll* and other secrets was supported by supernatural events which helped to cause forgetfulness in those not suited to hear them. A distinct difference, though, can be detected between the miracles that accompanied R. Nachman and that which occurred to R. Avraham. In the latter's case, he needed to pray that his interlocutor would forget that which he was told. It was not at all certain that his prayers would be answered. R. Nachman, however, was able to guarantee that nothing of his secret would be revealed (or remembered) by those not worthy. However, something of R. Nachman's power was passed along to R. Avraham, who knew his secrets, and he was himself privileged to be part of a supernatural experience which protected the secret Scroll.

R. Avraham's authority for the Breslav court extends well beyond matters of redemption and the messiah. The consensus opinion in the court is that he represents the sole and central authority for all transmission of the Breslav tradition to later generations. Here too we can note that his authority rests not merely on what he taught and said, but also on that which he refrained from teaching.

> R. Avraham possessed many things that he left concealed and did not leave his lips. Those close to him knew that these things were not mere stories, but things which reached the heavens themselves which he had

93 See also Rav Chaim Menachem Kramer, *Toldot Moharnat: Be'aish Uvmayim* (Jerusalem: 1996), III 114.

94 *Siach Sorfei Kodesh*, vol. 1, 230.

> received from the most exceptional people who knew them. For the most part these were things that had to do with the end of days, some of which came to him from the *Scroll* which the Rebbe left to the most special of his students. As the inner circle used to say: 'In every generation there is but one who knows the contents of the wondrous *Scroll*.' Before him it was R. Aaron Libovetzski, the student of R. Naftali, the student of our Rebbe who knew the secrets of the end of days written therein. Afterwards, these were passed to the ear of R. Avraham the son of Nachman, who revealed nothing of what he kept in his heart.[95]

It seems, then, that the fact that R. Avraham became the guardian of the Scroll was one of the determining factors of his becoming the authoritative figure for Breslav which he was. He was the one who received 'the traditions of our Rebbe in their entirety.'[96] From here it was but a short step to the claim that 'the traditions of our Rebbe and his original path, with no embellishments at all, was transmitted **only** by R. Avraham son of Nachman to the following generations.'[97]

The unique level of secrecy attached to the *Scroll* created a Breslav ethos which described the transmission of the Breslav tradition in its fullest as belonging only to that unique individual to whom the *Scroll* itself had been entrusted. This meant that only this individual was qualified to lead the court and to be considered as the ultimate authority regarding all questions of its teachings and legacy.[98] The possession of the *Scroll* granted authority not only regarding the past, but also regarding the future – for only

95 Chazan, *Avneiha Barzel*, 31.

96 Ibid.

97 Ibid., 30.

98 It is worth noting that despite his unique position, R. Avraham son of R. Nachman never held any official position in the Breslav court. A good portion of his life was lived in abject poverty – often without a home of his own. He subsisted by living with others and off of their charity.

the *Scroll* carried the full description of the entire messianic process and a depiction of the end of days.

Alongside of the normal social and religious institutions, the system of secrets and secrecy which was part of the Breslav ethos created another way of shaping the court and community. The question whether an individual was worthy of knowing the secrets which properly belonged only to the inner circle or whether he was still a 'stranger' was one of the fundamental ways in which the community assembled itself. Which secrets could be revealed to whom? The answer to this question determined the hierarchy within the seemingly leaderless Breslav court. The secrecy surrounding the *Scroll* helped to form a model of leadership which was based not on expertise in the known Breslav oeuvre, but rather viewed he who had been crowned with the knowledge of and responsibility for the court's esoteric works as its head. Knowledge of the *Scroll* was the jewel in this crown for it not only represented knowledge of the end of days, but knowledge of the very persona and mission of R. Nachman himself.

CHAPTER NINE
The Messianic Revolution and the Echoes of the Scrolls among the Breslav Chasidim Today

By 2006 exactly 200 years had passed since the *Scroll*'s predictions of the messianic age were first revealed. For most of these years the Breslav court enjoyed a marginal existence at best. They were persecuted and pursued both by other Chasidic courts as well as the non-religious maskilim. A small minority, they suffered a diasporic life with small groups scattered here and there. Their yearly attempt at uniting in Uman for the Jewish New Year brought them more strife, as they were met with rocks and curses from all sides. Even when the harsher attacks subsided, they still did not gain legitimacy in the eyes of the rest of the Chasidic world.[1] The beginning of the twentieth-century saw some easing of their situation, as their ranks slowly grew. New members joined their community in both the Ukraine, their birth-place, and Poland. However, the tragic events of two world wars, and the horrors of the Holocaust and Communism, soon threatened to erase any memory of their court.

Surprisingly, it was in Israel that the court managed to reorganize, and since the 1970s even thrive. Their standing and R. Nachman's status increased substantially throughout the Jewish world and began to seize a unique niche in Israeli culture. Thousands of new Chasidim, many of

1 See David Asaf, " *The Causeless Hatred is Ongoing: The Struggle against Breslav Chasidism in the 1860s*," *Zion* 59 (1994): 465-6 and fn. 1.

whom had no previous connection to the court, joined their ranks. Yeshivot were opened and communities established both in Israel and elsewhere. The court broke into different branches, each with its own leadership and philosophy. During this time, the court became, for the first time since its founding, something more than a small, marginal group. It grew into a large, influential community.

The status of R. Nachman has undergone even more radical change. From an insignificant nobody, known only to his closest followers, he has become known as a *tzadik* – accepted by thousands not even attached to Breslav. The most obvious expression of this change is the massive pilgrimage to Uman that now takes place every year at Rosh Hashana. Tens of thousands arrive each year at the Rebbe's tomb – religious and secular, Ashkenazi and Sefardi, Chasidim and not – all come to celebrate Rosh Hashana with R. Nachman. Most do come from Israel, but America, Canada and France are also well represented. Aside from those who see R. Nachman as a religious authority, there are many others who see in him a source of inspiration for their own very different lives and life's-work. R. Nachman's presence in Israeli society has grown by leaps and bounds and is found in literature, theatre, cinema and music.

It is no wonder, then, that many Breslav Chasidim feel that the age of R. Nachman's anonymity has passed and the age for which all had hoped has, in fact, commenced. The time when those who believed that R. Nachman represented the ultimate *tzadik*, preparing the way for final redemption and the coming of the messiah, were forced to live with a reality in which he was barely noticed, has ended. No longer is the site of the Rebbe's tomb hidden by others; no longer are his teachings ridiculed. Thousand come to his grave; thousands more drink from his words. The fact that in the Breslav oeuvre itself much is made of the connection between their acceptance and the dawning of the messianic age has led many to see the Breslav renaissance as heralding the long awaited messianic end of days itself: a messianic revolution. We know the claim made that 'We have a tradition from our Rebbe that he said: When my book is accepted in the world it will be possible to prepare for the messiah.'[2] Today when R. Nachman's works have become bestsellers, well loved in all of Israel, perhaps preparations should, in fact, begin.

While the feeling of renewal has permeated all layers of Breslav society, it is perhaps most noticeable among those branches of the court which came into being in the second half of the twentieth century. The messianic expectations, in a variety of ways, have become one of their major foci. While a full investigation of this phenomenon would require its own book-length treatment, I would like to offer just two examples of the ways that messianic fervor has made its presence felt in the Breslav world and attempt to gauge the role that the *Scroll* has played in this.

The first example is taken from the court of R. Israel Odesser, known as 'The Saba' by his followers. This is a neo-Breslav branch, small in size, and not accepted by other parts of the court. Nonetheless, it garners a good amount of attention in the Israeli public sphere. R. Odesser (1888-1994) claimed that he happened to find a note in a book – a note that was sent to him personally by R. Nachman. Among other things written in the note was the line – *N(a), Nach, Nachm(a), Nachman of Uman* – which became a sort of mantra and charm among his followers. Another line – *My fire will burn until the coming of the messiah* – was understood as R. Nachman's song of the future. They call it the 'song of redemption.' At first it was believed that in the note was the suggestion that R. Israel would not die before the coming of the messiah. As he aged, reaching 106 by his death, this belief became stronger. With his passing, though, the belief underwent a revision: the wide-spread publication of this note would hasten the coming of the messiah. This explains the great efforts

2 *Siach Sorfei Kodesh*, vol. 1-5 (Jerusalem: 1994), vol. 3, 83. Similar claims appear elsewhere, as well. 'We heard from his holy mouth that his holy book, *Likutei Moharan*, which was published was the beginning of the redemption ... and he said that the study of his holy writings was the beginning of the redemption' [*Chayei Moharan Im Hashmatot*, (Jerusalem: 2000), 314-19]. Also: 'The copyist said: The concealment of the wonderous great light of our Master ... may it be Your will that the truth will be revealed in the world and his holiness made known throughout the world. Then redemption will come speedily in our day' (ibid., 344-5).

made by R. Israel's followers to spread the 'N(a), Nach, Nachm(a), Nachman of Uman' throughout the land. It has spread well beyond the normal borders of the Chasidic world and there is probably no one in Israel who has not heard or seen it.[3]

In this branch's literature we find different references, direct and oblique, to the *Scroll.* One of them, while not the most direct, is important as it shows us something quite important regarding the messianic hopes of the Breslav sect. R. Israel Yitzchak Bezonson, one of it leaders, mentioned that the well-known note was not the only one which the Saba received from heaven.

> 'The time of redemption is near!' Thus the Saba saw in one of the notes. Once in Uman he told his student, R. Aaron, my friend: 'The wonder child will come to Uman. He will enter the tomb of R. Nachman. He will resurrect R. Nachman's son from Feige in order to bring him to Jerusalem. He will install him in the House of the Holy of Holies in order to serve there forever!'[4]

The Saba told two different versions of how the note reading 'The time of redemption is near' came into his hands. In one of them he received it like he did the famous note: 'I opened a book and there was a piece of paper upon which was written "The time of redemption is near."'[5] The other version describes a scroll which he received from his teacher, R. Israel Cardoner. In one section he found 'written in large beautiful letters in this language – "The time of redemption is near."'[6] According to descriptions

---

3 On the success of this campaign, Garb wrote: 'A visitor from another planet might take a look at the city centers of Israel and conclude that this slogan was one of the central religious tenets of Judaism' [Jonathan Garb, *The Chosen Will Become Herds: Studies in Twentieth Century Kabbalah* (Jerusalem: 2004), 153].

4 Rav Yisrael Yitzchak Bezanson, *Ga'aguim* (Tel Aviv: 1995), 160-1.

5 Hasaba Yisrael Ber Odesser, *Sichot Metoch Chayei Hasaba Yisrael Ber Odesser* (Jerusalem: 1998), 425.

6 Ibid., 287.

of the scroll mentioned elsewhere, it is clear that R. Israel understood that this was the *Scroll of Secrets* itself.[7]

Even though it seems that the text related in the other 'heavenly note' which he received was not based upon existing Breslav traditions, the influence of the *Scroll* is still apparent – especially regarding the matter of a 'wonder child'. As mentioned above, the tradition of a messianic child is found already in the prophecies of Isaiah – 'A child will be born to us, a son given us – leadership placed upon his shoulders. And he will be called Pele Yoetz, of the warrior Aviad Sar Shalom.'[8] In the narrower Breslav context, it is clear that when such statements are made with reference to R. Nachman's grave the connection to the 'wonder-child' of the *Scroll* is quite manifest.

We can also note that there does seem to be a connection between R. Odesser's view of himself as a figure who is a continuation of R. Nachman and the literary motif found in R. Nachman's writings which bring together the very old with the very young: the grandfather with the infant. R. Odesser (the elder-infant) himself attempted to bring R. Nachman's remains from the Ukraine to Israel. His followers have made other similar attempts since.

Another neo-Breslav group which has focused much energy and publicity on messianism of late is that group led by R. Eliezer Shlomo Schick. R. Schick divides his time between two Breslav concentrations – one in the Israeli Galil town Yavnael, and the other in New York. Mendel Piekarz has produced a detailed study of this group and its leader[9] showing that R. Schick sees himself as the leader of a religious messianic renewal movement. This movement began in 1965 and had been already predicted by R. Avraham Chazan fifty years previously. It was in this year that R. Schick began to gather large numbers of youth to the Breslav camp and to distribute tens of thousands of copies of R. Nachman's various writings – 'one of the hints

---

7 Compare to what appears on p.280-3.

8 Isaiah 9:5.

9 Mendel Piekarz, *Studies in Bratslav Hasidism*, expanded ed. (Jerusalem: 1995), 199-218.

that our salvation is near'.[10] The year 1976 was also noteworthy, according to R. Schick, as a year which could have been that in which the messiah revealed himself. However, the Breslavian model of missed chances, well-known from both the days of R. Nachman and R. Natan,[11] was repeated as harsh criticism against R. Schick erupted from other branches of the Breslav court. This prevented 'a great chance in the year 1976 for the revelation of the messiah and the light of R. Nachman.'[12]

The crowning glory[13] of all of R. Schick's work is the monumental responsa project which he initiated. In over ten thousand letters he anwers a huge range of queries from his followers. These letters have been collected and printed in a series of books called *Asher Banachal* (That Which is in the Riverbed). So far, 51 volumes have been published, and according to the publisher they have enough material for another 250! Since the collection of R. Natan's letters, *Alim Letrufa* (Healing Leaves) was published, such works are not strange to the Breslav community. However, the incredible volume of R. Schick's epistolary output, as well as the attention given to this project by his followers, is novel. Some have wondered what has spurred this seeming obsession.

Perhaps the answer lies in the *Scroll*. The very beginning of the messiah's public career is described as answering queries from and writing letters to all of Israel.

> And he will send epistles to all of the wise-men and they will send him the sons of the kings and each one will write to his father....[14]

---

10 Rav Eliezer Schick, *Pe'ulat Hatzadik* (Jerusalem: 1944), 722. See also 611.

11 See above, chapter 1 the text adjacent to note 33.

12 Rav Eliezer Schick, *Asher Banachal*, vol. 3 (Jerusalem: 1976), 43. This is also discussed in Piekarz, *Studies in Bratslav Hasidism*, 217.

13 Piekarz, *Studies in Bratslav Hasidism*, 201.

14 Section I, lines 13..

At the outset he will send [responsa?][15]

Initially he will be accepted as the halachic authority throughout Israel as he
begins to scrutinize the Torah until he attains deep insights. They [will] begin to send him queries until it is accepted by all that he is the premier halachic authority
in all of Israel.[16]

This seems to be the model for R. Schick's own project. The writing and receiving of letters is the very method by which the messiah is able to be accepted by all of Israel. Once his status is established, he will be able to lead all to 'prayer and contemplative introspection … enabling all to become Breslav Chasidim.'[17] This in turn will enable 'the revelation of the messiah and the light of R. Nachman.'[18]

Finally, it seems that our own time, especially 2006 – 200 years after the *Scroll* was originally related – may have its own interesting messianic potential. In the year 1806, after the death of the child Shlomo Efraim, R. Nachman stated that due to the great conflicts surrounding him, the messiah's arrival was delayed by 100 years.[19] The conflicts and persecutions which later engulfed R. Natan brought him to claim that these pushed off the messiah's arrival for another 100 years.[20] If we may be a bit radical, perhaps we should see in the publication of the *Scroll* here for the first time in 2006 something of a fin de siecle – as each of the two hundred year periods spoken of by R. Nachman and R. Natan have expired. Perhaps the revelation of what had been the most closely guarded secret of

15 Ibid.,

16 Section II, line 9.

17 Schick, *Asher Banachal* 3, 47.

18 Ibid., 43. This is also discussed in Piekarz, *Studies in Bratslav Hasidism*, 217.

19 *Siach Sorfei Kodesh*, vol. 2, 112.

20 Rav Avraham Chazan, *Yemei Hatlaot* (Jerusalem: 1933), 50. See note 11 above.

the Breslav court exactly 200 years after its initial recitation has its own messianic meaning. Perhaps this publication will itself help to fan the expectations for the messiah in our own day.[21]

However, the Scroll's real strength does not lie in its applicability to certain dates, but in its ability to present its reader with a unique messianic vision. The messianic age described by the *Scroll* is a time full of love of man and peace, prayer and wisdom. The reader of the *Scroll* is met by a world renewed through the longings created by song and melody. Reading the *Scroll* and listening to its unique voice may indeed instill in us a yearning to hear for ourselves the long awaited song of the redeemer.

---

21 This calculation seems to have served as the basis for the prediction of R. Eliezer Berland, the head of Yeshivat Shuvu Banim (the largest Breslav yeshiva today), that the Hebrew year 5766 (2005-6) was to be the year of redemption. This is connected to what he called the 'secret of the sixes': Every hundred years, the 66th year was especially auspicious for the arrival of the messiah. This itself is based on the Zohar's text which reads, 'In 66 the messiah-king will be revealed' (119a). R. Berland mentioned this in a sermon which he delivered in the spring of 2005 (recorded on CD no. 434, Machon Har Tzion).

CHAPTER TEN
EPILOGUE

Our Rebbe said: I am an enigma, which even after uncovering remains a secret.[1]

Despite having removed the veil covering much of the *Scroll*, many of its secrets remain unsolved. A number of lines of text are still encoded[2] and our attempts at deciphering them cannot be checked against any verifiable source – rather they are merely our best guesses. The difficulty in deciphering the *Scroll* is not only a result of the way in which the text was written – using abbreviations and acronyms – but also of its unique transmission history. The oral discourses of R. Nachman describing the coming of the redeemer were transcribed in shorthand. Regarding the first recitation of the *Scroll*, we know that 'most was forgotten.'[3] It is reasonable to assume that taken together these factors contributed to a wide discrepancy between that which R. Nachman actually said and that which was recorded.

It is my hope that the publication of the *Scroll* will serve to raise interest in its secrets such that as others begin its study, some of its still puzzling textual difficulties will be solved. Furthermore, I hope that the exposure of this once secret text will lead to a willingness to reveal other manuscripts and materials still unknown[4] which will help to fill in the many textual and

---

1 "Pnu Lachem Tzefona," *Or Haorot* 14. This statement is also found with slight variations in Avraham Zagdon, *Eilu Yadativ Hiyativ* (Beitar Elite: 2002), II 420; *Siach Sorfei Kodesh*, vol. 1-5 (Jerusalem: 1994), vol. 2, 15; vol. 4, 114; vol. 6, 78.

2 To the best of my knowledge no members of the Breslav court know their meaning.

3 Rav Natan of Nemirov, *Yemei Moharnat* (Jerusalem: 1982), I 21.

4 These include the manuscript of the *Scroll* mentioned in *Neveh Tzadikim* and the tape-recording of R. Yitzchak Levi Brand, one of the previous generation's leaders of the Breslav

conceptual gaps remaining in our understanding of the *Scroll*. The possibility that new textual evidence will help us to better understand the *Scroll*, as well as the hope that the publication of the *Scroll* will open scholarly debate of its themes, led me to think that this book may need to be understood as a first edition – a first attempt at deciphering the mysteries of the *Scroll*. My hope is that future versions of this work will be able to take advantage of texts and ideas which have yet to be discovered, thus granting us a fuller picture of the *Scroll*'s actual text and concerns.

Any messianism is by definition a collection of hopes and beliefs focused on the future. However, these hopes also reflect upon the continuation of the present as well. The specific characteristics of messianic hopes form the future ideal around which present-day life is centered. The *Scroll* is a miniature, packed with detail, presenting a future vision which helps us to understand the goal towards which the Breslav ethos aspires. The *Scroll*, which affords a glimpse into a Breslavian future based upon the messiah, is another piece of R. Nachman's colorful spiritual-literary mosaic – one which colors the rest of his works. Teachings, discourses, sermons and speeches – the behavioral models of the *tzadik* – all these are cast in a new light when seen not only as descriptions of the present, but also as harbingers of the messianic vision which R. Nachman spread out before us in the *Scroll*.

The connection of this messianic vision to the present is also an expression of the unique role-model which R. Nachman presented to his followers throughout his life. He represented for them the Moses-messiah of the future – allowing his Chasidim to taste the heady draught of the end of days in their own lifetimes. The mission-based consciousness of R. Nachman was passed on from him to his followers, continuing to echo throughout the court to this day. The flowering of the Breslav court (and consciousness) over the past few decades has heightened the messianic dimension found in R. Nachman's works as their wide-spread distribution is in itself one of the harbingers of messianic times described therein. The widespread fascination with the spiritual world of R. Nachman and the feelings of renewal which accompany it have not been limited to

---

Court, discussing the *Scroll*.

Breslav Chasidim and scholars alone. The world of Breslav has overflowed its banks and reached thousands for whom R. Nachman's ideas have become part and parcel of their lives. It would not be surprising, then, to venture that the study of the *Scroll of Secrets* – the key to the Breslav messianic vision – within whose words we find a vision filled with Torah, wisdom and prayer – searching and longing, music and song, fraternity and love – will itself grow until that day when the messiah himself finally arrives – speedily in our day, amen.

Appendix One

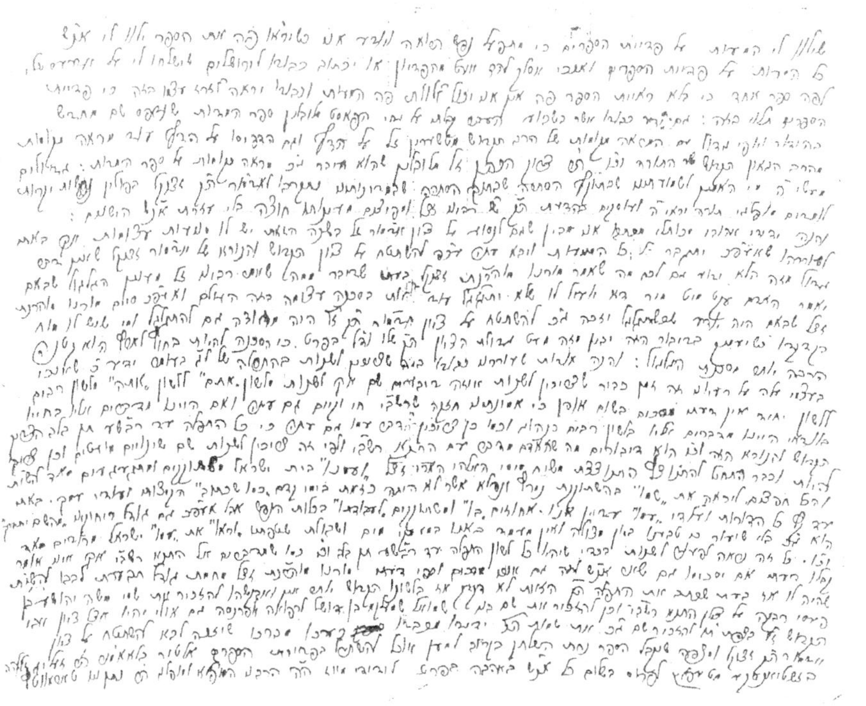

PICTURE ONE

From the letter sent by R. Alter Tepliker to R. Yisrael Halperin. His signature is visible in the second to last and last lines.

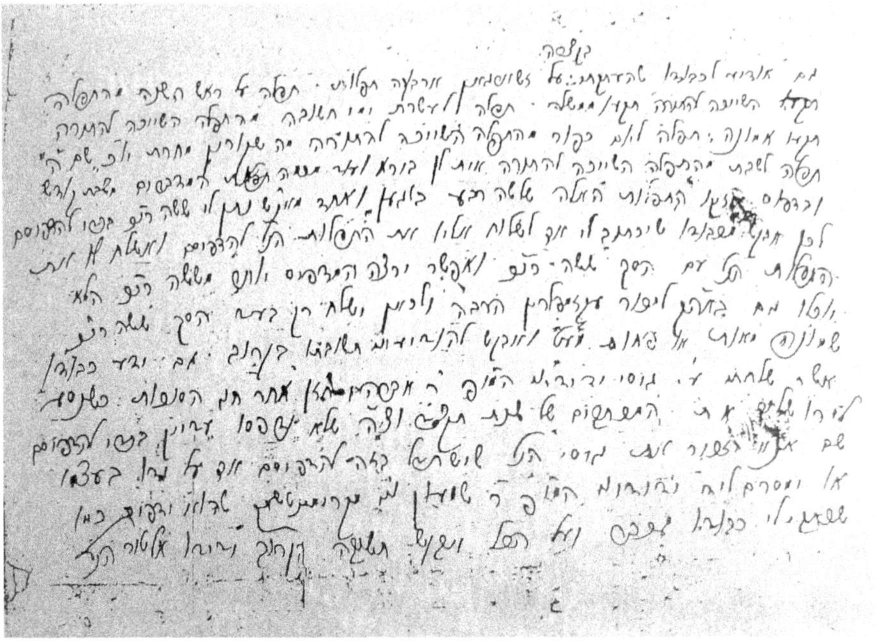

PICTURE TWO

An addition to R. Alter's letter regarding the copying and printing of Breslav works. He mentions his brother-in-law, R. Avraham Chazan. His signature is visible at the end of the last line.

Appendix Two
Further Testimony Concerning the Scroll and its Transmission

R. Natan Zvi Koenig attempted to resolve the contradiction between the reported loss of the *Scroll* (as detailed in *Yemei Moharnat*) and the fact of its continued existence among the Breslav court. 'It is possible that they found the writings afterwards or in the time of R. Nachman of Tulchin.'[1] The assumption behind this explanation is that in R. Nachman of Tscherin's generation there was only one copy of the *Scroll* and that this copy was lost. Therefore, if we find another extant copy at a later time, it must be because the *Scroll* was somehow rediscovered. We should also recall the Breslav tradition which held that only one individual in every generation was to be privy to the secret of the *Scroll*. Ensuring that only one copy of the *Scroll* existed at any given time was one way of ensuring that this tradition was upheld.

However, this assumption may not be true. It is quite possible that already in R. Natan's time there were two distinct copies of the *Scroll*: one in his possession and the other in the hands of R. Naftali to whom the secret of the *Scroll* was also originally revealed.[2] The first copy that was among R. Natan's papers and which was handed on to R. Nachman of Tscherin may have been lost. However, the second copy, R. Naftali's copy, may very well have made its way into the hands of R. Avraham son of R. Nachman and R. Alter Tepliker. According to R. Koenig's own account at least two copies

1 Rav Natan Zvi Koenig, *Neveh Tzadikim* (Bnei Brak: 1969), 78-9.

2 It seems that there were two distinct copies of the same text – each written by R. Natan – and not two different summaries of what was revealed by R. Nachman.

of the *Scroll* were extant in the days of R. Avraham son of R. Nachman: one in R. Avraham's possession, but, also his brother-in-law, R. Alter, 'possessed writings as well'.[3]

R. Koenig's suggested solution to the problem of the extant *Scroll* (its passage from R. Nachman of Tulchin, R. Avraham Chazan's father, to his son and son-in-law) is not the only history of transmission of which we know. In fact, this account is somewhat disputed by a passage found in the book *Avneiha Barzel*.

> Once R. Nachman of Tulchin asked R. Natan why he didn't give the Master's *Scroll* to his son R. Yitzchak and to R. Efraim, R. Naftali's son. He answered: 'I am upset with them for engaging in business. If they refrained from business, God would provide from them.'[4]

This tradition reveals that even the sons of R. Naftali and R. Natan were not deemed suitable to receive the *Scroll*. Now if we combine what we find here with the tradition that only one individual in every generation merits keeping the *Scroll*'s secret, we may assume that at the time of the telling of this story R. Nachman of Tulchin did not yet possess the *Scroll*. If he had, he would not have suggested revealing it to another. (However, it may be that the entire episode is meant to exhibit R. Nachman of Tulchin's modesty. His suggestion/question was actually after the fact – a demurral regarding his own worth vis-à-vis the sons of those who first received the secret.)[5]

---

3 According to R. Koenig the chain of transmission went through R. Nachman of Tulchin. He passed it on to his son-in-law, R. Alter, and he also passed it on to his son, R. Avraham Chazan.

4 R. Avraham Chazan, *Avneiha Barzel* (Jerusalem: 1983), 81. R. Avraham Chazan attempted to temper this criticism somewhat by explaining that despite working, these two spent much time in study as well. See R. Avraham Chazan, *Sichot Vesipurim (Printed with Kochvei or)* (Jerusalem: 1983), 285-6.

5 It is worth noting that in a later and corrected version of *Avneiha Barzel* published under the supervision of R. Yitzchak Levi Brand, this episode is not recorded. According to R. Avraham Weitzhandler (see the introduction note 26), this deletion was not an attempt to supress criticism of the two, but rather regarding the authenticity of the tradition itself. R.

R. Nachman of Tscherin mentioned in *Yemei Moharnat* a surprising suspicion concerning the *Scroll*'s fate. He claims that it was not lost, but rather stolen.[6] If this is indeed the case, then we may assume that such an act was not that of any ordinary thief with the usual interest in financial gain. Rather, the thief may very well have been a Breslav Chasid, who thirsted after the precious words of his Rebbe. It was through his thievery that the *Scroll* survived until our day.

According to R. Koenig's account, the *Scroll* belonged to R. Natan, found its way to R. Nachman of Tscherin among his writing, was lost, then once again found and made its way somehow to R. Nachman of Tulchin. The latter then passed it on to his son R. Avraham Chazan and, it appears, also to R. Alter of Teplik. This reconstructed tradition does not take into account the copyist's comments that the transcription was made from a copy of *Chayei Moharan* which belonged to R. Naftali.

R. Koenig quotes from the *Scroll* 'a line or two upon which R. Nachman's admonition [against publication] does not apply.'

> Happy will be the strong of faith in those days.... The general rule: Despite what has transgressed during the near 2000 year exile, we expect that he will arrive any day. Even if he should tarry, we await him [for] he will surely come and not be late. Even though all the ends [of days] have come and gone, he will certainly come and be beautiful and very pleasant. Happy is he who merits this - may he strengthen his faith then.[7]

He also added the following.

> Also there from the words of R. Avraham son of R. Nachman of Tulchin (obm): The matter of the Josephian messiah is [because] of

---

Yitzchak Levi Brand did not feel that R. Nachman of Tulchin would suggest that these two figures could have been the ideal persons to receive the *Scroll*.

6 Rav Natan of Nemirov, *Yemei Moharnat* (Jerusalem: 1982), I, 21.

7 Koenig, *Neveh Tzadikim*, 79.

> that which will happen to the Davidian messiah. He will need the merit of those *tzadikim* who have died. The Josephian messiah will die before him. Our Rebbe said ... for our Rebbe was completely pure regarding sexual matters... Our Rebbe said ... until after some time he reached the higher levels and saw until where the defect itself reached. He wanted to repair this completely, but it is not possible to change nature ... akin to the Joseph regarding keeping the covenant ...and the messiah ... May the truth be revealed in the world, quickly in our day, amen.[8]

This passage, marked by numerous ellipses, is not part of the *Scroll* itself. It is taken from the additions added by R. Avraham Chazan. It is quoted by R. Koenig because it appears together with the *Scroll* and refers to the same messianic matters. In the 'Sichot Me'anash' manuscript this section appears in full immediately following the text of the *Scroll.* (This manuscript is the subject of Appendix 4).

R. Natan's Biography

R. Chaim Kramer wrote an extensive biography of R. Natan which mentions the *Scroll* and describes those events which preceded its second revelation.

> On Friday, the eighth of Menacham Av 5669 our Master revealed the *Scroll* for a second time... At that time when he was prepared to reveal it again he did not desire to do so to any except for R. Natan and R. Naftali. He was at the time in the synagogue together with R. Natan, R. Naftali and R. Aaron, the rabbi of Breslav. Our Master waited and the minute that R. Aaron left the room – he rose and locked the door. Even though R. Aaron was a holy man, he [R. Nachman] did not want to reveal the *Scroll* to him, but only to these two of his followers.

8 Ibid.

> Therefore when R. Aaron was outside, our Master revealed it to R. Natan and R. Naftali.[9]

Regarding the Tepliker manuscript, including the *Scroll*, found in the contemporary Breslav court, Kramer writes:

> As mentioned, the *Scroll* was written in acronyms so that no one would understand it. There the entire sequence of the arrival of the messiah is recorded. It is worthwhile to copy the end of the manuscript as it appears in the copy belonging to one of the great Chasidim, R. Alter of Teplik: 'The general rule, despite what has transpired during the near 2000 year exile, we expect that he will arrive any day. Even if he should tarry, we await him [for] he will surely come and not be late. Even though all the ends [of days] have come and gone, he will certainly come and it will be beautiful and very pleasant for he who strengthens his faith then, for there will be great trials at that time'. (This is the conclusion of the *Scroll*.)[10]

This is quite similar to the quote found in *Neveh Tzadikim* with a few minor changes. It may be that these differences stem from the fact that the text was not copied from *Neveh Tzadikim*, but rather from a copy of the *Scroll* itself – another Tepliker manuscript. In his notes on this chapter, Kramer adds a few more details:

> A few pages from some book written in barely legible acronyms found among a few Breslav Chasidim and known as the '*Scroll of Secrets*' is contained in the pamphlet of the writings of R. Alter of Teplik.[11]

---

9 Rav Chaim Menachem Kramer, *Toldot Moharnat: Be'aish Uvmayim* (Jerusalem: 1996), III, 169.

10 Ibid.

11 Kramer, *Toldot Moharnat: Be'aish Uvmayim*, 584, note 7.

The description of the *Scroll's* transmission in *Toldot Moharnat* is based upon that which appears in *Siach Sorfei Kodesh*. However, the author also adds the following story:

> R. Hirsch Leib Lippel[12] once told that on the night of R. Natan's yartzeit, the tenth of Tevet, he was in the house of R. Avraham Sternhartz.[13] Due to the cold stormy weather on that same night, no one else had ventured out and so the two of them were alone. He heard from him parts of the *Scroll* and he also showed him a manuscript of *Chayei Moharan* which contained a section of the *Scroll*. (Told by R. Nachman Borshtein[14])[15]

No details concerning how the *Scroll* came in to the hands of R. Sternhartz are mentioned. Neither are any attempts made to square this episode with the tradition that the *Scroll* was passed on to R. Avraham Chazan.[16]

---

12 He died in 2000. For information on him, see Gedaliah Fleer, *Against All Odds* (Jerusalem Breslav Research Institute 2005), 151-9.

13 He was the great-grandson of R. Natan and the grandson of R. Nachman of Tscherin. He was also known by his Hebrew name, R. Avraham Sofer Kochav Lev. He authored Tovot Zichronot (Bnai Brak, 1978) which included much previously unpublished Breslav material. He came to Israel in 1935 and established the Breslav New Year's gathering at Mt. Meron. He expired in 1956. For more on him, see Kramer, *Toldot Moharnat: Be'aish Uvmayim*, 620-1.

14 One of the Breslav elders, may he live long.

15 Kramer, *Toldot Moharnat: Be'aish Uvmayim*, 584, note 7.

16 Some members of the court have told me that a recording exists of R. Lipel asserting that he possessed a copy of Chayei Moharan written by R. Natan and that R. Avraham Sternhartz had a copy in the hand of R. Naftali. I hope to study these manuscripts in the future.

Peulat Hatzadik[17]

Another source which offers evidence that the *Scroll* was, in fact, extant is a Breslav hagiography on R. Nachman written by R. Eliezer Shlomo Schick.[18] It is important to note before discussing this work, however, that Schick's standing in both the Breslav and scholarly communities is problematic. Among the first (except for his own followers), his work is disparaged as 'imaginary'. His critics maintain that he makes up for his lack of knowledge by inserting claims which have no basis in either Breslav tradition or texts. The main Breslav court in Jerusalem has several times sought to censure him and his writings.[19] Among the scholarly community, on the other hand, Schick is criticized for his use of scholarly materials (whose influence is noticeable in his writings) without proper attribution.[20]

As a result of these questions concerning his work, it is not possible to see his writing as an accurate reflection of Breslav traditions. Rather it seems to be more a reflection of various studies which he has read. Despite this, we cannot dismiss his actual deep familiarity with the Breslav oeuvre and the fact that he possesses a number of authentic Breslav manuscripts.

Regarding the *Scroll*, he claimed:

> I have in my possession a copy of the Tepliker manuscript – the two sections of the *Scroll of Secrets*. The first section describes what was related on Sunday the fifth of Av 5566, and the second section describes what was related on Friday, Sabbath-eve the eighth of Av 5569... Due to our Master's warning that it be kept secret, even though it is written in undecipherable acronyms, I have kept from publishing it and have kept it to myself in manuscript.[21]

---

17 The first edition was published in New York in 1978.

18 This is discussed above.

19 See for example the notice censuring him found in David Assaf, *Breslav: An Annotated Bibliography* (Jerusalem: 2000), 84-5.

20 See Piekarz, *Studies in breslav Hasidism*, expanded ed. (Jerusalem: 1996), 200, note 1.

21 Rav Eliezer Schick, *Pe'ulat Hatzadik* (Jerusalem: 1944), 344.

R. Schick reveals here that which the inner circle and the Jerusalem court keep hidden.[22]

He offers other details from the *Scroll* as well.

> At the end of the first section it is written: 'At first they will not recognize that he is the one, afterwards each one will come to acknowledge that he is the messiah until all know this. And [it] concludes: 'Much has been forgotten and never transcribed for the telling of all this took two hours and he prohibited us from discussing the matter and ordered us to write it in code. Immediately the majority was forgotten for it was not transcribed immediately.'[23]

> After the second section it is written as follows: At first there will be a mighty argument. And they will say, 'This is the messiah?!' They will say in these words, 'The messiah isn't a fancy hat!' (That is, he goes about with such a hat or such clothing). The general rule: Despite what has transpired during the near 2000 year exile, we expect that he will arrive any day. Even if he should tarry, we await him [for] he will surely come and not be late. Even though all the ends [of days] have come and gone, he will certainly come and be beautiful and very pleasant. Happy is he who merits this - may he strengthen his faith then for there will be great trials.' This is the conclusion of the second section of the *Scroll*.[24]

R. Schick, beyond revealing a few of the *Scroll*'s lines, also offers a description of its transmission which differs in a number of important ways from that held by the rest of the Breslav world.

---

22 See Zvi Mark, "*The Tale of the Bread – A Hidden Story of R. Nahman of Braslav*," *Tarbitz* 72, no. 3 (1993): 419-20.

23 Schick, *Pe'ulat Hatzadik*, 344.

24 Ibid., 504.

> It is well known among the inner-circle that R. Natan passed the *Scroll* (that is what is written therein) to his closest follower, R. Nachman of Tulchin. Once R. Nachman of Tulchin asked R. Natan why he didn't give the Master's *Scroll* to his son R. Yitzchak and to R. Efraim, R. Naftali's son. He answered: 'I am upset with them for engaging in business. If they refrained from business, God would lead them and provide for them.' R. Nachman of Tulchin passed it on to his son, R. Avraham. R. Avraham at first saw how R. Ezekiel of Uman gave of himself so to further our Master's works – and he gave him the *Scroll*. However, afterwards he came to greatly regret revealing it to him, for he saw that he wasn't truly as he thought. Even though he gave a great deal of charity, it was forbidden to have revealed the *Scroll* to strangers. Therefore, he prayed for a full year that R. Ezekiel would forget that which had been revealed to him. And so it was – the next year when R. Avraham arrived from the Land of Israel for the New Year, he began to question R. Ezekiel and understood from his words that he knew nothing. Then R. Avraham passed it on to … and he to …. May God grant us good tidings, amen, may it be His will.[25]

R. Schick claims that R. Natan passed the *Scroll* on to R. Nachman of Tulchin and it was transmitted on from there. This, of course, stands in contradistinction to the tradition presented in *Siach Sorfei Kodesh* and in the *Sichot Me'anash* manuscript. According to that tradition R. Natan did not transmit the *Scroll* to anyone. As it was to be entrusted to only one person in every generation, he was content to let it stay in the hands of R. Naftali who survived him. It also contradicts the tradition according to which R. Naftali passed the *Scroll* on to R. Aaron of Lipvotsk. Here it was R. Nachman of Tulchin who became the recipient who then passed it on to his son, R. Avraham Chazan.

The question that R. Nachman of Tulchin asked R. Natan concerning his refusal to pass the *Scroll* to his own son is now understood as wondering why the *Scroll* was not passed on to *others as well*. It is asked after the *Scroll* has been already revealed to R. Nachman of Tulchin.

---

25 Ibid., 344-5. The ellipses are in the original.

Who Heard the Scroll in its Second Telling?

In R. Schick's telling, the second revelation of the *Scroll* differs from what we have seen until now.

> Friday, 8th of Av: R. Naftali was together with our Master. (R. Natan was absent for our Master had sent him to his brother-in-law, R. Zvi, in the town of Berditchev so that he could collect a debt which was owed him). Our Master discussed with him matters of faith... and continued to discuss this in depth. During this [discussion] our Master began to reveal to him the second section of the *Scroll*.[26]

In a note R. Schick adds:

> And because R. Naftali knew that R. Natan had been privileged to hear the first section of the *Scroll* – he therefore revealed to him the second section of the *Scroll* afterwards. It stayed sealed and was transmitted only orally.[27]

It was not, then, R. Nachman who revealed the second section of the *Scroll* to R. Natan, and it was not even upon his instructions to R. Naftali that he came to know of it. Rather, R. Naftali, on his own initiative decided to tell him what had been revealed to him.

I know of no other Breslav source which excludes R. Natan from the second telling of the *Scroll*. The only such source for this is an argument made by the scholar Joseph Weiss. It seems that this is R. Schick's source as well. However, before turning to Weiss' claim, it is worth recounting the other traditions concerning the second telling of the *Scroll*.

In *Yemei Moharnat* we find the following description: 'Afterwards it is written there[:] that which they heard again about this matter today on

26 Ibid., 502-4.

27 Ibid., 504, note 90.

Friday Sabbath eve, 8 Menachem Av 5569 here in the town of Breslav, etc.' As the preceding description detailing the first telling is in the first-person plural, and the speaker is R. Natan, we may assume that the 'they heard' in this second description also includes R. Natan once again as one of those who heard the second telling of the *Scroll*.

The description in *Avneiha Barzel* is even clearer regarding R. Natan's inclusion in the second telling. 'Afterwards he called them [referring to R. Natan and R. Naftali who were mentioned previously] ... and related the *Scroll* to them for a second time.'[28] R. Chaim Kramer also included both R. Natan and R. Naftali in the second telling.[29] So too did the account in *Siach Sorfei Kodesh* and Fleer in *Against All Odds*.[30]

Joseph Weiss understands the above quote from *Yemei Moharnat* differently, however. According to his interpretation, as the first telling is described by R. Natan using 'we' and in the second, which we may assume is also described by R. Natan, he used 'they' – Weiss concludes that R. Natan excluded himself from those who were present at the second telling in Breslav.[31] However, Weiss' logic may be faulty here. There is no doubt that the beginning of the quote in *Yemei Moharnat* is not a direct quote in the words of R. Natan. It begins, 'Afterwards it is written there.' It is clear that 'there' means in the *Scroll* and this is the language of one describing the *Scroll* – here R. Nachman of Tscherin and not R. Natan. The words of the former may very well be included in the continuation of the sentence, 'which they heard again about this matter.' Only in the next part of this sentence, where it states, 'here in Breslav' is it apparent that the *Scroll* itself is being quoted. However, it is not clear that the end of the sentence and its beginning are

---

28 Chazan, *Avneiha Barzel*, 31; *Siach Sorfei Kodesh*, vol. 1, 230. Although Weiss shows how the text from Avneiha Barzel is corrupted and what refers to the second section of the Scroll actually relates to the first section, there seems to be no reason to doubt their authenticity once placed correctly. See Joseph Weiss, *Studies in Breslav Chassidism* (Jerusalem: 1995), 205-13.

29 Kramer, *Toldot Moharnat: Be'aish Uvmayim*, 169.

30 *Siach Sorfei Kodesh*, vol. 1-5 (Jerusalem: 1994), vol. 2, 82-3; Fleer, *Against All Odds*, 173.

31 Weiss, *Studies in Breslav Chassidism*, 201.

from the same source. The words, 'which *they* heard' may very well be the words of R. Tscherin introducing the second section of the *Scroll.*

Now that we have the *Scroll* itself, we see that the version of the introductory phrase which appears therein is also in the first-person plural: 'That which *we* heard again'. If this was written by R. Natan, it is clear that he himself was present at the second telling as well.

Weiss offers an explanation for R. Natan's absence from Breslav on the fateful day that R. Nachman chose to relate the *Scroll* again. This is hinted at in R. Schick's telling which we quoted above. Weiss argues that from the text of *Yemei Moharnat* we can conclude that R. Natan was in Berditchev.[32]

> In the summer of 5569 our Master sent me to Berditchev to collect a debt from his brother-in-law and over that summer and the following winter I went five times until I collected the debt, thank God... During that summer his daughter, Miriam, journeyed to the Land of Israel... In the summer of 5569 she went with her brothers-in-law, the sons of the rabbi from Voltshisk and our Master accompanied her himself far from the city going on foot some distance from the city. He did not wish to alight upon the wagon saying that one must travel to the Land of Israel by foot. All of the townsfolk walked with him to accompany her with joy and celebration. Wondrous things from his holy mouth were heard then, but I was not privileged to be there because I was in Berditchev on his business.[33]

From this passage alone we cannot know whether R. Natan spent the entire summer of 5569 away from Breslav. R. Schick relates that ten days after the second telling of the *Scroll*, on the 18th of Av, R. Natan and others of the inner circle 'stood before our Master in his house'.[34] This would rule out his having been away from Uman for the entire summer.

---

32 Ibid., 202.

33 *Yemei Moharnat*, 67-9.

34 Schick, *Peulat Hatzadik*, 512.

Other sources can aid us in ascertaining more exact dates of R. Natan's travels in the summer of 5569. In *Chayei Moharan* we find that 'in the year 5569 in the time between the 17th of Tamuz and the 9th of Av his daughter Miriam traveled to the Land of Israel.'[35] In a letter written by R. Nachman to another daughter Sarah on Tuesday the 12th of Av in that same year, the Rebbe related that 'a letter arrived from your sister Miriam from Odessa from where she sailed on Thursday the 7th of Av.'[36] We may surmise that the trip from Breslav to the port of Odessa took several days. Since we know that R. Natan was not in Breslav when Miriam departed for the port – where she arrived on the 7th, it is questionable whether he arrived the day after in Breslav – on Friday the 8th. While this is logistically possible, it would be something of a coincidence if it did occur.

As we have no record of any other discourses from that summer, we may surmise that the 'wondrous things from his holy mouth' which R. Natan missed out on hearing due to his being 'in Berditchev on his business'[37] relates to the second telling of the *Scroll* on the 8th. At that time R. Natan had still not returned from his travels.

These are the sources which led both Weiss and R. Schick to maintain that R. Natan did not hear the second telling of the *Scroll* from R. Nachman himself. However, the description in *Yemei Moharnat* does not agree with this assumption. The language 'we heard' found in the *Scroll* itself also argues against this. It is true that R. Natan was not in Breslav the entire summer. However, we should also recall that as there was no direct regular water route between Odessa and Israel at that time, anyone wishing to travel to Israel needed to arrive in Odessa some time in advance in order to attain passage on a ship setting sail for Israel.[38] This may have taken days or even weeks. Miriam may have left Breslav some weeks earlier – and R. Natan may have returned some time after her departure, yet still easily

---

35 *Chayei Moharan Im Hashmatot* (Jerusalem: 2000), 392.

36 Rav Natan of Nemirov, *Alim Letrufah* (Jerusalem: 1981), 10.

37 *Yemei Moharnat*, 66-67.

38 For a description of the wait needed for passage to Israel, see Ibid., from 182 onwards.

arrived before the 8th. Seen in this light the entire matter of a fortuitous coincidence of these two Breslav travelers just missing each other seems much less important.

Appendix Three
The Manuscripts

1. A comparison of the Tepliker manuscript with those described in Neveh Tzadikim, Peulat Hatzadik and Against All Odds.

The description in Neveh Tzadikim

The description of the *Scroll* given by R. Koenig seems to match that of the actual Tepliker manuscript. According to R. Koenig the manuscript was copied in 'a special volume together with the rest of the deletions from *Chayei Moharan* and other works from which material had been removed'.[1] Both of the introductions, that to the *Sefer Hahashmatot* and that to the *Scroll* were published by R. Koenig.[2] However, a few details raise some questions as to identifying the work described by Koenig with the Tepliker manuscript of the *Scroll*.

There are a number of differences between the printed introductions and what is found in the actual manuscript. These include changes in word order as well as missing words.[3] Perhaps Koenig had in his possession a slightly corrupted copy of the manuscript and not the actual manuscript itself. Alternatively, these changes may only indicate errors that occurred between the time of his copying the manuscript and its printing.

1 Rav Natan Zvi Koenig, *Neveh Tzadikim* (Bnei Brak: 1969), 78.

2 Ibid., 78 9 and 193 4.

3 See the comparison of the different versions latter in this chapter.

Koenig also describes a special addition to the manuscript from which he worked.

> Although the pamphlet, the *Scroll of Secrets,* was written in acronyms as mentioned above, in any case, in the copy that belonged to R. Alter many of these acronyms are deciphered. In the pamphlet, above the acronyms their full meanings are written. It is possible that R. Alter copied this [as well] or that the deciphering is his own from what he heard orally.[4]

In the manuscript in my possession there appears no such apparatus above the acronyms of the *Scroll.* It seems, then, that this is a different manuscript than that which R. Koenig possessed. The possibility that the additions which he described were later additions to the manuscript is not raised by Koenig. In his eyes these were either written or copied by R. Alter himself. This suggests that he recognized the handwriting in the additions as identical to that of the rest of the manuscript itself – both belonged to the same copyist: R. Alter.

The extant manuscript in my possession settles the question as to whether the additions were added by R. Alter or copied by him. As these do not appear in the manuscript which was copied, 'letter for letter,' it seems that they did not appear in the original either. This would mean, then, that R. Alter himself added the additional superscript.[5] If this is all true, then, the differences between our manuscript and that described by R. Koenig would mean that our manuscript is either an earlier copy of the Alter manuscript (written before the additions) or that there are two different versions. R. Koenig possessed one with the additions and we have another, slightly different, version.

---

4 Koenig, *Neveh Tzadikim*, 79.

5 It is not completely clear that R. Alter himself wrote the superscript in the manuscript. R. Koenig may have seen a later manuscript in which both the text and the superscript were written by a later copyist. Alternatively, R. Koenig may have recognized the hand-writing of R. Alter from other sources and felt that the text was entirely his work. The question as to whether the author of the superscript followed an oral tradition or whether he worked on his own is also open to debate.

Our version does not contain the words of R. Avraham Chazan from *Neveh Tzadikim* which he quoted, 'Also there from the words of R. Avraham son of R. Nachman of Tulchin....' This is another piece of evidence suggesting that we are dealing with two different versions. The version which R. Koenig saw had additional things lacking from ours. This is usually an indication of a later version. I will bring other evidence below to strengthen the presumption that our version is, in fact, the original Tepliker manuscript.

A Comparison with the Manuscript described in Peulat Hatzadik

It seems that R. Schick did not possess the original Tepliker manuscript as he writes: 'I have in my possession a copy of the Tepliker manuscript'[6] – a copy and not the original. Our version is a photocopy of the original itself. As he wrote that his manuscript contained 'only acronyms,'[7] we know that it was not the same manuscript as R. Koenig's which contained additional text. Our manuscript contains the exact same text at the end of the *Scroll*'s first section as does R. Schick's. The endings of the second section differ only slightly – this may be due to more to copying errors than to actual textual variations.

As opposed to the description in *Peulat Hatzadik*, it is clear that according to our manuscript R. Natan did hear the second telling of the *Scroll* directly from R. Nachman. The introduction to the *Scroll* tells us that it contains 'that which our Master, our rabbi R. Natan heard from the holy Master....' The second section opens with the text 'that which *we* heard...' as we discussed above. While R. Schick did maintain that R. Natan was not present for the second telling of the *Scroll* (as we discussed above), the similarities between his description of the *Scroll* and our manuscript are sufficient to enable us to assume that he was also referring to the Tepliker manuscript.

---

6 Rav Eliezer Schick, *Pe'ulat Hatzadik* (Jerusalem: 1944), 344.

7 Ibid.

A Comparison to the Manuscript Described in *Against All Odds*

The text described by Fleer is obviously the same manuscript in our hands. He provides a picture of the text in his book with the caption, 'The frontispiece of the book of R. Alter Tepliker'[8] in which the introduction to the *Sefer Hahashmatot* found in our manuscript is clearly shown. Curiously, Fleer calls the *Scroll* pictured in his book 'the short *Scroll of Secrets*'.[9] Now while we know that the *Scroll* contains two sections – the first much shorter than the second – it does not seem he was referring to only one section of the *Scroll*. Our manuscript (which is the same as that referred to by Fleer) contains both of these sections, not just the shorter first section. It may be that the odd form of the *Scroll* – its shorthand and acronyms – makes it appear to the untrained eye and to one unschooled in its history as a shortened version of a longer text.[10] The term 'short' may also refer to some of R. Avraham Chazan's sayings concerning the coming of the messiah which were attributed to the *Scroll*. As Fleer may have known of these sayings and did not find them in his copy of the *Scroll*, he may have assumed that he had a shortened version of a longer, more inclusive text.[11]

Other details mentioned by Fleer also lead us to believe that his copy of the *Scroll* was the Tepliker manuscript as well. It is contained in a book along with other works, some of them unpublished.[12] Most important, though, is that he describes it as lacking any interpretive apparatus; it consists only of shorthand and acronyms. Fleer tells us that he asked R. Hirsch Leib if he knew the meanings of the acronyms. R. Leib told him that when he gave the book to R. Avraham Sternhartz in Kriminshok, the latter 'sat all night

---

8 Gedaliah Fleer, *Against All Odds* (Jerusalem Breslav Research Institute 2005), 101.

9 Ibid., 173.

10 Fleer himself claimed not to understand the text.

11 For other examples of his knowledge of the future see *Siach Sorfei Kodesh*, vol. 1-5 (Jerusalem: 1994), vol. 3, 172, 92 and 200.

12 Fleer, *Against All Odds*, 100.

and deciphered the *Scroll*. He then came and told R. Leib all of the words.'[13] R. Leib added that he was too weak to go over all the acronyms' meanings, but that in any event, even if the text was deciphered, 'the book was still incomprehensible'.[14] Some time later, when he was feeling better he did go over the acronyms, but Fleer agreed with him that this really did not add much to understanding the text itself.[15]

It is clear from this tale that this was not the same text which R. Koenig saw. This manuscript contained only the acronyms and nothing else. It is noteworthy that both R. Leib and Fleer agreed that even after deciphering the actual words of the text it remained quite inscrutable.

2. DIFFERENCES IN THE INTRODUCTIONS FOUND IN NEVEH TZADIKIM AND THE TEPLIKER MANUSCRIPT[16ß]

Sefer Hahashmatot – Neveh Tzadikim

The Book of Deletions from Chayei Moharan contains texts which were deleted at the time of printing and were not printed. Gathered here are entire subjects and also the endings of works of which the beginnings were printed but whose endings were deleted and not printed. One should know that the page numbers and the letters which I wrote in this volume of Chayei Moharan accord with those of the Lemberg edition of the year 5636 [1875]. Also here are copied some of the deletions from the book Yemei Moharnat published in Lemberg in the same year.[17]

---

13 Ibid., 173.

14 Ibid.

15 Ibid., 174.

16 ß [Translator's note: The differences in the actual introductions are only in the way in which the Hebrew text is written – sometimes using one form of acronym, sometimes another. However, the words and meanings are identical. I have translated these texts extremely literally in order to preserve the actual word content in spite of it making for poor English.]

17 Koenig, *Neveh Tzadikim*, 193-4.

Sefer Hahashmatot – Manuscript

The Book of Deletions from Chayei Moharan which were deleted at the time of printing and were not printed. Gathered here are entire subjects and also the endings of works of which the beginnings were printed but whose endings were deleted and not printed. One should know that the page numbers and the letters which I wrote in this volume of *Chayei Moharan* accord with those of the first Lemberg edition printed in the year 'this will comfort us for our deeds' – 5636. Also here are copied some of the deletions from the book *Yemei Moharnat* published also in Lemberg in the same year.

Copied in the year 5658 [1897] here in Lemberg.

3. THE SCROLL OF SECRETS – THE SICHOT ME'ANASH MANUSCRIPT[18]

[Paragraph] 101 A copy of the work called the *Scroll of Secrets* from the hand of our teacher, our teacher, the rabbi, R. Natan, of blessed memory letter for letter as heard by our teacher, the rabbi, R. Natan of blessed memory, from the mouth of our leader, teacher and rabbi, the holy – the fount of flowing wisdom – the entire order of the coming of the righteous redeemer, may he come speedily in our day, amen.

This copy was made from a copy made from a volume of the book *Chayei Moharan* which had been in the hands of R. Naftali, of blessed memory. This volume was in the handwriting of our teacher and rabbi, R. Natan, of blessed memory until here.

5) That which we heard again about this matter today on Friday Sabbath eve, 8 Menachem Av 5569 in the town of Breslav twelve-(years) and one day old on this day, that is the day mentioned above, then he will become

18 All of the notes in parenthesis which appear in the text are in the original excepting those marked with asterisks which are my own. The following mark --- is used in places where the text was illegible. [Translator's note: ellipses (…) are used where the Hebrew is legible but the meaning is so unclear as to render translation impossible].

sole emperor (alef-yud-peh)[19] over the entire world and on that day he will enter under the wedding canopy.[20] They will give him a sermon-gift. Every half-year something else will happen, as explained above as we have already heard. Initially he will be accepted as the halachic authority throughout Israel who will work hard in this matter until he attains deep insights. They [will] begin to send him queries until it is accepted by all that he is the premier halachic authority in all of Israel.
3) Initially he will be king of Israel[21] and afterwards sole emperor[22] over all[23] until finally all will surrender themselves to him due to the favor, glory, love and yearning that they will all feel towards him until they will completely nullify themselves before him.
6) He will be great in wisdom and accepted by the wise men of the nations[24] as great in wisdom until all come to him. And all the sons of the kings all will come to him to receive wisdom from him. And he will travel to all the emperors in all the places and each will send a royal command to all the ministers that they shall receive him and honor him greatly in every place where he will pass. Any minister who cannot receive him on his journey's path will ready himself in the emperor's city and there he will receive him. Each of the kings will give him a present – or a country or a people. And some will give him a stipend. He will exchange with each of them until he receives through barter the Land of Israel for he will give to each the country near his border and receive for this a country closer to the Land of Israel until he receives through barter the Land of Israel. In that same year in which he will travel to the Land then he will be a great emperor[25]

19 These letters may be the initials of the copyist. Parts of parantheses are missing in the original.

20 Fifteen words found in the Tepliker manuscript are missing here.

21 The Hebrew is not clear.

22 The Hebrew is not clear.

23 The Hebrew is not clear.

24 The Hebrew is not clear.

25 The Hebrew is not clear.

and then all will travel to the Land of Israel and the Land of Israel will have room for all. Afterwards the Land of Israel will expand. At the time that he will travel to the Land of Israel he will be the only king[26] of Israel and he will send ahead a map to the nations of the world that is [vav?] instructing to build there palaces near his own palace for all the kings according to his wisdom. From the four corners of the world artisans will arrive to build these palaces mentioned above. Because everyone will live nearby him due to their great yearning for him such that they cannot be without him. He will build his palace in accord with the future, according to the children he will have. There will be a unique use for each room this room will be used for such, etc. and in this room he will sermonize. That is, before his children are born he will use them as mentioned above. By lot and by high standing the building of the palaces[27] will be ordered for everyone will be near his palace[28] but the absolute proximity, this will be according to lot and high standing. The messiah himself will die but he will have many children. Ten generations will he see, and then will pass on, while still alive, the em' [apparently empire] to his first-born son. His first-born son and his son will sire also a first-born son and so too the son of his son will sire also a first-born son for ten generations. Then … but before this … he himself the em' [sole emperor?] over all. And all will be appointed. There will be a host of soldiers for every king and he will give them orders like the order of the stars and planets. And he will make new musical instruments and songs, for his genius in song will be very great. He will innovate in this art such that the souls of those who hear his songs will faint, etc. He will announce what he will do each day - at this hour such an activity, etc. For three hours he will deal with the soldiers[29]that come to him as even then there will be illnes … an ill person will come to him and he will instruct them [sic] to take from the orchard which he will make …

---

26 The Hebrew is not clear.

27 The Hebrew is not clear.

28 The Hebrew is not clear.

29 The Hebrew for *sick* and for *soldiers* is very similar.

never before. He will go among the sick and instruct each of them to take that which he knows according to the powers of the appointed angels who daily visit each blade of grass. All will surrender themselves to him with neither war nor struggle in light of his beauty and their longing for him. He will fix for everyone practices and make for them prayer. Thus he will do until all turn to one clear tongue. When he will be in the Land of Israel, they will search for a match for him even though it is proper that his match be made through divine knowledge. However, just as one who has lost an object [seeks] its return, etc.[30] They will search for a match for him. She will be eleven and one day, on that day, will enter under the wedding canopy with him. They will not know at first that he is the one. Afterwards, each will reach his own conclusion and will consider that it is possible that this is him etc. (Happy will be the strong of faith and in study in those days.) Once I heard that he said concerning the messiah there will be a mighty argument. And they will say, 'This is the messiah?!' They will say in these words, ['The messiah isn't a fancy hat!'] There will be the evil inclination and etc. and the Sanhedrin and all those things that were but each thing will be much more pleasant than before. Each and every one according to his station will have his eyes opened in wisdom and will gain new understanding better than before each in accord with his station. Of the days of the messiah there is much discussion in the Tractate Sanhedrin in the chapter 'Portion' [-] how long they will be. There are opinions that it will only last forty years and there are other opinions concerning this.) His traveling wardrobe, what his attire will be, what will be his name. Before the messiah will arrive, the grandchild/ren of the Baal Shem Tov will come before all the kings. Their written and spoken language will go.

[The entire thing: Despite what has transpired during the near 2000 year exile, we expect that he will arrive any day. Even if he should tarry, we await him [for] he will surely come and not be late. Even though all the ends [of days] have come and gone, he will certainly come and be beautiful and very pleasant. Happy is he who merits this – may he strengthen

30 See TB Kiddushin 72b.

his faith then]. Regarding his being a halachic authority mentioned above, it seems that he said that he will be three years old and then he will be accepted as the authoritative teacher in all of Israel. Also, the text is missing what he discussed ... much more we discussed was forgotten. The Blessed One grant us to see speedily soon in our day. He said that regarding this matter everyone knows a bit, but he knows everything. [Until here the '*Scroll* of Secrets'].

... these things in round parentheses I did not find in the manuscript of R. Natan, may his memory be a blessing, only in that of R. Zalman of Medvedevkah.

Appendix Four
R. Avraham Chazan on the Scroll of Secrets: The Sichot Me'anash Manuscript

Immediately following the *Scroll* in the *Sichot Me'anash* manuscript there is a paragraph detailing oral traditions concerning the *Scroll* and R. Nachman's role in the messianic process. This tradition is related by R. Chazan and was written down for the first time apparently in the beginning of the 20th century. As such, it is not part of the *Scroll* itself, but an addition which adds more context.

> I heard from R. Avraham son of R. Nachman of Tulchin who said in the name of his father, that his father said in the name of R. Natan that his [the messiah's] son will be a greater innovation than him and his son than him, for he will have spiritual capacities of [both] his father and grandfather. The messiah will [arrive] in approximately 600 years for they will live long lives. He also said that regarding the Josephian messiah: why is he needed? He answered that because of what will happen to the Davidian messiah he will need the merit of those tzadikim who have died and the Josephian messiah will die first. Our Master said, 'I have prepared a nice place for him,' for he was the Josephian messiah – completely free of sexual impurity. Our Master said that he did not know of this thing until after he rose to great heights and saw to where the defect reached. He wanted to repair this completely, but it is impossible to change nature. He said regarding the Baal Shem Tov that he had sexual intercourse twice and once had an 'accident'. He had two children: his daughter Adel and his son Hirsch-Ber. This was because he needed to repair 'once the text

and twice the translation'. For an 'accident' is akin to the translation as explained in discourse 19 of section I. But our Master was like the first strength of Yaakov[1] – he never saw an accidental spilling of seed in his lifetime. Therefore he was like Joseph who was pure. The messiah will need to make use of his merit and reveal the truth in the world – amen, speedily in our day.

There are a number of messianic themes concentrated in these few lines. I will expand on each of them below.

The Transmission of the Scroll

As opposed to the tradition which held that R. Natan did not reveal anything of the *Scroll*, here we see clear evidence (at least according to R. Avraham Chazan) that he did in fact share its details with R. Nachman of Tulchin. The tradition described here also differs from that reported by R. Aaron Lipvotzker's daughter Tziril. She claimed that R. Avraham received the *Scroll* from her father, while here it seems that it was passed on by his own father who received information concerning it directly from R. Natan.[2]

It is possible to reconcile these two traditions, however. R. Avraham Chazan may have received the *Scroll* (or information concerning it) from two distinct sources – both R. Aaron Lipvotzker and his own father. This of course, though, conflicts with the tradition that only one individual in each generation was privy to any knowledge of the *Scroll*.

We should note that the 'Lipvotzker tradition' is also found in the *Sichot Me'anash* manuscript. This seems to indicate that this manuscript is a collection of different traditions and does not represent only one specific Breslav thread concerning the *Scroll*.

---

1 See TB Yevamot 76a.

2 It may be that R. Avraham is referring only to additional explanations of the *Scroll* and not the *Scroll* itself which he received from his father.

The Messiah's Stature

In contrast to claims that the 'the greatest of men is the Davidian messiah,'[3] this tradition indicates that the messiah's children will outdo him. His son will be greater than him, his grandson even greater. While the messiah himself will head the new dynasty of Israeli kings and *tzadikim*, he is surpassed by the spiritual prowess of his own offspring.

The Length of the Messianic Era and the Longevity of the Messiah

In the *Scroll* we find mention of the messianic era's length only in R. Zalman of Medvedevkah's handwriting and not in that of R. Natan's.

> '[Of] the days of the messiah there is much discussion in the Tractate Sanhedrin in the chapter 'Portion' [-] how long they will be. There are opinions that it will only last forty years and there are other opinions concerning this.)'[4]

From this it seems that the actual length of the messianic age is still an open question. However, the forty years mentioned in the *Scroll* (as one option) is quite different than the 600 mentioned in the *Sichot Me'anash* manuscript. It is not clear, though, whether this longer time refers to the entire messianic era or to a miraculous longevity of the messiah himself.

Our Master was the Josephian Messiah

The identification of R. Nachman with the Josephian messiah is made here directly. No 'akin to' or 'messiah-like' is used to create a comparison. This is identification and not merely a comparison. R. Nachman *is* the

---

3 Rav Yehudah Halevi, *Sefer Hakuzari*, trans. Yehudah Even Shmuel (Jerusalem: 1973), III:72

4 Section II lines 85-7.

Josephian messiah; the first messiah who lives and then dies clearing the way for the Davidian messiah's arrival.

This statement though is only the assertion of R. Avraham himself. He separates the claim made by R. Nachman, 'I have prepared a nice place for him,' from the clear identification that he reads as this statement's implication. He offers his own explanation for the identity – that R. Nachman was 'completely free of sexual impurity'. As R. Avraham took great pains throughout his writings to base his assertion that R. Nachman was the Moses-like or Josephian messiah, it seems that if he was aware of a direct statement to that effect made by R. Nachman himself, he surely would have mentioned it.

Sexual Purity

R. Avraham sees a clear connection between R. Nachman's sexual purity and his identification as the Josephian messiah.[5] The point that from a very early age R. Nachman was pure is often found throughout the Breslav writings.

> I heard from R. Yudel, who said that he heard from our Master how he was proud of having broken the chains of lust completely even at an early age. This was something unique never before found. For there are those tzadikim who have abandoned [sexual] cravings, but not before their old-age – and he gave examples of this. However, a young man like me, still in the fullness of his youth – to break the chains of lust completely like me, this is something altogether unique.[6]

---

5 The connection between Joseph and sexual purity is based upon the Biblical tale in which he succeeded in refusing the advances of Potiphar's wife. It is found throughout the kabalistic literature in which Joseph represents 'Yesod' – the place of the *brit* and the sphere of *tzadik*. R. Nachman uses these themes frequently in referring to the Josephian messiah. See Arthur Green, *Tormented Master* (New York: Schocken, 1987), 187-98.

6 *Sichot Haran*, (Jerusalem: 1995), 316.

> He was very proud of his strength in breaking this lust. He was truly an awesome holy-man in this regard. He said that in this matter he had absolutely no desire. For him, male and female were alike. That is, he faced no struggle of desire when he saw or spoke with a woman, for all were alike for him.[7]

This spiritual tranquility that R. Nachman was so proud of was not characteristic of him from an early age. There was a long period in which he underwent a number of trials regarding desire. However, he did not seek to avoid these trials, but even sought them out – praying that God would send them his way.

> He was a great hero and bested his natural inclination and desire many times. Even so, he would not distance himself from such challenges. On the contrary, he wanted them and would pray that God send him such trials … even though during these trials it was extremely difficult for him. Several times, beyond count, God came to his aid and he merited overcoming his inclination and breaking the heat of the flames of desire.[8]

His ability to overcome natural desire brought him to great spiritual heights and was predicated on the purification of his physical being.[9] The expression which R. Avraham used, 'completely free,' seems to have been chosen in light of some of the sources that I will share below.

---

7 *Shibchei Haran*, (Jerusalem: 1995), 16:18-9

8 Ibid. See also *Chayei Moharan Hamenukad*, (Jerusalem: 1995), 198-9;Green, *Master*, 38-40; Zvi Mark, *Mysticism and Madness in the Work of R. Nachman of Breslav* (Jerusalem: 2003), 59-69; Zvi Mark, "*The Formulation of R. Nachman of Breslav's 'Tikkun ha-kelali', the 'Tikkun for Nocturnal Pollution', and Pilgrimage to the Tomb of R. Nachman, and their Relationship to Messianism*" *Da'at* 56 (2005): 130-1.

9 See Zvi Mark, "*The Tale of the Bread – a Hidden Story of R. Nachman of Breslav*" *Tarbitz* 72, no. 3 (2003).

'He wanted to repair this completely'

The background behind R. Avraham's statement that 'Our Master said that he did not know of this thing until after he rose to great heights and saw to where the defect reached. He wanted to repair this completely, but it is impossible to change nature,' is found in a discussion held between R. Nachman and his followers, R. Natan and R. Naftali, concerning the establishment of the special ceremony which R. Nachman initiated for those who suffered nocturnal emission.

> Know that these ten chapters of Psalms are extremely effective for repairing nocturnal emission – they effect a complete cure and are extremely effective.... There were many great tzadikim who wanted to deal with this and searched for a complete cure. There were others who knew nothing of this and some who began to discover things about this, but passed away before completing it. But God has helped me so that I have merited [the chance] to deal with this problem completely. The cure is through the saying of the ten chapters of Psalms mentioned above. This is something new and wondrous. ... He said: this has not been known since the beginning of time. Actually, I wanted to destroy this completely, but this is not possible – either physically or spiritually. Physically, because one would have to change human nature forever – something not possible. Even Moses who did this was only able to do so for a given time – like the parting of the sea or the Jordan which only lasted for a given time. However, to change human nature completely, such that each and every individual's nature would be permanently altered, this is impossible. Also spiritually, this is impossible ...But these ten Psalms are a precious, wondrous, effective thing.[10]

10 *Sichot Haran*, 178-9.

R. Nachman felt that he had 'completely'[11] dealt with the problem of impurity through the creation of his *Tikkun*.[12] It seems that R. Avraham used the same terminology not as a description of one of his rebbe's spiritual projects, but of his rebbe himself in this regard.

The Baal Shem Tov

> 'He said regarding the Baal Shem Tov that he had sexual intercourse twice and once had an 'accident'. He had two children: his daughter Adel and his son Hirsch-Ber. This was because he needed to repair 'once the text and twice the translation'. For an 'accident' is akin to the translation as explained in discourse 19 of section I. But our Master was like 'the first strength of Yaakov – he never saw an accidental spilling of seed in his lifetime. Therefore he was like Joseph who was pure.'

In this text, which records the most intimate of details concerning the founder of the Chasidic movement, it is unclear where the great-grandson's, R. Nachman, words end and those of R. Avraham Chazan begin.[13] The reference to one of R. Nachman's discourses would seem to indicate that at least this section is no longer quoting R. Nachman himself. Only the first section of *Likutei Moharan* was published in R. Nachman's lifetime – and as such, the book was not yet divided into sections I and II. Additionally, the words, 'but our Master' are clearly not a quote, but R. Avraham's own words. Perhaps the entire section is only a reworked paraphrase of R. Nachman's own words – including the reference to *Likutei Moharan*. In this case, the question as to whether R. Nachman himself asserted that he had never

11 This description is but one of many that detail R. Nachman's exceptional status in this area. See R. Natan's description in Likutei Moharan I: 114 where he exclaims that R. Nachman's achievements were 'impossible to describe in writing'.

12 See Mark, "*The Formulation of R. Nachman of Breslav's 'Tikkun ha-kelali', the 'Tikkun for Nocturnal Pollution', and Pilgrimage to the Tomb of R. Nachman, and their Relationship to Messianismi*," *Da'at* 56 (2005): 130-1.

13 Before this section the words, 'our Master said' appear.

spilled his own seed or whether this was only an oral tradition here quoted by R. Avraham remains unsettled.[14]

We can learn a bit more about this tradition from a letter written by R. Avraham which is printed in a number of works, including the deletions from *Nachalei Emunah.* (There are several versions of this letter, but it seems that the manuscript in my possession contains its most important content).

> I heard from my father, who heard from R. Natan in the name of the Baal Shem Tov and also some from our Master himself, that the Baal Shem Tov was proud and said, etc., etc. Our Rebbe merited to [understand] the secret of the Torah reading on the Sabbath and wrote in the holy tongue, etc. (This too I heard from my father who heard from R. Natan in the name of our Master). … regarding the matter of completing the reading as obligated by our Sages and according to R. Luria specifically on the Sabbath eve.) Much can be explained in the paths of interpretation which God has helped me to comprehend regarding this discourse, but I have no time to discuss this now any longer.
> …signed your friend R. Avraham Chazan….[15]

Beyond the additional strengthening of this tradition, as we learn that this letter was written by R. Avraham himself and not by one of his students, we also find more information about this tradition itself. It appears that the description of the Baal Shem Tov's intimate life is a quote from the Baal Shem Tov himself. R. Nachman was but one of those who knew of this tradition concerning his great-grandfather ('also some from our Master himself'). It was transmitted by R. Natan, who heard it from others. We

14 The fact that the Baal Shem Tov suffered once from an unwanted emission is mentioned in order to establish R. Nachman's superiority. However, the Baal Shem Tov did not see such accidental emissions, if not tied to feelings of desire, as necessarily evil. They were part of the mystical process of repair – in this case of 'once the text and twice the translation'. See *Likutei Torah,* (Bnei Brak: 1953), 85.

15 Natan Zvi Koenig, ed., *Nachalei Emunah* (Bnei Brak: 1967), 26-7.

also find that the parallel tradition concerning the intimate conduct of R. Nachman was likewise transmitted by R. Natan.[16]

The great abstinence practiced by the Baal Shem Tov is described in *Shibchei Habesht*. The author writes how after the rebbe's wife died and his followers suggested that he remarry, he replied, 'I need a wife? I was celibate for 14 years and my son Herschel was born through "the power of speech"'.[17] R. Nachman added his own praise of his ancestor's holiness and celibacy:

> It goes without saying how he praised the Baal Shem Tov beyond all praise. When he spoke (Likutei Moharan II 72) of the how the leader must be holy and celibate akin to those qualities of Moses himself, he said, in our own time we had the Baal Shem Tov ....[18]

The merit of those Tzadikim who have died

The way in which R. Nachman will help to prepare the way for the coming of the messiah qua Josephian messiah described here differs from the usual understanding of his contribution to the hastening of the messianic age. Here the emphasis is not on spreading words of Torah and the like, but rather by somehow helping to balance mystical metaphysical accounts which need to be settled for the sake of the Davidian messiah. This messiah will need the spiritual 'points' accrued by R. Nachman in order to overcome those obstacles which he will face in his own time. It may be that the more ordinary religious activities of R. Nachman – bringing the masses back to the path of God – are also included as part of that which will, in good time, serve to aid the Davidian messiah.

---

16 The content of this letter is not all that clear. Without being able to read it in its entirety (it apparently is still held by the Koenig family) it will not be possible to fully understand this matter.

17 *Shibchei Habesht*, Avraham Rubenstein ed. (Jerusalem: 1992), 311-2. The expression 'the power of speech' may not be meant literally, but rather, as it does elsewhere, against one's will. That is – one is coerced by God. The Passover Hagadah, for example, tells us that the Jews went down to Egypt, 'by the power of speech' – that is against their will.

18 *Chayei Moharan Im Hashmatot*, (Jerusalem: 2000), 438.

Appendix Five
The Return of the Baal Shem Tov as the Messiah

The possibility that the Baal Shem Tov will return to life as the messiah has already been broached throughout Chasidic tradition. In the work *Shibchei Habesht*, this tradition is attributed to the Baal Shem Tov himself.

> I also heard that the Besht said that if the righteous redeemer will not arrive within sixty years, I will arrive [back] in this world.
>
> Our community rabbi said that he heard from his grandfather who spent a Shabbat with the Besht before the holiday of Shavuot on which he died. He said that he had one doubt. The rabbi said that he had two doubts: he did not know whether he said in fifteen or in fifty years; or sixteen or sixty years. I heard from others specifically sixty years. I asked R. Aaron of Mezibush and he told me that he would certainly return to this world, but that 'I will not be like I am now'. The meaning is not known, for who would [dare] ask the meaning of this thing.[1]

The expression used for 'return' here – is the same used when discussing reincarnation – *gilgul*. The meaning, then, may be that the return of the Baal Shem Tov is meant as his reincarnation and not as an actual physical return – 'like I am now'.

The tradition of Chernobyl Chasidism preserves a tale regarding the Baal Shem Tov's return as well.

---

1 "*Shibchei Habesht* (Manuscript)," (1992), 124.

> The holy rabbi R. Yaakov of Techarkas[2] related that his grandfather, R. Nachum of Chernobyl,[3] … told them … even though the Besht has not been and will not be until the coming of the redeemer, when the messiah arrives he will be. He repeated himself three times – when the messiah arrives he will be. The holy R. Yaakov said that the meaning of his grandfather's words was that the Besht will be the messiah.[4]

There is a glaring similarity between the tradition that holds that 'the Besht has not been and will not be until the coming of the redeemer' and that which holds that from the time of R. Nachman's death until the coming of the messiah nothing new will be revealed.[5] This similarity would be even more impressive if we accepted the thesis that R. Nachman himself is destined to return as the messiah.[6]

---

2 This is the son-in-law of Dov Ber of Lubavitch, the 'middle rebbe' of Chabad.

3 This is the founder of the Chernobyl Chasidic dynasty and the author of *Meor Eneyim* and *Yismach Lev*. He was considered to be close to the Baal Shem Tov.

4 *Maasiot Vemaamarim Yikarim* (Jerusalem, 1984), 35. For more on this source, see David Berger, *The Rebbe, the Messiah and the Scandal of Orthodox Indifference* (New York: Littman Library of Jewish Civilization, 2001), 62-3.

5 *Siach Sorfei Kodesh*, vol. 1-5 (Jerusalem: 1994), vol. 3, 172.

6 Regarding both R. Nachman and the Baal Shem Tov we can assume that what is meant here is reincarnation.

Appendix Six
Where is the Golden Tree?

In *Avneiha Barzel*, R. Shmuel Horowitz mentions, in the name of R. Avraham Chazan, a few of the subjects which R. Nachman discussed during that fateful wagon-ride when he first revealed the *Scroll*. 'Our Rebbe began to tell of us of Russia and what would transpire until the coming of our redeemer and from then until the resurrection of the dead.'[1] In the Scroll itself, we find no such mention of Russia. Other things may have been discussed in the wagon, but the Scroll only records that part of the conversation that pertains to the coming of the messiah.

We are also told that later on when R. Natan wanted to discuss the Scroll with R. Yoske, R. Nachman's son-in-law, who was on the wagon with him he found that R. Yoske knew nothing of the Scroll but had only heard something about a 'tree with golden leaves'.[2] This tree is also not mentioned in the Scroll. It may be that this is also part of another discussion. However, it may be that the mention of this tree is actually an expression of R. Yoske's own misunderstanding of what was discussed concerning the messiah. R. Yoske was not meant to hear the Scroll. His mention of a wondrous tree might actually be the equivalent of admitting that he really did not understand anything of it. The trees used to create medical compounds described in the Scroll are all 'natural' – not miraculous. It would seem that no such tree was actually mentioned by R. Nachman. Rather, R. Yoske simply misheard or misunderstood.

---

1 R. Avraham Chazan, *Avneiha Barzel* (Jerusalem: 1983), 30.

2 Ibid.

BIBLIOGRAPHY

Haencyclopediah Hatalmudit Jerusalem, 1987.

"*Breishit Rabbah*." edited by Theodor & Albeck. Jerusalem, 1965.

Chayei Moharan. Warsaw: Rav Aaron Tzikalmon, 1928.

Chayei Moharan. Jerusalem, 1983.

Chayei Moharan (Hashmatot Chadashot). Beit Shemesh: Hanekudot Hatovot, 2005.

Chayei Moharan Hamenukad. Jerusalem, 1995.

Chayei Moharan Im Hashmatot. Jerusalem, 2000.

"*Eicha Raba*." edited by Shalom Buber. Vilna, 1899.

Emek Hamelech. Amsterdam, 1648.

Hashmatot Mechayei Moharan. Jerusalem, 1893.

Hashmatot Mechayei Moharan - Typed Manuscript.

Imrei Pinchas Hashalem: Otzar Torat Pinchas Mekorvitz Vetalmidav. Bnei Brak, 2003.

Keter Shem Tov. Brooklyn, 1987.

Likutei Torah. Bnei Brak, 1953.

Megaleh Amukot Al Hatorah.

"*Midrash Breishit Rabati Nosad Al Sifro Shel R. Moshe Hadarshan*." edited by Chanoch Albeck. Jerusalem, 1967.

"*Midrash Rabbah*." edited by M. A. Merkin. Tel Aviv, 1987.

Midrash Tanchuma Hashalem. 2 vols. Jerusalem, 1988.

Psikta Rabati. Meir Ish Shalom ed. Tel Aviv, 1963.

"Pnu Lachem Tzefona." *Or Haorot* 14: 2.

Seder Eliyahu Rabbah Veseder Eliyahu Zuta. Meir Ish Shalom ed. Jerusalem, 1969.

Seder Olam Raba Hashalem Latana Rabi Yosi Ben Chalafta. Bnei Brak, 1990.

Sefer Hazohar. Reuven Margolit ed. Jerusalem, 1984.

Sefer Sipurei Ma'asiot Hamenukad. Jerusalem, 1985.

Shibchei Habesht. Rav Yehoshuah Mondshine ed. Jerusalem, 1982.

Shibchei Habesht. Avraham Rubenstein ed. Jerusalem, 1992.

"*Shibchei Habesht* (Manuscript)." 1992.

Shibchei Haran. Jerusalem, 1995.

Shir Hashirim Rabba. Jerusalem, 1994.

Shir Yedidut Hamenukad. Jerusalem, 1981.

Siach Sorfei Kodesh. Vol. 1-5. Jerusalem, 1994.

Siach Sorfei Kodesh. Vol. 6. Jerusalem, 2000.

Sichot Haran. Jerusalem, 1995.

"*Sichot Me'anash* (Manuscript)."

Sifrei Al Sefer Devarim. Finkelstein ed. New York, 1993.

Tikunei Zohar. Translated by Rav Yehudah Edrei. Jerusalem, 1998.

Tzva'at Haribash. Brooklyn, 1996.

Yalkut Shimoni. Jerusalem, 2000.

"*Zohar Chadash*." Chamad, 1991.

Agnon, Shmuel Yosef. *Elu Ve'elu*. Tel Aviv, 1997.

————. *Timol Shilshom*. Tel Aviv, 1945.

Alter, Rav Avraham Issakar Meir Eliyahu. *Me'ir Eynei Hagolah*. Pietrakov, 1925.

Altschuler, Mor. *The Messianic Secret of Hasidism*. Haifa, 2002.

Anshin, Rav Natan. "*Harav HeChasid Hamuflag Rav Naftali...*" *Mebo'ei Hanachal* 56-7 (1998): 17.

————. "Rav Avraham Ben Rav Nachman..." *Mebo'ei Hanachal* 4, no. 37 (1985): 25-26.

Assaf, David. "*The Causeless Hatred is Ongoing: The Struggle against Bratslav Hasidism in the 1860s*." *Zion* 59 (1994): 465-506.

———. *Bratslav: an Annotated Bibliography*. Jerusalem, 2000.

———. *The Regal Way: the Life and Times of R. Israel of Ruzhin*. Jerusalem, 1997.

Azoulay, Rav Avraham. *Chesed Le'avraham*. Vilna, 1917.

Berger, David. *The Rebbe, the Messiah and the Scandal of Orthodox Indifference*. New York: Littman Library of Jewish Civilization, 2001.

Bezanson, Rav Yisrael Yitzchak. *Ga'aguim*. Tel Aviv, 2005.

Biale, David. *Eros and the Jews*. Berkeley, CA: University of California Press, 1997.

Breiter, Yitzchak. *She'arit Yitzchak*. Jerusalem, 1990.

Buber, Martin. *Bepardes HaChasidut*. Jerusalem, 1945.

Buber, Rav Menachem. *Yemot Hamashiach: Hageulah Uviat Hamashiach Bemekorot Hayahadut*. Kfar Chabad, 1992.

Bultman, Rudolf. *Theology of the New Testament*. Vol. I. New York, 1951.

Chaim.

Chazan, R. Avraham. *Avneiha Barzel*. Jerusalem, 1983.

Chazan, Rav Avraham. *Biur Halikutim*. Jerusalem, 1993.

Chazan, R. Avraham. *Chochma Vebina (Bound with Kochvei Or)*. Jerusalem, 1983.

Chazan, Rav Avraham. *Chochmah Utvunah (Printed Together with Sipurei Maasiot)*: Hanekudot Hatovot, 2004.

———. *Kochvei Or*. Jerusalem, 1961.

———. *Kochvei Or*. Jerusalem, 1983.

———. "*Ma'asiot Umeshalim*." In *Kochvei Or*, edited by Rav Avraham Chazan. Jerusalem, 1983.

Chazan, R. Avraham. *Sichot Vesipurim (Printed with ~~Kochvei Or~~)*. Jerusalem, 1983.

Chazan, Rav Avraham. *Yemei Hatlaot*. Jerusalem, 1933.

———. *Yemei Hatlaot*. Jerusalem, 2000.

Chernobyl, Rav Menachem Nachman of. *Me'or Enayim*. Jerusalem, 1999.

Dan, Joseph. *Apocalypse Then and Now*. Israel, 2000.

———. *The Modern Jewish Messi*anism. Israel, 1999.

Demitrovsky, Chaim Zalman. "Al Derech Hapilpul." In *Sefer Hayovel Lechvod Shalom Baron Lemelot Lo Shemonim Shana*, edited by Shaul Liberman, 111-64. Jerusalem, 1975.

Dresner, Samuel H. *The Zaddik: The Doctrine of the Zaddik According to the Writing of Yaakov Yosef of Polnoy*. New York, 1974.

Elior, Rachel. *Hasidic Thought – Mystical Origins and Kabbalistic Foundations*. Tel Aviv, 1999.

Eliyahu, Rav Yosef Chaim ben. *Ben Ish Chai*. Jerusalem, 1986.

Epstein, Rav Kolonimus Kalman. *Me'or Veshemesh*. New York, 1976.

Etkes, Immanuel. *Ba'al Hashem: The Besht – Magic, Mysticism, Leadership*. Jerusalem, 2000.

———. *The Beginning of the Hasidic Movement*. Tel Aviv, 1998.

Even-Shmuel, Yehudah, ed. *Midrashei Geulah*. Tel Aviv, 1954.

Feiner, Shmuel. "*Sola fide! The Polemic of Rabbi Nathan of Nemirov Against Atheism and Haskala*." *Jerusalem Studies In Jewish Thought* 15 (1999): 124-89.

Fenton, Paul B. "*Sacred Dance in Jewish Spirituality: Hasidic Dance*." *Da'at* 45 (2000): 135-45.

Fishbane, Michael. "'*The Mystery of Dance' according to Rabbi Nahman of Bratslav*." In *Within Hasidic Circles,* edited by Emanuel Etkes, 335-49. Jerusalem, 1990.

Fleer, Gedaliah. *Against All Odds*. Jerusalem Breslov Research Institute 2005.

Frank, Rav Mordechai. "*Mevo*." In *Biur Halikutim*, edited by Rav Avraham Chazan, 1-48, 1993.

Garb, Jonathan. *The Chosen Will Become Herds. Studies in Twentieth Century Kabbalah*. Jerusalem, 2004.

Goldreich, Amos. "*Birurim Beriato He'atzmit Shel Ba'al Tikunei Hazohar*." In *Massu'ot: Studies in Kabbalistic Literature and Jewish Philosophy in memory of Prof. Ephraim Gottlieb*, edited by Michal Oron and Amos Goldreich, 459-96. Jerusalem, 1994.

Green, Arthur. *Tormented Master*. New York: Schocken, 1987.

———. "The Zaddiq as Axis Mundi." *Journal of American Religion* 45 (1977): 327-44.

Gruenwald, Ithamar. "*Mezricha Leshkiah: Ledmutan Shel He'escatelogia Vehameshichiut Beyahadut*." In *The Messianic Idea in Jewish Thought*. 18-35. Jerusalem, 1982.

Gries, Ze'ev. *Conduct Literature (Regimen Vitae). Its History and Place in the Life of Beshtian Hasidism*. Jerusalem, 1989.

Halbertal, Moshe. *Concealment and Revelation: The Secret and its Boundaries in Medieval Jewish Tradition*. Jerusalem, 2001.

Halevi, Rav Yehudah. *Sefer Hakuzari*. Translated by Yehudah Even Shmuel. Jerusalem, 1973.

Hallamish, Moshe. *Introduction to the Kabbalah*. Jerusalem, 1991.

Haran, Rayiah. "*The Doctrine of R. Abraham of Kalisk*." *Tarbiz* 66, no. 4 (1971): 517-41.

Heinemann, Joseph. "*The Messiah of Ephraim and the Premature Exodus of Ephraim*." *Tarbiz* 40 (1971): 450-61.

Heller, Rav Mehsulam Feibush. *Yosher Divrei Emet*. Jerusalem, 1998.

Hellner-Eshed, Melila. *A River Issues Forth from Eden: on the Language of Mystical Experience in the Zohar*. Tel Aviv, 2005.

Horowitz, Rav Shmuel. *Tzion Hamitzuyenet*. Jerusalem, 1990.

Horowitz, Rav Yeshayahu. *Shnei Luchot Habrit*. Jerusalem, 1975.

Hundert, Gershon David. *Jews in Poland-Lithuania in the Eighteenth Century: A Geneology of Modernity*. Berkeley, 2004.

Idel, Moshe. *Hasidism Between Ecstasy and Magic*. Tel Aviv, 2001.

———. "*Hitbodedut*: On Solitude in Jewish Mysticism." *Enisamkeit, Archaeologie der Literarischen Kommunikation* VI (2000): 189-212.

———. "*Hitbodedut as Concentration in Jewish Philosophy*." Jerusalem *Studies in Jewish Thought* VII (1988): 39-60.

———. "*Hitbodedut qua Concentration in Ecstatic Kabbalah*." *Da'at* 14 (1985): 35-81.

———. *Messianic Mystics*. New Haven, 1998.

Jung, Carl Gustav. "The Psychology of the Child Archetype." In *Essays on a Science of Mythology: The Myth of the Divine Child and Mysteries of Eleusis*, edited by C. G. Jung & Caroly Kerenyi, 70-100. Princeton, 1969.

Klein-Braslavy, Sara. "*Prophecy, Clairvoyance and Dreams and the Concept of 'Hitbodedut' in Gersonides' Thought.*" *Da'at* 39 (1997): 23-68.

Kloizner, Rav Yisachar David. *Meshiach Bekol Dor*. Kiriat Malachi, 1992.

Knohl, Israel. *The Messiah Before Jesus*. Israel, 2000.

Kochav-Lev, Rav Avraham. *Tovot Zichronot (Bound with Yerach Eitanim)*. Bnei Brak, 1978.

Koenig, Natan Tzvi, ed. *Nachalei Emunah*. Bnei Brak, 1967.

Koenig, Rav Natan Tzvi. *Neveh Tzadikim*. Bnei Brak, 1969.

Koenig, Rav Tzvi. *Yekarah Dechai (Printed with Sha'arit Yisrael)*. Bnei Brak 1963.

Kolish, R. Zvi Yehudah Halevi Momlok of. *Abir Haro'im*. Pietrakov, 1935.

Kramer, Rav Chaim Menachem. *Toldot Moharnat: Be'aish Uvmayim*. Jerusalem, 1996.

Liebes, Yehuda. "*The Novelty of Rabbi Nahman of Bratslav.*" *Da'at* 45 (Summer) (2000): 91-103.

————. "*Hamashiach Shel Hazohar: Ledemuto Shel R. Shimon Bar Yochai.*" In *The Messianic Idea in Jewish Thought*, 87-236. Jerusalem, 1990.

————. "*Hatikun Haclali Shel R. Nachman Mebreslav Veyachaso Leshabta'ut.*" In *On Sabbateaism and its Kabbalah*, 238-61 and 429-48. Jerusalem, 1995.

————. "*Jonah as the Messiah ben Joseph.*" In *Studies in Jewish Mysticism Philosophy and Ethical Literature,* edited by J. Dan and J. Hacker, 269-311. Jerusalem, 1986.

Lintz, Rav Gedaliah of. *Teshuot Chen*. Brooklyn, 1982.

Lublin, Rav Yitzchak Meir Korman of. "*Ma'aseh Mehalechem* (Manuscript)." In *Machon Schocken*. Jerusalem.

————. "Sefer Chayei Moharan (Manuscript)." In *Machon Schocken.*

Magid, Shaul. "Through the Void: The Absence of God in R. Nachman's of Bratslav's Likuttei Moharan." *Harvard Theological Review* 88 (1995): 495-519.

Maimonides, Rav Moshe ben. *Shalosh Hakadmot*. Jerusalem, 1940.

Margolin, Ron. *The Human Temple: Religious Interiorization and the Structuring of Inner Life in Early Hasidism*. Jerusalem, 1995.

Mark, Zvi. "*The Tale of the Bread – a Hidden Story of R. Nahman of Braslav.*" *Tarbiz*

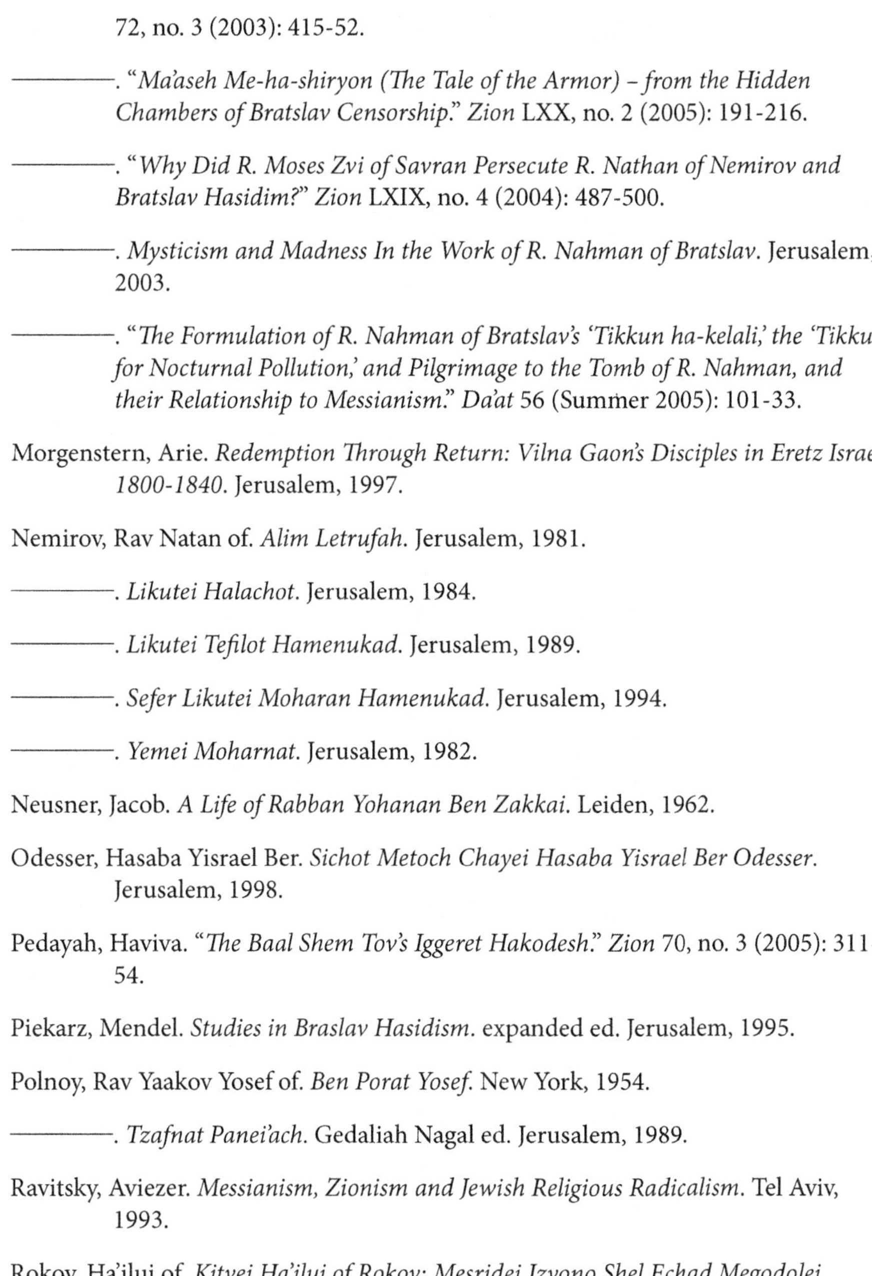
72, no. 3 (2003): 415-52.

————. "*Ma'aseh Me-ha-shiryon (The Tale of the Armor) – from the Hidden Chambers of Bratslav Censorship.*" *Zion* LXX, no. 2 (2005): 191-216.

————. "*Why Did R. Moses Zvi of Savran Persecute R. Nathan of Nemirov and Bratslav Hasidim?*" *Zion* LXIX, no. 4 (2004): 487-500.

————. *Mysticism and Madness In the Work of R. Nahman of Bratslav*. Jerusalem, 2003.

————. "*The Formulation of R. Nahman of Bratslav's 'Tikkun ha-kelali,' the 'Tikkun for Nocturnal Pollution,' and Pilgrimage to the Tomb of R. Nahman, and their Relationship to Messianism.*" *Da'at* 56 (Summer 2005): 101-33.

Morgenstern, Arie. *Redemption Through Return: Vilna Gaon's Disciples in Eretz Israel 1800-1840*. Jerusalem, 1997.

Nemirov, Rav Natan of. *Alim Letrufah*. Jerusalem, 1981.

————. *Likutei Halachot*. Jerusalem, 1984.

————. *Likutei Tefilot Hamenukad*. Jerusalem, 1989.

————. *Sefer Likutei Moharan Hamenukad*. Jerusalem, 1994.

————. *Yemei Moharnat*. Jerusalem, 1982.

Neusner, Jacob. *A Life of Rabban Yohanan Ben Zakkai*. Leiden, 1962.

Odesser, Hasaba Yisrael Ber. *Sichot Metoch Chayei Hasaba Yisrael Ber Odesser*. Jerusalem, 1998.

Pedayah, Haviva. "*The Baal Shem Tov's Iggeret Hakodesh.*" *Zion* 70, no. 3 (2005): 311-54.

Piekarz, Mendel. *Studies in Braslav Hasidism*. expanded ed. Jerusalem, 1995.

Polnoy, Rav Yaakov Yosef of. *Ben Porat Yosef*. New York, 1954.

————. *Tzafnat Panei'ach*. Gedaliah Nagal ed. Jerusalem, 1989.

Ravitsky, Aviezer. *Messianism, Zionism and Jewish Religious Radicalism*. Tel Aviv, 1993.

Rokov, Ha'ilui of. *Kitvei Ha'ilui of Rokov: Mesridei Izvono Shel Echad Megodolei Yehadut Lita*. Edited by Tzvi Kaplan. Jerusalem, 1963.

Roskies, David G. "The Master of Prayer: Nachman of Bratslav." In *A Bridge of Longing: The Lost Art of Yiddish Storytelling*, 20-55. Cambridge, MA, 1995.

Ruderman, David. "Three Contemporary Perceptions of a Polish Wunderkind of the Seventeenth Century." *AJS Review* 4 (1979): 143-63.

Saparin, Rav Yitzchak Yehuda Yechiel. *Megilat Setarim (First Published in Manuscript by Naftali Ben-Menachem)*. Jerusalem, 1944.

Sargai, S. Z. *Halichot Hageula Bemishnat Chasidut Izbetza-Radzin*. Jerusalem, 1991.

———. *Pa'amei Geula*. Jerusalem, 1967.

Scholem, Gershom. "*Al Mekorotav Shel 'Ma'aseh Rabi Gadiel Hatinok' Besifrut Hakabbalah*." In *Explications and Implications*, 270-83. Tel Aviv, 1975.

———. *Explications and Implications*. Tel Aviv, 1975.

———. "*HeChasidut Hashalav Ha'acharon*." In *Studies in Hasidism*, edited by Avraham Rubinstein, 31-52. Jerusalem, 1977.

———. *Shabbetai Zevi and the Shabbetaian Movement during his Lifetime*. 2 vols. Tel Aviv, 1987.

———. "*A Document by the Disciples of Isaac Luria Israel Sarug – Disciple of Luria*." *Zion* 5, no. 2 (1940): 133-60.

Sedlikolov, Rav Efraim of. *Degel Machneh Efraim*. Jerusalem, 1994.

Shapiro, Rav Kolonimus Kalman. *Aish Kodesh*. Jerusalem, 1960.

Shapiro, Rav Natan Netah. *Megaleh Amukot Al Hatorah*. Lemberg, 1884.

———. *Megaleh Amukot Al Parshat Ve'etchanan*. Bnai Brak, 1992.

Shatz Oppenheimer, Rivka. *Hasidism as Mysticism*. Jerusalem, 1988.

Schick, Rav Eliezer. *Asher Banachal*. Vol. 3. Jerusalem, 1976.

———. *Asher Banachal*. Vol. 6. New York 1978.

———. *Asher Banachal*. Vol. 14. Jerusalem, 1984.

———. *Peulat Hatzadik*. Jerusalem, 1944.

Shilo, Elchanan. "*The Use and Literary Function of Kabbalah in the Works of S. Y. Agnon*." Ph.D Thesis, Bar-Ilan University, 2005.

Shternfeld, Rav Noach Halevi. *Gidulei Hanachal*. Jerusalem, 1984.

Schwartz, Dov. *Messianism in Medieval Jewish Thought*. Ramat Gan, 1997.

Steinsaltz, Rabbi Adin. *Six Stories of Rabbi Nahman of Bratzlav*. Jerusalem, 1995.

Tamar, David. "*Luria and Vital as Messiah Ben Joseph*." *Sefunot* 7 (1963): 169-77.

Tscherin, Rav Nachman of. *Parparot Lechachma*. Jerusalem, 1983.

Tepliker, Rav Alter. "*Hashmatot Mechayei Moharan*." 1898.

———. *Hishtapchut Hanefesh*. Jerusalem, 1904.

Tishby, Isaiah. *Studies in Kabbalah and its Branches*. Jerusalem, 1993.

———. *The Doctrine of Evil and the 'Kelippah' in Lurianic Kabbalism*. Jerusalem, 1992.

Tzeitlen, Hillel. *Al Gvul Shnei Olomot*. Tel Aviv, 1997.

———. *Rav Nachman Mebreslav: Chaiyav Vetorato*. Warsaw, 1910.

Tzikernik, Isaiah Wolf. "*Ma'asiot Uma'amarim Yakarim* " In *Czarnobil Hasidism Tales*, edited by Gedalyah Nigal. Jerusaelm, 1994[!].

Urbach, Ephraim E. *The Sages: Their Concepts and Beliefs*. Jerusalem, 1998.

Vermes, Geza. *Jesus the Jew*. Philadelphia, 1981.

Vital, Rav Chaim. "*Arba'ah Meot Shekel Kesef*." New York, 1995.

———. *Etz Hada'at Tov*. Jerusalem, 1991.

———. *Sefer Halikutim*. New York, 1995.

———. *Sefer Hechizionot*. Eshkoli ed. Jerusalem, 1954.

———. *Sefer Pri Etz Chaim*. New York, 1995.

———. *Sha'ar Hagilgulim*. New York, 1995.

Walden, Menachem Mendel, ed. *Niflaot Harebi*. Bnei Brak, 1944.

Weiss, Joseph. "*R. Nahman of Bratzlav's Hidden Book of the Advent of the Messiah*." *Kirjath Sepher* 44 (1969): 270-79.

———. *Studies in Braslav Hassidi*sm. Jerusalem, 1995.

Wertheim, Aharon. *Halachot Vehalichot BeChasidut*, 1989.

Zagdon, Avraham. *Eilu Yadativ Hiyativ*. Beitar Elite, 2002.

Index

A

E

F

H

I

J

K

L

M

N

T

U

V

W

Y

Z

CPSIA information can be obtained
at www.ICGtesting.com
Printed in the USA
LVOW13s0007180118
563078LV00032B/1563/P

9 781934 843949